Energize
YOUR RETIREMENT

Energize YOUR RETIREMENT

Stories *of* Passionate Pursuits

Christine Sparacino

To Anabelle + Joe
Best wishes
Christine Sparacino

VIA VERDE PRESS
WALNUT CREEK, CA

Published in the United States of America by Via Verde Press.

Cover design by Barbara Aronica
Book design by Sue Balcer

First Edition

ISBN 978-0-9905669-2-2

Contents

Author's Note: What to Expect from This Book vii

Introduction 1

Part One: Animals and Nature 9

Chapter 1: Amateur Astronomer 11

Chapter 2: Beekeeper 23

Chapter 3: Bird Watcher and Conservationist 33

Chapter 4: Habitat Restorer 47

Chapter 5: Mushroom Hunter 59

Chapter 6: Service-Dog Trainer 71

Part Two: Arts and Letters 85

Chapter 7: Calligrapher 87

Chapter 8: Crossword-Puzzle Constructor 99

Chapter 9: Magician 111

Chapter 10: Performing-Arts Usher 123

Chapter 11: Fiction Writer 133

Chapter 12: Stone Sculptor 145

Part Three: Civic and Social Participation 157

Chapter 13: Disaster-Response Worker 159

Chapter 14: Medicare Counselor 171

Chapter 15: National Park Volunteer 183

Chapter 16: Nonprofit Board Director 195

Chapter 17: Ombudsman for Elder Care 207

Chapter 18: Youth Mentor 217

Part Four: Mechanics and Technology 227

Chapter 19: Blogger/Vlogger 229

Chapter 20: Craft Beer Homebrewer 241

Chapter 21: Ham Radio Operator 251

Chapter 22: Motorcyclist 263

Chapter 23: RV Traveler 277

Chapter 24: Woodturner 287

Part Five: Physical Activity and Sports 297

Chapter 25: Backpacker 299

Chapter 26: Dancer 311

Chapter 27: Softball Player 323

Chapter 28: Target Shooter 333

Chapter 29: Triathlete 345

Notes and Sources 359

Acknowledgments 379

Index 381

Author's Note:
What to Expect from This Book

Energize Your Retirement is the result of a conversation that began when I encouraged my husband to retire after thirty years from a business he built from scratch and join me in retirement. His answer was always the same "What would I do?" I started to explore the possibilities and found many fascinating people enjoying fulfilling activities that became their passionate pursuits. So many, in fact, that I wanted to chronicle these great stories and help those struggling with the concept of an energized life after decades of work.

This book is a collection of stories that shares what some people decided to do when they retired and asked themselves, *Now what*? It narrates how they designed a lifestyle to include activities that bring meaning to their lives. The retirees in this book tell their stories in their own words, radiating an enthusiasm for their pursuits that will encourage others to find satisfaction in their retirement years.

The pursuits are diversified, some purely physical, others thoroughly cerebral. The mix includes relaxing as well as invigorating activities. Some retirees interviewed pursue a solo endeavor, others participate with a partner, while still others form or join a group of fellow enthusiasts. Each retiree talks about a pursuit that grew and flourished into their passion. Some spend many hours at it; others enjoy activities that require a small amount of time. Some require a good-size monetary investment, while others require very little.

As a fellow retiree, I've taken on my own personal pursuit with all of the zeal of a Champagne cork released in flight. I pursue my passion for writing by chronicling the stories of energized retirees, people who embraced a pursuit that became their passion. I've interviewed both men and women about the focus of their time. How did they become interested in this pursuit? How did they get started? How much time do they devote to this activity; and most important, what satisfaction does it bring? Each interview includes a budget estimate of expenses one might expect if they were to take up each endeavor.

The pursuits presented interest both men and women. There are a few activities that some may think of as typically feminine or masculine, but passionate pursuits appeal to both genders and myriad personality types. For example, the majority of calligraphy group members may be women. However, I was surprised to learn that most calligraphy teachers are men. The woman target shooter I interviewed belongs to a shooting club whose membership is 80 percent male; the club president, however, was a seventy-year-old woman. Group activities and organizations are delighted with male and female helping hands. Many national support organizations' websites actively recruit both men and women participants with varying commitment levels and management styles; leaders and nonleadership workers are all welcomed.

There is a wide range of ages among this group of energized retirees. The youngest is fifty-nine and the oldest is eighty-four years old. The stories include retirees who are devoted to their chosen path and spend a lot of time on their favorite pursuit, while others limit the obligation to fit their lifestyle. The focus of this book is on activities that can be enjoyed throughout the United States, from Bangor to San Diego, from Seattle to Miami, including volunteer pursuits that are part of a national organization. Within each chapter is a collection of "Fascinating Facts" on each topic. Additionally, each chapter's "Resources" section cites informational sources including websites, apps, videos, and books and magazines.

The book is divided among five themes: Animals and Nature, Arts and Letters, Civic and Social Participation, Mechanics and Technology, and Physical Activity and Sports. Each chapter is dedicated to one passionate pursuit within that theme. This book can be enjoyed by reading the chapters in sequence or reading the chapters in any order you wish.

My hope is that you will enjoy learning about these retirees' energized worlds, and become acquainted with topics previously unfamiliar to you. I hope that you enjoy meeting these interesting people and that they will inspire you to energize your retirement years with a passionate pursuit of your own.

Introduction

I'm inspired by people who keep on rolling,
no matter their age.
—Jimmy Buffett

You Are Retired!

You've packed up the contents of your desk or tools of the trade. You've received congratulations from coworkers and off you go—off to begin a new chapter of your life. Amazon lists more than 37,000 titles on the subject of retirement. Most books concentrate on financial advice: how to save and how to manage those savings. We are told this is the key to a happy retirement.

Yes, financial preparation is critical, but equally important is deciding what to do with your time. Most retirement books don't mention the emotional effects of retirement or tell us how retirees fill their time after they leave the workforce. For many people, a career is their identity. You may be a CEO, teacher, or police officer, with many years of specialized training and decades of honing that knowledge into expertise. After retiring from the workplace, you may suddenly feel irrelevant. The title, corner office, perks, and administrative help are suddenly gone. You're on your own. You may be asking yourself this question: What I will I do to maintain a meaningful life?

If you are planning or beginning your retirement, it is important to decide how you want your retired life to look. If you are already retired, you may be ready to discover a new interest. You now have a new opportunity to turn the page and begin to write your life's next chapter.

The Tidal Wave

The full-time workplace exodus to retirement has begun. The first baby boomers turned sixty-five years old on January 1, 2011. Not only are people currently reaching the age of sixty-five at the rate of 10,000 a day, they will continue at this rate for the next twenty years! The age 65 and older population surged to 44.7 million in 2013, up 3.6 percent from 2012, according to the Census data. The existence of the baby boomer generation has had a tremendous influence on American society and will continue to affect both our medical system and retirement system.

- The first baby boomer turned 65 on January 1, 2011.
- Every 10 seconds a boomer turns 65 (this amounts to between 3 and 4 million a year).
- By 2015, those aged 50 and older will represent 45% of the US population.
- By 2030, the 65-plus population will double to about 71.5 million, and by 2050 will grow to 86.7 million people.
- Americans reaching age 65 today have an average life expectancy of an additional 17.9 years (19.2 years for women and 16.3 years for men).

In June 2013, the MetLife Mature Market Institute reported the data from interviews with more than 1,000 individuals born in 1946, the first year of the boomer generation. Boomers said that they intended to work past the traditional retirement age of sixty-five, but by age sixty-six retires outnumbered those still working by 2 to 1. More than half (52 percent) of the 1946 boomers are now fully retired, 21 percent remain employed full-time and 14 percent are working part-time. Only 4 percent are self-employed.

The problems with the economy in the past five years have created a tough job market, and many unemployed older workers are retiring earlier than planned. Compounding those numbers are those workers in their early to mid-fifties who are eligible to retire after thirty years of service. All together, the number of those fully retired or semi-retired is growing exponentially. What are these retirees doing with their time?

Transition

It is important to realize that your new job will be staying engaged and fulfilled. Retirement can be exciting and demanding, bringing new experiences, challenges, and uncertainties. This time can be an opportunity to reinvent yourself—the dawn of a new age. And time will be plentiful. What will you do with it?

After the first few months of "retirement high," you may not have a clear idea of what to do when you get up in the morning. After you've cleaned the attic, basement, and garage, you'll want to guard against depression, needless shopping, watching TV reruns, and frequent naps. Most of us plan our vacation trips carefully, listing where we want to travel and what we want to see. Your retirement journey requires the same thoughtful planning. You must decide on new goals and think about what gives meaning to your days and keeps you engaged and fulfilled.

Your workday structure has disappeared—no commute: no traffic jams or bus to catch; no coffee breaks and rushed lunches.

Your old schedule is gone. Social interaction with clients and co-workers is gone. This may be disturbing to the new retiree. Many retired men, especially, report feeling a strong loss of identity. A National Institute of Health study found that men, who heavily invested in their jobs as a source of well-being, are more apt to become depressed in retirement. Former professionals become accustomed to a certain level of credibility and respect that often evaporates in retirement. The challenge is to change your mental perspective and regain confidence in other areas.

Staying Healthy

A century ago, people who lived longer than age ninety were rare. Today, they're the fastest growing segment of the US population. Remaining physically fit, mentally alert, and emotionally connected are the three key ingredients of healthy aging. This is vital for a successful retirement. The Centers for Disease Control and Prevention (CDC) reports that successful aging is largely determined by individual lifestyle choices and not by genetic inheritance. The study found that having a physically active lifestyle was important for successful aging. The Harvard Study of Adult Development, one of the oldest and most respected studies on aging in the country, reported that exercise was the key to ensuring a long, happy life, protecting the heart and preventing disabilities.

Good mental health is the second key to healthy living. It's important to have a cognitively active lifestyle. A study reported in 2013 by Reuters Health suggests that people who spend time reading, writing, and processing new information maintain their thinking and memory skills longer. The study recommended that people engage in activities that are stimulating and challenging.

Emotional connection is the third key to healthy living and a positive force in any stage of life. Personal relationships and strong bonds with family and friends are crucial for happiness. A 2012 study by Bankers Life and Casualty asked 300 retirees, ages fifty-five to seventy-five questions about what they missed most about working. They reported that 65 percent missed the workplace interaction. Only 15 percent of the retirees said they missed the income. Retirement can leave a big void in social interaction. Be sure to include healthy habits that engage all three of the key ingredients of healthy living into your retirement lifestyle.

What Excites Me?

Retirement is the perfect time to become the person you would like to be and do the things you always wanted to do. But as homogeneous as the term "retirement" is, our choices of pastimes and passions are unique. Some people are extroverts looking for more connection, while others enjoy doing things that bring peace and solitude. Some have a list of goals to accomplish before "kicking the bucket." Others take a cosmic, spontaneous approach. The days ahead can be a learning process filled with trial and error as you search for what will best contribute to a fulfilling and exciting retirement.

Your schedule will be unique and no one pursuit is better than the other. The goal is to find out what excites you and feeds your spirit. Your well-being is enhanced when you feel vibrant and socially connected, and have a strong sense of purpose. Sometimes a hobby or activity takes on a life of its own. It brings so much enjoyment; it becomes a passion.

Stories of Passionate Pursuits

That's what this book is about. I have compiled stories from people who have used their pastime activities to adjust to their new reality of retirement, and these varied pastimes have become their passion. These stories introduce you to energized semi-retired and fully retired men and women who explored new opportunities and found their niche. They incorporate enrichment into their lives and are fascinating people. Meeting with them and having them share their passionate pursuits was enlightening, motivating, and fun.

Contagious Energy

While no one is immune to physical limitations at an advanced age, expressions like *young at heart* and *energized* epitomize the storytellers I present in this book. I was reminded of the famous Satchel Paige quote: "How old would you be if you didn't know how old you are?" All of those interviewed, whether they were in their fifties, sixties, seventies, or eighties were full of life, energy, optimism, inspiration, and joie de vivre.

A Variety of Interests

The book presents a variety of unique interests within the five themes. Each story represents only the perspective of the narrator and does not cover all aspects of the activity. The goal with this compilation of interviews is to introduce experiences that you may not have considered before. Each story explains how the storyteller began and how this pastime developed into his or her passion. But that doesn't mean they don't have other interests. In fact, many of the people I interviewed have multiple interests, such as travel and grandchildren, but one special pastime stands out that makes them feel vibrant, socially connected, and satisfies a sense of purpose.

By reading their stories, we can learn from their experience and avoid some pitfalls of idle time. The book contains personal accounts of how and why these storytellers do what they do. Additionally, I've added the resources to help you locate information that will start you on your way. My hope is that you will enjoy exploring a little bit of these retirees' energized worlds, become acquainted with a topic previously unknown to you, and learn and try something new. Perhaps this armchair presentation will be the first step and will inspire you to energize your retirement years with a passionate pursuit.

PART ONE

ANIMALS AND NATURE

CHAPTER 1

Amateur Astronomer

Astronomy compels the soul to look upwards and leads us from this world to another.
—Plato

Astronomy brings to mind multimillion-dollar telescopes, space stations, and an astrophysics degree. However, many amateur astronomers find planets, nebulae, stars, and satellites without expensive equipment and advanced degrees. *Night-sky watchers* and *stargazers* are other names for these hobbyists.

Many amateurs contribute to the scientific research in the field of astronomy. They provide valuable data to professional researchers by tracking asteroids, imaging variable stars and planets, and discovering comets in our vast universe.

Special Training Not Required

Enjoying astronomy does not require you to be a professional, and you don't need additional schooling to appreciate the heavens. People of any skill level or age can participate and gain a better understanding of the universe. An estimated 300,000 to 500,000 amateur astronomers live in the United States.

Urban Astronomy

Amateur astronomy isn't only for those living in rural areas. The Astronomical League, composed of more than 260 local amateur astronomical societies from all across the United States, has developed a program to support urban astronomy. The goal is to bring amateur astronomy back to the cities, back to those areas affected by heavy light pollution. The League's website recommends several tips to make viewing more enjoyable and rewarding. Here are some of those suggestions:

- Use a dew shield [an extension or cap that keeps the lens dry] on your telescope to shade it from stray light.
- Use a dark cloth to cover your head and eyepiece to shield them from stray light.
- Use earphones or a radio to mask neighborhood noise. Noise can be distracting.
- Observe during a new moon. Just like observing in dark skies, the moon adds light to the night sky and reduces contrast.
- Observe after a rainstorm. The skies appear darker as light is not reflected off dust particles in the air.
- Observe after 11:00 p.m. Many stores have closed by this time, and because they turn off their lights, a city's light glow is reduced considerably.
- Try to catch your target objects straight overhead. This is always the darkest part of the sky.

Theo with his telescopes

Theo is seventy years old and passionate about sharing his love of astronomy. His forty-year career in information technology included programming, software development, and many years of international travel connected with call centers for sales and support. He lives outside of Atlanta, Georgia.

Theo: I discovered astronomy as a young Boy Scout in the Netherlands. I lived and worked in Germany for many years before immigrating to New York. Years later, I settled in a suburb of Atlanta, Georgia. I was always fascinated with the night sky, but my international business travels kept me busy and away from it. When I retired, I started talking about it and my kids bought me a telescope for Christmas. That was the trigger point. I went to the Web, looked for astronomy clubs, and found one in my neighborhood. I am currently the Outreach Coordinator of the Charlie Elliott chapter of the Atlanta Astronomy Club.

What equipment do you use?

Theo: I started with my Christmas present, a four-and-a-half-inch reflector telescope. Then I moved up to a nine-and-a-quarter-inch reflector, which I feel is a good platform for imaging and observing. After a while, I traded that one in for an eleven-inch Cassegrain that I currently use. My advice: Don't buy a telescope when you first start. Rather, start with a good pair of binoculars. You will be surprised what you can see. Binoculars do not really require any training to use, do not need to be assembled, and can be used anywhere. They have a wide field of view, making it easy for beginners to find objects in the sky.

Visit an astronomy club and use the equipment they have available. Club members bring their own equipment to events and are open to sharing. You might meet twenty people with twenty different types of equipment. Some clubs may have additional equipment available and provide new users with refractor and reflector telescopes to try out. By working with the different equipment, it will give you a good idea of what kind of equipment you should get. As your interest in astronomy grows, telescopes that are more powerful can help you to observe objects in the universe with greater clarity and in larger variety.

Usually at club meetings, everybody observes many things together: nebulae, planets, star clusters, and galaxies. Once you start observing, then you can decide what you like. Clubs also have subgroups, which specialize in a specific area. For example, some planetary people observe how the storms on planets evolve. Many focus on Jupiter and Mars, while others may look at double stars, color distance between the stars, or half stars. You will develop your own favorites through active participation. That is why I suggest that you wait before you invest in a telescope. Give yourself time to decide what kind of telescope to buy. You can get a nice starter telescope for $400 depending on what you want to do.

Amateur Astronomy Clubs

Astronomy can be a tremendously social hobby. Joining an amateur astronomy club is a good way to exchange resources and information, receive tips, and meet others interested in the night sky. Most astronomy clubs schedule regular "safaris" to go out away from the lights of the city and get a good night of sky watching done. Going on such an outing with a big group of enthusiasts is the type of experience that will take a passive interest in astronomy and change it into a healthy obsession.

The Night Sky Network

The Night Sky Network (NSN) is a partnership between amateur astronomy clubs all over the country, NASA, and other expert organizations. The NSN is an important example of community outreach, bringing the science, technology, and inspiration of NASA's space missions to the community. As members of this coalition, amateur astronomy club members receive free training and tool kits when they share their knowledge, time, and telescopes in schools and community outreach events. In return, clubs must promise to present at least five events each year.

The tool kits help presenters explain topics such as the scale of the solar system and galaxies, how telescopes work, and even black holes. The kits provide activities for all ages, for use in small or large groups with hands-on activities, "telescope treasure hunts," PowerPoint presentations, and animations. Additionally, club members who are part of the Night Sky Network get exclusive access to teleconferences with leading NASA scientists and others presenting the latest developments in cutting-edge astronomy.

Outreach

Theo: When I joined the local amateur astronomy club, I met a fellow named John who became my best friend and mentor. He helped me, not only in understanding astronomy, but also in sharing his knowledge with others. John provided a lot of outreach to schools and the community and that really intrigued me. On a personal level, I really want to give something back. This country has been good to me and given me a lot of opportunity. I wanted to use my time to help the next generation. I also believe this country doesn't have enough scientists and we don't spend enough money to educate our kids in science.

Through outreach, presenters in the astronomy club bring several telescopes and go out to civic groups and schools in the area. Theo is the current outreach coordinator of his club and has been doing that for the past six years. The Charlie Elliott Astronomy Club held over 100 events last year, approximately 65 percent in the schools and 35 percent in other community venues. Theo was personally involved in sixty-three outreach events last year and will exceed that number this year.

Solar Specialty

Theo: Many of the astronomy club members like to specialize in one area. I like to make pictures of the sun every day, capturing it through imaging. I keep up a website and a blog called the Dutch Observatory. I document the sun's activity: sunspots, filaments, and prominences—it's fascinating. Filaments are dark, threadlike features; they are dense clouds of material. They are suspended above the surface of the sun by loops of magnetic fields. Prominences are the same things as filaments, except they are seen projecting over the limb of the sun. As the magnetic fields that support them change, they erupt and rise off the sun. They are thousands to millions of kilometers wide and tall. I also do planetary imaging, but I specialize in the sun. That's what I really like to do.

Solar Ambassador

Theo is a member of the Astronomical League and in 2010 became a NASA-JPL Solar System Ambassador. There are currently 516 Ambassadors in the United States. Ambassadors are space enthusiasts from various walks of life who are interested in providing greater service and inspiration to the community. As an ambassador, Theo traveled to California to help design the tool kit for sun observing used in presentations. Another benefit of being a Solar System Ambassador is receiving first-hand information updates on the different missions from NASA team members.

What is the most rewarding aspect of this activity?

Theo: The outreach to the community and schools from kindergarten through college is the most rewarding part. Introducing astronomy to children at an early age and then watching them continue their interest by joining the astronomy club brings me a great deal of satisfaction. If I see students who are interested, I invite them to come with their parents and use my equipment to make their own images of the sun. It is an involved process to produce a picture, capturing a thousand frames and removing noise to make an image. It's a lot of work. They do it themselves, which gives them ownership of what they did, how they did it, and why.

Astrophotography

Amateur astrophotography uses a film camera, such as a 35mm single lens reflex (SLR) camera or a digital camera to capture images of the night sky. As new technologies become cost effective, recreational astronomers are following the professional observatories in the switch from film to digital-charged coupled devices (CCDs) for astronomical imaging. These cameras are specially cooled to reduce noise, and are specifically made for scientific and imaging purposes. They are made to be used through a telescope, but adapters can be purchased that allow use with camera lenses for wide-angle shots. Astronomical equipment companies also now offer a wide range of purpose-built astronomical CCDs complete with hardware and processing software. Helpful books and software on astrophotography are listed in the Resources section at the end of the chapter.

How much time do you spend on this pursuit?

Theo: I spend a lot of time on my passionate pursuit. During the day, I am observing the sun, imaging, and keeping up the blog on my website. I also work on club activities coordinating the outreach events, and, of course, I spend a lot of time visiting schools and giving community presentations. Then there are club meetings, monthly observing sessions, and special events. I spend more than four hours a day [doing astronomy]. I am afraid it has become an obsession. I think of it as my full-time job. The more you get into it, the more you do.

Pro-Am Research

Theo believes astronomy is one of the few sciences that allows for a great deal of interaction between professionals and amateurs.

Theo: When you think about how vast the universe is, the professionals don't have time to look at everything, so amateur astronomers can play a key role in helping them. All over the world, amateur astronomers are performing valuable fieldwork, giving scientists the material to work with. They observe, track, make images, and then submit the data on specific areas for the professionals to analyze.

Many professional researchers work hand-in-hand with teams of amateurs to make discoveries that wouldn't be possible without this kind of collaboration. For example, the American Association of Variable Star Observers (AAVSO), an international nonprofit organization of professional and amateur star observers, produced a star catalog that measures the characteristics of more than 42 million stars. These observers measured and mapped mass, temperature, and internal structure for the first time in history.

Lowell Observatory in Flagstaff, Arizona, dedicates pages of their website to announce projects for amateur astronomer participation. These projects span a variety of activities requiring a range of technical skills and knowledge, from taking deep images of galaxies to monitoring small stars for transient events to data mining.

Sky & Telescope magazine has a dedicated Professional-Amateur (Pro-Am) section on its website, including details about an AstroAlert service. This is an e-mail news service to alert telescope users when significant celestial transients occur (or are predicted to occur) for which scientists are requesting CCD images or other observations from advanced amateurs.

Do you have any other advice for people interested in this pursuit?

Theo: I think the most important thing is to know there is a lot of help out there, so don't be afraid to ask. Join an astronomy club that is part of the Night Sky Network, so you can take part in outreach and bring the wonders of the universe to your community.

FASCINATING FACTS

- 1.3 million Earths could fit in the sun.
- You would have to travel 25,000 mph to escape gravity.
- When 3 celestial bodies align, as in an eclipse, it's called a *syzygy*.
- There are 88 official constellations, the same number as keys on a piano.
- It took the Apollo mission over 4 days to get from the Earth to the moon. Their radio transmissions made it back in 1.3 seconds.
- If you could travel to the nearest star in a car going 70 mph, it would take 356,908,917,036 years to get there.
- There is a crater on the moon called Hell. It is named after the Hungarian astronomer Maximilian Hell (1720–1792).

Resources

Websites

The Astronomical League: astroleague.org; Urban Program: http://bit.ly/WZ6pyj.

Astrophotography software (free): http://bit.ly/WIPIHr.

The Dutch Observatory (Theo's website and blog): http://ceastronomy.org/tramakers/.

Exploratorium's gateway to ten cool astronomy sites: http://bit.ly/1khA68x.

Night Sky Network astronomy clubs in the United States: http://1.usa.gov/1rqu5VC.

Star chart: http://skymaps.com/.

Stargazing basics: http://bit.ly/1lJHHHB.

Apps

Several subjects such as star charts, comet watch, and satellite guides are available at this site: http://bit.ly/1ziUvNI.

Videos

Amateur Astronomy for Beginners (fourteen videos by truemartian): http://bit.ly/1pkjxHO.

Amateur Astronomers—KQED QUEST: http://bit.ly/1lJHZya.

Reading

Guy Consolmagno and Dan M. Davis, *Turn Left at Orion: Hundreds of Night Sky Objects to See in a Home Telescope and How to Find Them* (Cambridge, UK: Cambridge University Press, 2011).

Michael A. Covington, *Astrophotography for the Amateur* (Cambridge, UK: Cambridge University Press, 1999).

Chet Raymo, *An Intimate Look at the Night Sky* (Washington, DC: WAMU, American University, 2001).

Sky & Telescope magazine: skyandtelescope.com.

Observatories

Arecibo Observatory, Arecibo, Puerto Rico. It houses the largest single dish radio telescope in the world and was featured in the James Bond movie Golden Eye.

Griffith Observatory, Los Angeles, California. Its namesake, Griffith J. Griffith, amassed a fortune in the mining business and in 1919 bequeathed funds to build Griffith Park and the Observatory, dedicated in 1935.

Kitt Peak National Observatory, southwest of Tucson, Arizona. Home to twenty-four optical and two radio telescopes representing eight astronomical research institutions.

Lick Observatory, San Jose, California. The University of California astronomical observatory has made several vital discoveries over the decades.

Lowell Observatory, Flagstaff, Arizona. Home of the Discovery Channel Telescope completed in 2012. After ten years of planning and construction and a cost of $53 million, it is one of the most technologically advanced.

Mauna Kea Observatory, Hawaii. It sits on the 4,200-meter-high summit of the inactive volcano. It houses the world's largest observatory for optical, infrared, and submillimeter astronomy.

McDonald Observatory, Fort Davis, Texas. Located in a rugged and desolate area, where visitors can gaze at the sky through some massive telescopes.

Palomar Observatory, San Diego County, California. Located near the Cleveland National Forest on Palomar Mountain in north San Diego County at an elevation of 5,500 feet, the observatory is home to five telescopes owned and operated by the California Institute of Technology.

Yerkes Observatory, Williams Bay, Wisconsin. Established in 1897, it has the world's largest refracting telescope and a collection of more than 150,000 photographic plates.

CHAPTER 2

Beekeeper

For to a bee a flower is the fountain of life;
And to the flower a bee is a messenger of love.
—*Khalil Gibran*

Known as the angels of agriculture, honeybees support one-third of the human food supply and 70 percent of all cultivated plants. Farmers rely on honeybees to pollinate crops such as blueberries, cranberries, apples, almonds, and squash. In addition to honey, bees produce beeswax that is used in candles and cosmetics. Bee venom is used in various parts of the world to treat health problems such as arthritis, neuralgia, high blood pressure, high cholesterol, and multiple sclerosis.

The Western or European honeybee is classified *Apis mellifera*, which in Latin means "honey-bearing bee." Beekeeping is known as *apiculture*, and a beekeeper is known as an *apiculturist*.

Beekeeping in the United States

The Virginia Company chartered by King James I of England brought European honeybees to the American colonies as early as 1622. The Shakers, a religious sect that migrated from England to the colonies in the late 1700s, were accomplished fruit growers, and recognized the importance of bees in ensuring a good crop. Many European immigrants fleeing wars, poverty, and religious persecution brought extensive beekeeping skills to the United States. Today, according to the 2012 Industry Survey by *Bee Culture* magazine, there are an estimated 115,000 to 125,000 beekeepers in the United States. The vast majority are hobbyists with fewer than twenty-five hives. Commercial beekeepers are those with three hundred or more hives.

Ed, the apiculturist

Ed is sixty-four years old and the owner of a commercial construction firm. He is semi-retired and when he's not working on a renovation project, he enjoys beekeeping.

Ed: One day, while on a government project, I got to talking to a fellow who was retiring and going to be keeping bees. That interested me, so I started looking into it. Before I established my construction company, I taught math and science in high school. I think the science of beekeeping was the draw. Plus, I always enjoy honey in my tea, so the idea of producing my own honey appealed to me.

How did you get started?

Ed: Some people learn by reading, but I'm a visual learner. I searched on YouTube and found a series by a professor at the University of Georgia on "A Year in the Life of a Beekeeper." The professor covers all aspects of beekeeping. He starts by buying packages of bees and takes you all the way through the nectar flows, when the bees generate the honey. There are other free videos on the subject on YouTube as well.

Zoning Regulations

Beekeeping can be a hobby whether you live in a rural or urban area. Many municipalities permit beekeeping to do their part to help with the effects of colony collapse. Beekeepers are thriving in cities across the nation utilizing rooftops, patios, and small plots of land. Although cities such as Detroit, Chicago, and New York City permit beekeeping, not all urban and suburban areas are bee-friendly. Sometimes residents object to the idea of their neighbors having beehives. Before taking up this hobby, double-check your city ordinances to make sure you are allowed to keep bees.

Ed: A speaker I heard at the State Bee Convention this year recounted that West Virginia takes an interesting approach to encouraging the growth of the bee population. Instead of planting grass to cover the scars of strip-mining operations, state agencies sowed wildflowers, thereby encouraging pollinators. Kentucky also encourages bee growth with wildflowers along their highways instead of grass. The money saved from not having to mow the grass pays for the wildflower seeds. Because these states have sufficient rain throughout the spring and summer months, the wildflowers germinate themselves, creating a beneficial ecological cycle.

How much time do you spend in your pursuit?

Ed: The amount of time I spend depends on the season. Springtime is the busiest time for the bees. During that time, I look in on my hives at least once a week. I check for the amount of brood [eggs] produced and their different stages. I look for a buildup of honey. I locate the queen to make sure she is still there. I scrape and discard "burr comb" or comb that is not neatly formed on frames, which keeps the hive orderly and accessible. I look for additional queen cells that will produce a new queen, which, when she hatches, will push out the old queen and cause her to lead a swarm from the hive. If that happens, I lose my bees, so I destroy the additional queen cells before they produce a new queen.

The summer is the busiest time for me. I look for a buildup of honey and start the harvest and extraction process. In the winter, I will look in on the hives every two to three weeks to check on numbers. I don't want to disturb them too much during the cold weather. If the number of bees is low, there is a good chance the hive will not make it through the winter.

Most beekeepers will "smoke" the hive area while they perform housekeeping tasks. I burn strips of burlap, pine needles, or eucalyptus bark because they are slow-burning. The smoke dulls the bees' alarm pheromones and they stay calm. I find it interesting to watch the bees, measure the growth of the hive, and compare the production from hive to hive.

Honey

Ed: When the honey comes in and it's time to harvest, it is time-consuming. It's similar to the canning process—sterilizing, filling bottles, sealing caps, and attaching labels. The honey is pure raw honey; nothing is added. Honey doesn't spoil and lasts indefinitely; bacteria won't grow because of the low pH and moisture content.

Honey can be dark or light, depending on the climate and the flower nectar the bees collect.

To make honey, the bees collect the nectar from flowers and store it in their "honey stomachs," separate from their true stomachs. On their way back to the hive, they secrete enzymes into their honey stomachs that begin converting the nectar into honey.

According to the National Honey Board, the color, flavor, and aroma of honey depend on the flower from which the bee gathers the nectar. Color may range from nearly colorless to dark brown. There are more than three hundred unique types of honey available in the United States, each originating from a different floral source. As a rule, the flavor of lighter-colored honeys is milder and the flavor of darker-colored honeys is stronger.

Swarms

Ed: I haven't bought packaged bees since the first hive I purchased when I started. I increase my hives by collecting swarms. Depending on where you live, bees can swarm in late March or early April and throughout the summer months. It is a natural reproductive division. They overpopulate their current space and new queens hatch. When a new queen takes over the hive, the old queen leaves with her followers to go find another place to live, thus creating a swarm.

Swarms can settle anywhere—on tree limbs, on chimneys, in roof rafters. I've even seen them on the side of a car. They stop in a temporary location, and send out scouts to look for a permanent home. Surprisingly, bees are in their more docile state when they swarm because they are not defending a hive and they are full of honey.

I think bees in swarms are stronger than packaged bees—they are survivors. If a resident finds a swarm of bees, the best thing to do is call a local beekeeper association rather than a pest-control company. You save the expense and at the same time keep the environment free of more pesticides—a real threat to the honeybee. Beekeepers will gladly take the bees off your hands. I'm on the call list; that means if someone calls with a swarm to be removed, you have to stop everything and go. That can be time-consuming. There is no charge, but a donation is appreciated and it goes directly to the bee association for bee education programs.

What expenses are involved?

Ed: I bought my first package of bees for $100 and set up my hive in the backyard. I'm handy with tools, so I built the hive boxes and frames that hold the honeycomb myself. You can also purchase fully assembled boxes at a bee supply store.

I bought a bee suit, which is an absolute must for this hobby, soft leather gloves, a smoker, and a small tool used for prying open the boxes. Figure start-up costs to be $300 to $400. Additionally, for my first honey harvest, I purchased an electric extractor, which is a centrifuge device for removing the pure honey from the frames. Those can run $500 to $750, but totally worth it, as the alternative is a tedious hand-crank system.

I bought plastic honey bottles, self-sealing caps, and my wife ordered professional-looking labels. Those costs vary depending on how much honey you have. The production of my bees surprised me. My first year, I had forty pounds of honey, the second year over a hundred pounds. I give a lot of it away to my family, friends, and commercial construction clients. I do sell some to help defray the costs, but so far, I haven't turned it into a business.

Be sure to check the zoning laws in your town or city. My hives grew and I picked up swarms in the spring. In fact, I had to find two additional locations for my growing hives. Then my first winter hit, and I lost half of my hives. So, be prepared for the cycle.

Do you belong to an organization connected with your hobby?

Ed: Yes, I belong to a local beekeeper association. It is one of the largest in the state of California, with over four hundred members coming from surrounding counties. The meetings are once a month and have a set format, beginning with a question-and-answer forum, which is helpful. Old-timers, both recreational and commercial, give a great deal of helpful information freely.

Each meeting usually has a lecturer on a variety of topics, such as biology, disease prevention, or special techniques. We are lucky to have many university researchers close by and they are generous with their time as presenters. Also, major companies such as Häagen-Dazs and Costco are strong supporters of local beekeepers.

What are the most rewarding aspects of this passionate pursuit?

Ed: I like the final packaging of honey. It's extremely rewarding. The production process, and the mechanics of how the colony functions as a superorganism, also fascinates me. The bees work as a team and most of them will never see the results of their work because the average life-span of a worker bee is four to six weeks.

Of course, the dark side of this pursuit is bee stings. And yes, I get "tagged," as the beekeepers call it. The most I've gotten is six stings at a time. I keep the Benadryl in stock. If you don't know if you are allergic to bee stings, you *should have a physician test you, and if you are allergic, this is definitely not the hobby for you.*

What do you see evolving in the future for your pursuit?

Ed: I've always had an entrepreneurial bent, so I probably will transfer that in my full retirement. I might like to try the commercial angle. There are approximately six thousand almond growers in my state and they produce a hundred percent of the domestic supply and 70 percent of worldwide production. Every year, farmers pay beekeepers to supply the bees needed to pollinate their orchards and crops. I live close to one of the most prolific agricultural areas in the nation, so I might try it. That is probably my next step.

Colony Collapse Disorder

Honeybees have received a lot of attention lately. The *New York Times* reported in October 2010 that in the United States alone, 20 to 40 percent of the bee colonies since 2006 have suffered *colony collapse*. In Canada, 35 percent of bee colonies have disappeared over the past three years, and according to the UK's Bee Farmers' Association, up to 50 percent of bee colonies in Britain were lost over the 2012–2013 winter season. Many other pollinators, such as butterfly species are in serious decline too.

Neonicotinoids

The name of this new class of insecticides literally means "new nicotine-like insecticides." They are much more toxic to invertebrates, like insects, than they are to mammals, birds, and other higher organisms. One thing that has made neonicotinoid insecticides popular in pest control is their water solubility, which when applied to the soil, are absorbed by the plants.

Ed: I read an article on Yahoo! News recently that in Europe, an international panel of twenty-nine scientists called the Task Force on Systemic Pesticides found there was clear evidence of harm to honeybees, butterflies, and other species from neonicotinoids. The task force said these pesticides can persist in soil for more than a thousand days, and the compounds into which they break down can be more toxic than the original, active ingredients. Neonicotinoids are five thousand to ten thousand times more toxic to bees than DDT, a pesticide that is banned for agricultural use.

Do you have any advice for interested readers?

Ed: One of the most important things I would like people to be aware of is the toxic effect the use of neonicotinoid pesticides has on bees.

FASCINATING FACTS

- There are 20,000 different species of bees in the world.
- Honeybees fly up to 15 mph and their wings beat 200 times per second or 12,000 beats per minute. They fly the equivalent of more than twice around the world in their lifetime and tap 2 million flowers to gather a pound of honey.
- Archaeologists found 2,000-year-old jars of honey in Egyptian tombs.
- The average person in the United States consumes 1.3 pounds of honey per year.
- The top five honey-producing states for 2012 in order of production are North Dakota, South Dakota, Florida, California, and Minnesota.
- In 2010, the United States produced only 39% of the honey needed for domestic consumption and imported the rest.
- August 17 is National Honey Bee Day in the United States and Canada.

Resources

Websites

American Beekeeping Federation: abfnet.org.

Beekeepers associations (Bee Culture magazine's website has a link to many of them): http://bit.ly/1owuRRS.

Bee clubs and associations throughout the United States by state: http://bit.ly/1AmmsFJ.

The Bee Source originated in 1997 by a hobbyist for beekeepers and beekeeping. It has more than 14,000 registered members and is the most active online beekeeping community of its kind in the world: http://bit.ly/1ziXOUU.

List of bee-friendly plants: http://bit.ly/1q4HmlI.

The National Honey Board: honey.com.

Videos

There are many videos on beginner beekeeping on YouTube, such as *A Year in the Life of a Beekeeper*: http://bit.ly/1owvwmj.

Reading

Alethea Morrison, *Homegrown Honey Bees: An Absolute Beginner's Guide to Beekeeping Your First Year, from Hiving to Honey Harvest* (North Adams, MA: Storey Publishing 2013).

Roger A. Morse, *The ABC & XYZ of Bee Culture: an Encyclopedia Pertaining to the Scientific and Practical Culture of the Honey Bees*. Medina, Ohio: A.I. Root Co, 1990.

Diana Sammataro and Alphonse Avitabile, *The Beekeeper's Handbook* (Ithaca: Comstock Pub. Associates, Division of Cornell University Press, 2011).

Michael Schacker, *A Spring Without Bees: How Colony Collapse Disorder Has Endangered Our Food Supply* (Guilford, Conn: Lyons Press, 2008).

American Bee Journal: http://bit.ly/1rJi417.

Bee Culture magazine: beeculture.com.

CHAPTER 3

Bird Watcher and Conservationist

When we try to pick out anything by itself, we find it hitched to everything else in the Universe.
—John Muir

According to the US Fish and Wildlife Service, there are currently 51.3 million birders in the United States. Some people make a distinction between the terms *birders* and *bird watchers*; however, in this chapter the terms are used interchangeably as the activity of observing wild birds.

Bird watching is a good way to appreciate nature and the outdoors. Birds are common throughout the United States and offer an easy opportunity to observe a wide variety. There are 981 species of birds found north of the Mexican border that are accepted by the American Birding Association (ABA) as North American birds. Some birds are colorful and highly visible, while others conceal themselves within nature and are harder to find. It's easy to get started: all you need is a pair of binoculars and a good guidebook.

Bird Watching Basics

The National Audubon Society's website gives a detailed primer of the basics of bird watching. It involves the following elements: knowing where to look and what to look for, knowing how to listen, and knowing the appropriate etiquette when approaching bird habitats. The key to bird watching is to be attentive and aware of the bird's small expressive movements, the sounds it makes, and where it might be. When bird watching, observe wild birds in their natural habitat, learn to identify birds and understand what they are doing. Wherever you live, you'll probably discover many species that are easy to find in your area.

Bird Conservation

Bird conservation groups play a vital role in increasing awareness of the fragile ecosystem and the strain our human society places on many birds. Some problems these groups point to are habitat loss, overexploitation, chemical toxins and pollution, and diseases. Government agencies, research universities, nonprofit conservation groups, and ordinary citizens make collective efforts to address these problems and provide programs to reverse bird declines and maintain healthy populations. Conservation efforts identify population declines and their causes, and find biological solutions, such as habitat preservation, used to combat the underlying causes of bird population declines.

Photo by Deb Allen

John, birder and conservationist

John is seventy-three years old and a retired international banker who lives in New York City. He and his wife lived in Korea for two years and they travel extensively.

John: I grew up in the country on a lake in Wisconsin. I always liked wildlife. When I was a small boy, a family friend took me bird watching. I observed a woodcock and a goldfinch. The woodcock was totally camouflaged. I think a lot of children are taken early on by a parent or relative to discover the natural world. I have to say I wasn't overly fascinated the first time. Birds grew on me over time. They're beautiful and they're everywhere.

How did you get started?

John: I was in international banking and charged with opening an office in Seoul, South Korea. It was there that I became deeply involved with cranes. Cranes are magnificent birds. They are stunningly beautiful. They are large, and you can't go wrong in finding them. Cranes are an important symbol in several Asian cultures and in the Native American culture too.

Crane Symbolism

In Korean culture, the red-crested white crane symbolizes longevity, spirituality, and nobility. It was considered the bird of the immortals. It is said that people who lived noble, solitary lives became cranes when they died.

Cranes are associated with good luck in many Native American tribes. Native fishermen used to consider it a good omen to see a crane while fishing. In some Native American folklore, the crane plays the role of peacemaker. In others, he is notable for his vanity. To the Native American Anishinabe (Ojibwa) tribes, cranes represent leadership and skill at speaking, and the Cheyenne associate Sandhill cranes with lightning.

John: *One day while living in Korea, I saw a newspaper with a picture of a crane on the front. I asked the secretary to translate the story for me. She told me that a famous American scientist, Dr. George Archibald, would be talking at the university nearby. So my wife and I attended the lecture.*

Dr. Archibald, the cofounder of the International Crane Foundation, was involved in research work on cranes in the Demilitarized Zone, which is a strip of land running across the Korean Peninsula that serves as a buffer zone between North and South Korea. The DMZ is a critical habitat for cranes. During his talk, he showed a map of various worldwide locations of crane populations. One crane he discussed was a Tibetan black-necked crane. I had done some trekking in Nepal years before and, after his presentation, I told him that I had seen such a crane. He got excited because he said visitors were no longer able to get permission to go into the area to see them. And that's how my conservation efforts began. Dr. Archibald asked me to set up a crane conservation group in South Korea. I've been a board member for the ICF for twenty-five years.

The International Crane Foundation (ICF)

The foundation that John became involved with was founded in 1973, and combines research, captive breeding and reintroduction, landscape restoration, and education to safeguard the world's fifteen crane species. In the United States, ICF is advancing efforts to understand our native Sandhill cranes better and is working to restore the endangered whooping crane to protect this species from extinction.

Describe a setting where your activity takes place.

John: I live across the street from Central Park and I can walk into one of the top ten birding "hot spots" in the country. New York City is right in the flight path of the eastern migration. The best seasons for birding are spring and fall because of migration. You can find a hundred species in the spring.

There are bird walks conducted all the time in Central Park. Recently, a group I joined spotted a long-eared owl and a pair of Baltimore orioles. It is unusual to see those birds there. I walk around the park and really enjoy myself. I always bring a pair of binoculars with me on my walks.

You can "bird" anywhere throughout the United States, from Cape May, New Jersey, to Point Reyes, California. My wife and I traveled to Los Angeles recently. While there, I saw yellow Chevron parakeets and hummingbirds in Pershing Square, downtown L.A. If you go to the Platte River in Nebraska in March, you'll see one of the greatest sights in nature: five hundred thousand Sandhill cranes stopping off on their migration from Canada to Texas. It rivals an African safari in magnificence. The Sandhill crane and the whooping crane are the only two cranes found in the US.

What equipment and expenses are involved?

John: Start simply. Join a couple of bird walks. The National Audubon Society has local chapters all over, and many local museums offer bird walks. If you enjoy it, invest in a good $200 pair of binoculars. Don't spend too much. I use Swarovski binoculars, 10 x 42. My wife has binoculars that are 8 x 32, which aren't as heavy. For a starter, use 8 x 32; or if you're more advanced or by the ocean, the 10 x 42s are good.

Choosing Binoculars

Look for binoculars that have a wide enough field of view to locate a bird and then follow its movements. The instrument must provide a bright enough image to allow you to distinguish subtle features, particularly in dim light, and also focus quickly so that you can get a sharp image of a fast-moving bird.

Binoculars are described using two numbers for example 8 x 32, or 10 x 40, or 8 x 21. The first number tells you the magnification, while the second tells you the size of the objective lens, in millimeters. Binoculars that have a bigger ratio between the magnification and the objective lens size will always give a sharper, brighter image than ones with a smaller ratio. (For instance, 8 x 42 provides a brighter, sharper image than an 8 x 32 or a 10 x 42.)

John: Just wear old clothes, a hat, and sunscreen. Invest in a good field guide. Sibley's guide is an easy one to use. It is detailed and has a lot of how-to information. When I'm traveling, I use the National Geographic Field Guide to the Birds of Eastern North America or Western North America.

Locating Birds

John: Good birders pick up a species by its calls; for example, identifying a blue jay scolding an owl. I know maybe thirty calls. Some enthusiasts can pick the sound out first and then locate the bird. Some can even differentiate between twenty-five different warblers' calls in the spring.

A lot of bird field guides now have apps that you can download onto your iPhone or Android. I was with a serious birder in a marsh in Wisconsin and we observed some tundra swans. I thought they were trumpeter swans, which are quite rare. The other fellow activated his app, which brought up a picture and he lined up the picture with the actual bird, and you could see it was a tundra. Then, later in the marsh area, he downloaded the call of the Virginia rail and he played the call. You can download the different species' calls, pick the one you think it is, play it, and see if it replicates the one you hear. Bird watching has gotten increasingly "techno."

How much time do you spend on this pursuit?

John: It depends. Like most retired people, I get busy and find I never have as much time to do things as I think I'm going to have. On a Saturday morning, I'll spend three hours birding. I've traveled for long weekends to Montana or Oregon with my wife and fit in a little bird watching. I've also traveled to places exclusively to see birds with organizations such as the American Bird Conservancy.

Last summer, I spent three weeks in a remote high desert of Mongolia with Earthwatch. I worked with the Denver Zoo Foundation on their research project to study the breeding ecology, developmental biology, and movement patterns of Cinereous vultures, which are the largest raptor in Eurasia.

Do you have a "life list"?

John: Many people do keep a "life list," counting all the species that they've seen in their lifetime. I don't do that. I keep what I call a "year list." I use the American Birding Association checklist for North American birds for some favorite locations that I frequent. I've used that for years.

The ABA Checklist

The American Birding Association assigns codes 1 through 6 to identify the frequency of sightings of North American species of birds: 1) regularly occurring in the locale and widespread; 2) regularly occurring in the locale but somewhat affected by lower densities or difficult to detect; 3) rare (annual but in low numbers); 4) casual (not annually seen); 5) accidental (seldom recorded in that area); and 6) cannot be found (probably extinct or in a captive breeding program).

John: So far in this early part of the year I have seen 115 species, 3 of which I would term as "lifers" because I had never seen them before. By checking the eBird report, which is an online database of reported sightings managed by the Cornell Lab of Ornithology and National Audubon Society, I learned, for example, of the sighting of a common poorwill at a location I happened to be visiting.

Earthwatch

Earthwatch is a nonprofit organization that combines volunteer travel opportunities for individuals from all walks of life with scientific research expeditions to conserve wildlife and the environment. Earthwatch sends volunteers on expeditions all over the world.

John: Earthwatch puts laypeople like you and me together with scientists and researchers. It's not only birding. You're part of a team project that may continue for eight to nine years. Expeditions center on archeology and culture, climate change, ocean health, and wildlife and ecosystems. You pay your own way, and costs for an expedition are around $3,000. My first expedition involved research on Orca whales off the San Juan Islands, Washington. Another trip involved leatherback sea turtles in Saint Croix, Virgin Islands.

What is the biggest danger to birds?

John: The American Bird Conservancy has developed the Strategic Bird Conservation Framework, a pyramid, which builds capacity, eliminates threats, conserves watch-list species, and halts extinctions. The biggest cause of bird deaths is collisions with glass. Each year 700 to 900 million birds die from collisions with picture windows in homes and windows in skyscrapers. You can help by putting a translucent tape on the windows during migration season. A German company is testing a glass embedded with prints and patterns that are undetectable to the human eye but prevent birds from flying into windows.

The second biggest danger is feral cats and pets that wander outdoors. Cats kill a couple hundred million birds per year. They kill ground-nesting birds. Other hazards are pesticides and habitat destruction. One example of a threat to a species by habitat destruction is the fragmentation of the Florida scrub jay's habitat. The land is carved up into neighborhoods and houses built. The birds don't want to move from their home, and this land development is one of the reasons for the jay's population decline.

Citizen Science

John: There are many opportunities for citizen involvement. People move over from bird watching; there's a progression to conservation. One of the best studies done on White-crown sparrows was by a woman at home watching from her picture window. She recorded their behavior and their activities. She was a citizen scientist. Cornell Laboratory of Ornithology has a huge citizen bird-watch program.

Annual Events

The National Audubon Society conducts the Christmas Bird Count (CBC) between mid-December and early January, involving more than 50,000 participants each year. The all-day count takes census of early-winter bird populations and the results are compiled into the longest running database in ornithology.

The Great Backyard Bird Count is conducted every February and is similar in purpose to the CBC. The four-day event engages bird watchers of all ages in counting birds to create a real-time snapshot of bird populations. The data collected helps researchers at the Cornell Lab of Ornithology and the National Audubon Society learn more about how birds are doing, and how to protect them and the environment we share.

Project Feederwatch, organized by Cornell, goes on all winter, surveying the birds that visit feeders at backyards, nature centers, community areas, and other locales throughout North America. In combination with other events, Feederwatch helps scientists track broad-scale movements of winter bird populations and long-term trends in bird distribution and abundance.

What is the most rewarding aspect of this activity?

John: To me it's the beauty of being in nature, of being surrounded by nature and the contribution I can give. I prefer to go on trips where I can mix enjoying the cultural aspects of the area and birding. I've been to some beautiful places, such as to Bhutan with its extraordinary people. I've also been to Cape May, New Jersey, one of the best places in the country for bird-watching.

Conservation is important to me. In the 1940s, there were less than twenty whooping cranes left in the US. Now, because of conservation efforts, we're up to over five hundred cranes. I've worked very hard with the National Crane Foundation and they've made a huge, critical difference.

Any advice for beginners?

John: Don't be frustrated. There are six hundred to seven hundred species in the typical field guide. Start in your own neighborhood. You might be able to identify a robin or a cardinal or a sparrow already, but you might not know that there are five or six species within that group in your yard. Learn to take binoculars with you when you go out hiking or for a walk. If you really enjoy birding, think about the future of those creatures.

FASCINATING FACTS

- Birds have hollow bones, which helps them fly.
- A group of larks is called an *exaltation*, a group of geese is a *gaggle*, a group of crows is a *murder*, and a group of owls is referred to as a *parliament*.
- Mockingbirds can imitate many sounds, from a squeaking door to a cat meowing. Thomas Jefferson kept a pet mockingbird and taught the bird to ride on his shoulder and take food from his lips.
- Peregrine falcons may reach speeds of 200 mph when diving for prey. They use their balled-up talons to knock out their prey, and then catch the hapless, falling bird before it hits the ground or water.
- The golden plover flies 2,400 miles from North American breeding grounds to South American wintering grounds and arrives with only a two-ounce weight loss.

Resources

Websites

American Birding Association: aba.org/.

Bird cams: http://bit.ly/1khCjAE.

Cornell Laboratory of Ornithology: allaboutbirds.org.

Earthwatch Environmental Volunteer Expeditions: http://bit.ly/1mSbPAj.

eBird Report: ebird.org.

Identifying birds: whatbird.com.

International Crane Foundation: https://www.savingcranes.org.

National Audubon Society: audubon.org.

Apps

iBird Pro Guide App; Peterson Birds of North America Birding App; Sibley eGuide to the Birds of North America App; Audubon Birds Field Guide App; National Geographic Birding App: http://bit.ly/1k2k7uD.

Reading

Les Beletsky, *Global Birding: Traveling the World in Search of Birds* (Washington, DC: National Geographic Society, 2010).

Jon L. Dunn and Jonathan Alderfer, *National Geographic Field Guide to the Birds of Western North America* and *National Geographic Field Guide to the Birds of Eastern North America* (Washington, DC: National Geographic, 2008).

Pete Dunne, *Pete Dunne on Bird Watching* (Boston, MA: Houghton Mifflin, 2003).

Stephen Kress, *National Audubon Society Birding Handbook* (London, UK: Dorling Kindersley, 2000).

David Sibley, *Sibley's Birding Basics* and *Sibley Guide to Bird Life and Behavior* (New York, NY: Knopf, 2013).

Bird Watchers Digest: http://bit.ly/1tQ5pqY.

Citizen Science Events

Christmas Bird Count: http://bit.ly/1khCCvA.

The Great Backyard Bird Count: http://bit.ly/1td2ZVO.

Project Feederwatch: http://bit.ly/1rMPhqJ.

CHAPTER 4

Habitat Restorer

We do not inherit the land from our ancestors;
we borrow it from our children.
—Native American proverb

An ecosystem includes all of the living things (plants, animals, and organisms) interacting with one another. In the twenty-first century, we have developed an increased awareness of this interaction and the major challenges affecting our codependence. Healthy habitats preserve our water, increase our food supply, and protect our quality of life and economic interests. By restoring lost habitats, wildlife regains its ability to provide food, water, cover, and places to raise young.

Habitat Loss

Habitat loss is a serious threat to ecosystems. There are three major kinds of habitat loss, according to the National Wildlife Federation: (1) habitat destruction, resulting from clearing old-growth forests for timber or draining wetland areas to use the land for raising crops; (2) habitat fragmentation caused by dams and water diversions affecting aquatic species; and (3) habitat degradation caused by pollution or invasive plant species. The current world population must find a balance between the need for resources and the condition of the ecosystems for the next generations.

Habitat Restoration

The goal of habitat restoration is to identify disturbed habitats and restore the native flora and fauna to ensure the continued use of the land by both wildlife and humans. Healthy forests control erosion and maintain good water quality in our lakes and rivers. Returning disturbed land to health adds to existing habitats, helps to protect many species, and restores the balance of our ecosystem. As good citizens of this planet, we have a responsibility to maintain and preserve our natural resources for future generations.

Janie, cataloging and preserving plants at Great Smoky Mountain National Park

Janie is sixty-six years old and lives west of Knoxville, Tennessee. She and her husband built their home on a half acre of land amid oak and hickory trees and lots of tulip poplar trees. The tulip poplar is the state tree of Tennessee. Through a program sponsored by the National Wildlife Federation, Janie's backyard is a "Certified Wildlife Habitat," one of more than 150,000 sites designated as such across the country. In addition to working on her backyard habitat restoration, she drives fifty miles each way to Smoky Mountains National Park, where she volunteers to help park botanists with native-plant restoration work.

Janie: I graduated from the University of Tennessee with a natural science degree, a major in botany. Originally, I was an English major, but I took one course, Botany 101, and switched majors. The professors and the field trips opened my eyes and I developed a love for all of nature, especially wildflowers. When I couldn't find a full-time teaching position in my field, I got a job in banking and stayed there for thirty-three years. Now I'm using my botany. I've come full-circle.

How did you first get interested in restoring habitats?

Janie: Many contacts I've made started me on the road to my passionate pursuit. When I retired, my friend of forty years approached and asked me to go with her to a garden club. We both ended up joining. Through further networking, I was introduced to the Smoky Mountain National Parks group.

I've have the opportunity to work with specialists in the botany field through my volunteer work at the Twin Creeks Science and Education Center. I work on a variety of projects, replanting stolen native plants.

Poaching Problems

American ginseng is a native plant in the Smoky Mountains. These wild roots are a highly prized tonic, especially in Asian markets. Dried ginseng root is used in medicines, teas, and other health products. Ginseng harvesting in the park has always been illegal. But the National Park Service reported that in 2013, law enforcement rangers seized more than 800 illegally poached ginseng roots in Great Smoky Mountain National Park.

Janie: The rangers have a lot to do. They usually find poachers when they stop them on a driving violation, then find a trunk full of ginseng. Poachers sell wild ginseng roots for up to $1,000 per dry pound. The plant has a lot of medicinal uses.

The park plants ginseng in order to ensure the continuity of the species. For the last five years, I've assisted the botanists by weighing, aging, and dyeing the ginseng roots before we plant them. We take a "short, three-mile walk" straight up a mountain up to the eight-hundred to thousand-foot elevation to plant the ginseng. Since the average age of the team is half my age, it's challenging for me.

The park also has problems with people poaching ramps and galax. Ramp is a wild leek native to North America and very popular in haute cuisine. Ramps are endangered plants in the park and need to be protected.

Galax is a small, cool-weather plant with broad, waxy, heart-shaped leaves. It is a popular plant used in floral arrangements because the leaves hold their green color for an extended time. The larger the leaf, the more desirable it is. Several web-based wholesale floral supply companies sell galax for as high as 80 cents to $1.70 per leaf, depending on the size. The US Fish and Wildlife Service estimates that as many as 3 billion galax leaves are harvested each year from the southern Appalachians—some taken with a valid permit, but much of it poached illegally. Law enforcement faces constant challenges to stop poachers and protect the galax plants.

Garden Habitat Restoration

Janie: As a member of a garden club, I automatically receive a subscription to Volunteer Gardener magazine. The magazine had an article on qualifying a garden through the National Wildlife Federation as a certified wildlife habitat. The article discussed how few certified gardens the state of Tennessee had, so I started providing information on how to establish a garden as a certified wildlife habitat in my garden club. It's a learning process. Many people don't realize that by joining groups such as the NWF, it helps reintroduce different species of animals that are endangered or extinct.

The Certified Wildlife Habitat Program

The information on the National Wildlife Federation website helps people recognize what good habitats their property already has, and what they can add to encourage nature and make welcoming habitats to attract wildlife such as birds and butterflies. Use of the NWF online assessment and planning guide is free. The website details the process of creating a habitat and then applying for certification.

Creating a Wildlife Habitat

The first step in the certification process is creating a wildlife habitat by providing food, water, cover, and a place for wildlife to raise their young. A wildlife habitat must have the following elements:

Food Sources: There must be at least three sources of food. Examples include seeds from a plant, berries, nectar, foliage/twigs, nuts, fruits, sap, pollen, suet, a bird feeder, a squirrel feeder, a hummingbird feeder, or a butterfly feeder.

Water Supply: Wildlife needs sources of clean water for many purposes, including drinking, bathing, and reproduction. Your habitat should have at least one of these two water sources: natural sources such as ponds, lakes, rivers, springs, oceans and wetlands; or human-made sources such as birdbaths, puddling areas for butterflies, installed ponds, or rain gardens.

Cover: Wildlife needs at least two places to find shelter from the weather and predators and that shelter should come from the following sources: wooded areas, a bramble patch, ground cover, a rock pile or wall, a cave, a roosting box, dense shrubs or thickets, evergreens, brush, log piles, a burrow, a meadow or prairie, a water garden, or a pond.

A Place to Raise Young: Creating a wildlife habitat is about creating a place for the entire life cycle of a species to occur, from tadpole to frog, from caterpillar to butterfly. There must be at least two places for wildlife to engage in courtship behavior, mate, and then bear and raise their young. It is necessary to set up a nesting box, a birdhouse, or a brush shelter. Many habitat features that serve as cover can double as locations where wildlife can raise their young.

Wildlife Habitat Certification

After creating the wildlife habitat, the second and last step is to pay a $20 fee, which includes a personalized certificate, a one-year membership in the National Wildlife Federation and a subscription to the NWF magazine. There is also the option to order a sign that designates the area as a certified wildlife habitat.

How did you get started?

Janie: After we were married, my husband and I built a house and the contractor's secretary gave me wildflowers for my garden. I developed a beautiful collection. That's how it started. I went online and read about the habitat program. I already had many of the elements required, such as the wooded area and flowers. I built a pond with Shubunkin, which is a cross between a goldfish and a carp. They look a lot like Koi.

I had to eliminate a few invasive plants. I added native plants and perennials that attract and provide for the pollinators: bees, flies, hummingbirds and butterflies. During the evaluating process, I found I needed more ground cover. I piled small rocks up against the potting shed for a shelter area for small critters.

I didn't have an owl house or a bat house. My husband gave me those for Christmas. He put them way in the back of the yard thirty feet up in a tree. I put wood chips and shavings in the owl house because they don't bring nesting materials to their nests. I can hear the owls back behind the house.

What special equipment and tools do you use, and what expenses are involved?

Janie: If you have a backyard or a garden, you probably have many of the tools needed to develop a wildlife habitat. You need a shovel, rake, trowel, and scissors to begin. You can buy tools inexpensively at garage sales and discount stores. For clothing, I wear my red paisley boots and heavy socks to keep my feet warm. I usually wear long-sleeved shirts and gloves.

I buy forty pounds of birdseed that will last three months. Birdseed with sunflower seeds attracts songbirds. You can have twenty-five to thirty songbirds on a feeder if it's big enough.

I try different nurseries. I no longer buy annuals, just natives and perennials, and I like to buy from people who grow their own plants. I plant Nigel thistle because the American goldfinches love it. I grow herbs and tomatoes. I have them in elevated gardens to keep out the rabbits. I have a compost pile. I don't buy mulch anymore; I just grind up leaves. The plants love it and it's recycling.

I kept my start-up costs low by adding to my yard gradually, building my own birdhouses and birdbath. The birds don't like to get very deep in the water. A dish with a couple of stones is all that is needed.

The Garden Shed

Janie: My husband is very supportive. He bought me a twelve-by-eighteen-foot potting shed to keep all my gardening tools. It has electricity, shelves and a ceiling fan. *My sister made me curtains for the window. I put my Wildlife Habitat plaque on my shed.*

How much time do you spend on this pursuit?

Janie: My husband and I love to be outdoors, weather permitting. When it's nice out, we're out all day. After we get the yard prepared for the winter, my husband and I will spend an hour or two there every other day. We start in March with lime, fertilizer and grass seed and work out in the yard straight through until November.

What is the most rewarding aspect of this activity?

Janie: Being one with nature is rewarding. I like just kicking back and relaxing. I sit down on my bench by the pond and put my feet in on a hot summer day and watch the birds. I think it's important to give back to nature. I can influence others by setting a good example. My neighbor just bought her daughter a bluebird house and a bird feeder; she's going to certify her house as a wildlife habitat.

I also have lots of fun with my garden. I have a fairy garden, in which everything is in miniature. A fairy garden appeals to the whimsical side in gardeners. I hang chimes and little swirly things in my fig tree and close to windows to keep the birds from flying into the glass.

I planted lantana to encourage the butterflies to come into the garden. The Monarch is becoming extinct in this area of Tennessee. They aren't migrating to this part of the country anymore. Naturalists are encouraging people to plant milkweed to encourage the butterflies. The Monarchs migrate from Mexico and the milkweed is their host plant. There are many people out there using pesticides to kill the milkweed, which creates a risk to the Monarch as well.

Most people buy annuals because of the color, but it is important to plant native plants. People should avoid buying invasive plants and using harmful pesticides. There are many organic products available today that are not harmful to plants or animals.

Do you have any plans that may evolve within this hobby?

Janie: One of my dreams is to become a Master Gardener. It's very difficult to gain entrance into the program in this area. I was accepted in the University of Tennessee Extension Program for January 2015. The program involves three months of study, January through March, and then forty hours of internship work, which I plan on doing at the Smoky Mountain National Park.

After I receive my certification as a Master Gardener, I can give presentations at garden clubs and teach courses. Certain classes are required every year to keep certification up to date.

Other Habitat Conservancy Groups to Investigate

American Rivers

This is a nonprofit organization involved in protecting and restoring rivers nationwide. Their programs focus on dam removal and other river-related issues. Since 2001, more than 100 fish-passage restoration projects have been funded under this partnership with the National Oceanic and Atmospheric Administration (NOAA).

BAMONA

The Butterflies and Moths of North America (BAMONA) project is an ambitious effort to collect and provide access to quality-controlled data about butterflies and moths for the continent of North America from Panama to Canada. Citizen scientists of all ages and experience levels participate by taking photographs of butterflies and moths and then submitting their observations.

Earthwatch

Earthwatch combines volunteer travel opportunities for individuals from all walks of life with scientific research expeditions to conserve wildlife and the environment. The nonprofit sends volunteers, at their own expense, on expeditions all over the world. Expeditions center on archeology and culture, climate change, ocean health, wildlife and ecosystems.

The Nature Conservancy

The Nature Conservancy is the leading conservation organization working around the world to protect ecologically important lands and waters. Founded in 1951, the Conservancy has protected more than 119 million acres of land and thousands of miles of rivers worldwide, operating more than 100 marine conservation projects globally. The Conservancy works in all fifteen states and more than thirty-five countries.

Pheasants Forever

Pheasants Forever (PF) is dedicated to the conservation of pheasants, quail, and other wildlife through habitat improvements, public awareness, education, and land-management policies and programs. Pheasants and quail share a common need for flowering plants, such as sunflowers and milkweed, with pollinating insects like honeybees, butterflies, beetles, and bats. PF members work together with many other organizations to create thriving wildlife habitats.

FASCINATING FACTS

- It can take a minimum of 500 years to make 1 inch of topsoil.
- A tablespoon of soil has more living organisms than there are people on Earth right now.
- The United States has more than 250,000 rivers. That's 3.5 million river miles. Sixty five percent of drinking water comes from rivers and streams
- Butterflies can see red, green, and yellow. Worldwide, there are approximately 28,000 species of butterflies. There are about 725 species in the United States and Canada.
- You can tell the temperature outside by listening to a cricket. Count the number of chirps in 15 seconds, and then add 37. The sum will be the approximate temperature in degrees Fahrenheit.
- According to the US Department of Energy, planting just three shade trees around your home can save between $100 and $250 per year in energy costs.

Resources

General Information

Environmental conservation organizations: http://abt.cm/UDi442.

The National Oceanic and Atmospheric Administration (NOAA) Restoration Center has restored more than 2,000 projects nationwide. See collective restoration efforts around the country: http://1.usa.gov/1nvO5Hh.

The National Wildlife Federation: nwf.org.

The Nature Conservancy: nature.org.

Pheasants Forever: pheasantsforever.org.

Xerces Society: xerces.org.

Volunteer Programs

Certified Wildlife Habitat Program: http://bit.ly/1nvQXUr and http://on.fb.me/1lJTxl8.

BAMONA: butterfliesandmoths.org.

Native Plant and Wildlife Websites

Top 10 Native Plants by Region: http://bit.ly/WZrKaK.

Lady Bird Johnson Wildflower Center's Native Plant Information Network. Search for native plant information by traits or names: wildflower.org.

Plants that attract butterflies to your garden: http://bit.ly/1tQbJPb.

To obtain a list of butterflies in your state or county: butterfliesandmoths.org.

Projects

Build a bat house: http://bit.ly/Uvvtve.

Build a bee house: http://bit.ly/UDkDTJ.

Videos

Hundreds of videos on butterflies, dragonflies, hummingbirds, birds, frogs, and wildlife gardening: http://bit.ly/UDkGPt.

The Volunteer Gardner, produced by Nashville Public Television, features local experts who share gardening tips, upcoming garden events, recipes, and visits to private gardens: http://bit.ly/1pkpBzU.

Reading

Bill Birchard, *Nature's Keepers: The Remarkable Story of How the Nature Conservancy Became the Largest Environmental Group in the World* (Hoboken, NJ: John Wiley & Sons, 2005).

Eric Lee-Mäder, *Attracting Native Pollinators: Protecting North America's Bees and Butterflies* (North Adams, MA: Storey Publishing, 2011).

Douglas W. Tallamy, *Bringing Nature Home: How You Can Sustain Wildlife with Native Plants, Updated and Expanded* (Portland: Timber Press, 2009).

CHAPTER 5

Mushroom Hunter

All mushrooms are edible, but some only once.
—Croatian proverb

Mushrooms are fungi, a kingdom of organisms separate from plants, animals, and bacteria. *Mycology* is the branch of biology dealing with fungi, and a *mycophile* is a devotee of mushrooms, such as one whose hobby is hunting wild edible mushrooms.

People have been collecting mushrooms for at least 3,600 years for food and medicinal purposes. Archaeological history identifies ancient Greece and Rome, China, and parts of South America and Africa as locations where inhabitants valued the mushroom for diet and health. The fruiting body of the mushroom is found aboveground, leaving the root system belowground. This differs from the mushroom's elite cousin, the truffle, which is extremely difficult to find because it grows entirely beneath the ground with nothing growing above ground to signal its presence.

Mushrooms lack chlorophyll and must obtain their nourishment from the ground that they grow in. Mushrooms frequently grow at the bottom of trees, in the tree root zone. They can also be found on dead or fallen trees, in meadows, on live trees, and in forests. Since mushrooms are composed mainly of water, they materialize when days are moist and misty, usually in the spring and the fall.

Mushroom Myths

According to environmental educator, Terra Brie Stewart, myths about mushrooms have existed throughout history. Many ancient people believed that mushrooms were formed when bolts of lightning hit the ground. Others thought witches or evil spirits created them and you could catch a disease merely by touching them. Still others believed that *fairy rings*, which are the places where mushrooms grow outward in circles, were dangerous places where anyone who trespassed would face mortal consequences. These ideas all seemed to come from the ability of mushrooms to "appear out of nowhere," usually after a rainstorm.

Global Pastime

Mushroom hunting is prevalent in most of Europe, especially in the Baltic and Slavic countries, where it is a common family activity. It is widespread in the northwestern Indian subcontinent, as well as in Australia, Japan, Korea, and Canada. In the United States, mushroom hunting is popular in Appalachia, the Midwest, and the Northeast, and on the West Coast from Northern California through Oregon and Washington.

Harriet, the mycophile

After many vacations traveling throughout the Pacific Northwest, Harriet and her husband left Illinois and retired to Eugene, Oregon. Harriet had formerly worked as a garden consultant involved in the landscaping and maintenance of residential spaces.

Harriet: I always enjoyed my fingers in the soil. Since we didn't know many people in our new town, I joined the local hiking club and the Cascade Mycological Society to make new friends and enjoy the outdoors. In the past, I never paid much attention to mushrooms other than to eat them, but now I'm an avid mycophile.

Many Interests

Although some people who become mushroom hunters are pursuing the epicurean experience of good food, according to Harriet many are academics interested in the science of fungi.

Harriet: With DNA analysis available now, it has become apparent that many of the scientific classifications from the last decade of the twentieth century are no longer accurate. Some mushroom hunters are interested in the role mushrooms play in remediation of forests affected by logging. My club, the Cascade Mycological Society, works with the US Forest Service and the Bureau of Land Management on regional research and monitoring programs. Other mycophiles grow their own mushrooms commercially.

Still other mushroom hunters advocate for the study and use of fungi in fields such as medicine, pesticides, and pollution control. Paul Stamets puts forward these ideas in his 2005 book *Mycelium Running: How Mushrooms Can Help Save the World*. There are also enthusiasts who appreciate the artistic value of the mushroom: photographers, sketch artists, dye makers, and those who create spore prints—important diagnostic characters in most handbooks for identifying mushrooms. Some jewelry artists create mushroom earrings. Lastly, there are those who are looking for the magic mushrooms or "shrooms" that cause a hallucinogenic drug effect.

What is the most rewarding aspect of this activity?

Harriet: I enjoy the social aspect of the club that I belong to, the Cascade Mycological Society, and the forays to go out mushrooming. My trips to get mushrooms are very much a hunt. Hikers like to find a trail and follow it for some distance, but when mushroom hunting, you can wander around all day and only cover three miles. Sometimes you find a spot and never lose sight of your parked car. Mostly, I really enjoy the information gathering and the feeling of being in the woods. This is of great value to me. Many times the mushrooms are secondary to simply being in the woods. I'm a visual person, and it's a lot of fun just to look at the mushrooms. Mushroom people want to look at the details, studying all of the intricacies of each specimen, using a magnifying glass or, later at home, a microscope.

I dye fabric with mushrooms and make a variety of colorful scarves. The mushrooms used for that are, for the most part, not edible. Colors can be many shades of tans and browns but also pinks. This can be a social activity as well, and I enjoy learning from friends and teachers.

How much time do you spend on this pursuit?

Harriet: I like the fact that I am outdoors and this activity goes on all through the winter months, falling off in the dry summertime. I devote a full day each week to the outdoors in search of mushrooms. I use photography as a note-taking device and might keep a series of photos that show a mushroom and a distinctive feature of where it was found, knowing that the digital image contains the date and some other useful information.

I enjoy cooking with mushrooms. I send them to friends and family all over the country, either dried or cooked in sealed packs. I also spend time on membership duties for the Cascade Mycological Society.

I can identify and will eat about twenty-five species of mushrooms. Of course, some I like better than others. This is an individual choice. There are a few sought-after mushrooms that I don't like, but I will collect them if I know someone will want them. One year, I obtained a commercial collecting permit. I never sold any, but we picked so many that we required it.

Permit Requirements

In general, a Free-Use Permit is required in national forests for picking of mushrooms for personal use. This private use is limited, for example in the Pacific Northwest, to 1 gallon of a single species and 3 gallons of 3 separate species. Check your location for personal-use limitations. A Commercial-Use Permit is necessary for greater amounts, or if you intend to sell or trade mushrooms. Check with specific national forests and state lands agencies for rules. The local mycological society is a good source on permit requirements for your area.

What special clothes and equipment do you use?

Harriet: Basic mushroom-hunting supplies consist of boots, rain gear (when necessary), a stick, a knife, brush, basket, and most importantly, a field guide for identifying mushrooms. You can use the stick as both a walking aid and tool for checking under leaves and stumps. A sharp knife enables you to remove the mushroom from the ground, while the brush serves to remove the soil clinging to it. A basket transports what you find while providing ventilation. Wear long pants and a long-sleeved shirt for protection against the poison ivy or poison oak and bugs that are prevalent in the woods.

One concern I have is that many people get lost in the woods. Caught up in the activity of looking for mushrooms, they forget where they are. One suggestion is to use a GPS to help you find your way. And I bring an air gun as well, to scare away the cougars.

"Be Afraid"

Harriet: "Be Afraid" is a well-used phrase in mycological clubs and an important part of mushroom hunting. Before assuming that any wild mushroom is safe to eat, it should be identified as such. Using the full name of the mushroom is very important to make sure there is no confusion. A good field guide will help with the proper identification of a species. Start with the well-known ones, and be careful about the ones that look different. Never eat a mushroom that has not been checked by someone who is well recognized by *mycophile peers as knowledgeable. For every perfectly safe-to-eat mushroom in this world, there is another that looks very similar that can make you sick, or worse. Never, ever eat a mushroom if you're not 110 percent certain it is safe.*

Mushrooms must be correctly identified, since several types of mushrooms have similar appearances, including those that are safe to eat and those that are poisonous. *Toadstool* is a common nickname used to refer to poisonous mushrooms. Long ago, people believed that toads used certain mushrooms to sit on. They also believed that toads were poisonous creatures and so the mushrooms they sat on were thought to be poisonous too. While only a small number of mushroom species can be fatal if eaten, a greater number can make you sick.

The toxins in mushrooms are chemicals that are thought to have evolved to prevent animals from eating them. Symptoms of mushroom poisoning are sometimes delayed by hours or even days after eating, when the toxins have begun to attack the liver and other organs. Certain species can cause hallucinations, dizziness, drowsiness, dilated pupils, or muscle spasms. Other species cause severe vomiting and diarrhea, and sharp abdominal pain. If you suspect that you have consumed a poisonous mushroom, contact a physician, or your local poison control center. Once help has been secured, it is advisable to try to get the suspect mushrooms identified.

The Importance of a Support Group

Harriet: *We have experts in the Society that lead forays and give their time providing scientific information. Some volunteers are medical professionals, and the North American Mycological Association website is a good source for toxicology reports. Our monthly club meetings include presentations from scholars and field experts, many from* close-by University of Oregon in Eugene. Also, there are many classes available at the university and junior colleges in our area.

Joining a local club, attending a class, or meeting up with local residents are good ideas to prevent misidentification when mushroom hunting. People who have relocated and are new to the area sometimes make mistakes. They may be familiar with mushrooms in their former location, but not knowledgeable about species in their new surroundings.

Variety of Mushrooms

There are an estimated 40,000 species of mushrooms, and more are discovered all the time. Wild mushrooms, including, morels, porcini, chanterelles, and matsutake, and of course the famed truffles, attract people because of their unique flavors and aromas, which commercially cultivated species lack. What you see in your grocery store is only a fraction of the variety of mushrooms available. Mushrooms can look like a mini bird's nest, coral from the ocean floor, an octopus, balls of lace, little brown brains, orange peels, shelves on a tree trunk, or even big white soccer balls. They come in a wide variety of colors, and some even glow in the dark.

Gourmet Treat

The ability to identify and prepare safe-to-eat mushrooms is often passed down through generations. After a heavy rain, whole families often venture into the nearest forest, picking buckets full of mushrooms, which are cooked and eaten for dinner, or dried or marinated for later consumption. In California, the core of the mushroom-hunting culture was traditionally European immigrants and a small community of eccentric hobbyists. Now, foraging classes, guidebooks, Internet buzz, and even mushroom-identification smartphone apps have brought mushroom hunting into mainstream food culture.

Safe-to-eat mushrooms are used in delicious dishes throughout the world and are high in nutritional value. Many mushrooms are low in calories, and are a great source of essential vitamins and minerals as well as some protein. They can be a good source of B vitamins. There is some evidence that fresh crimini mushrooms may even have B12, a vitamin previously thought to be available only through meat. Although many varieties can now be purchased in stores, chefs of the slow food movement have touted the virtues of wild mushrooms as foods that are local, sustainable, chemical-free, and delicious.

Truffles

Although both mushrooms and truffles are from the fungus kingdom, the main difference between a truffle and a mushroom is where they grow. Truffles grow underground and are difficult to find, as opposed to mushrooms, which seem to pop up everywhere. Truffles are rare and therefore expensive, whereas mushrooms are easy to grow and inexpensive. Costwise, button mushrooms are probably the least expensive to purchase. Portobello mushrooms typically cost more than twice as much as buttons, and the harder-to-find mushrooms, such as enoki and chanterelle, have even higher costs. Truffles, on the other hand, are all expensive. The most expensive truffles, either the black perigord truffle or the white alba truffle, have been known to sell for as much as $250 per ounce.

Fungus Festivals

The popularity of mushroom picking in some parts of the country has led to mushroom festivals. The festivals are held between September and October, depending on the mushrooms available in a particular region. Fungus festivals feature displays of local mushrooms; showcase speakers on a variety of topics such as ecology, toxicology, and cultivation; and provide cooking demonstrations. Many books and mushroom-related items are available for sale. Fungus festivals are held annually in Alaska and the Flagstaff area of Arizona, as well as California, Oregon, Washington, Colorado, and New Mexico. The Resources section contains a list of fungus festivals.

FASCINATING FACTS

- The United States is the world's second largest producer of edible mushrooms, following China.
- A mature mushroom will drop as many as 16 billion spores.
- Charles Horton Peck was an American mycologist of the nineteenth and early twentieth centuries who described over 2,700 species of North American fungi.
- To date, penicillin, lovastatin, ciclosporin, griseofulvin, cephalosporin, ergometrine, and statins are the most famous pharmaceuticals that have been isolated from the fungi kingdom.
- Neither cooking, canning, freezing, nor drying will make a poisonous mushroom safe to eat.
- Chipmunks find truffles from their delicious smell and are responsible for spreading the spores.
- Pigs can be successfully trained to find truffles due to the pungent aroma truffles give.

Resources

Websites

David Fisher's American Mushrooms: americanmushrooms.com.

List of North American mycological societies: http://bit.ly/1rVjCm6.

The Mushroom Forager, a website focused on the northeastern United States: themushroomforager.com.

Apps

Audubon Mushrooms—A Field Guide to North American Mushrooms by Green Mountain Digital: http://bit.ly/1mSj5fp.

The Mushroom Navigator: http://bit.ly/1rJnxoC.

Other apps on mushroom hunting and foraging: http://bit.ly/1nvU3Id.

Videos

How to find Morel Mushrooms from eCountry Lifestyle.com: http://bit.ly/1rVk5Vm.

Paul Stamets: 6 Ways Mushrooms Can Save the World: http://bit.ly/1zjanQ0.

Search "Mushroom Hunting" or "Mycology" on YouTube: YouTube.com.

Reading

David Arora, Mushrooms *Demystified: A Comprehensive Guide to the Fleshy Fungi*. Berkeley, CA: Ten Speed Press, 1986).

Frank Evans, Matt Trappe, and James M. Trappe. *Field Guide to North American Truffles Hunting, Identifying, and Enjoying the World's Most Prized Fungi*. (New York, NY: Ten Speed Press, 2013).

Gary H. Lincoff, *National Audubon Society's Field Guide to North American Mushrooms* (New York, NY: Knopf, 1981). It is recommended because it is small enough to take with you on forays, not expensive, and covers all kinds of mushrooms.

Roger Phillips, *Mushrooms and Other Fungi of North America* (Buffalo, NY: Firefly Books, 2005), covers more mushrooms then most guides, in living color.

Fungi Magazine explores the world of mycology from many different angles—for example, toxicology, medicinal mushrooms, and photography, and contains book reviews: fungimag.com.

Festivals

Annual festivals in North America include those in Vancouver Island; Boyne City, Michigan; Washington's Long Beach Peninsula; Washington's Olympic National Forest; Mendocino County (north of San Francisco); Flagstaff, Arizona; Madisonville, Texas; Telluride, Colorado; Kennett Square, Pennsylvania; Girdwood, Alaska; Muscoda, Wisconsin; Eugene, Oregon; and Richmond, Missouri.

CHAPTER 6

Service-Dog Trainer

I think dogs are the most amazing creatures;
they give unconditional love.
For me they are the role model for being alive.
—Gilda Radner

The Americans with Disabilities Act (ADA) defines a service animal as "any dog that is individually trained to do work or perform tasks for the benefit of an individual with a disability, including a physical, sensory, psychiatric, intellectual, or other mental disability. These dogs must be permitted to accompany people with disabilities in all areas where members of the public are allowed to go."

Multiple Services

Service dog is the general term for a dog trained to perform some of the tasks that the individual with a disability cannot perform. Service dogs help the visually and hearing impaired, or can detect dangerously low blood sugar on a diabetic's breath. A service dog may alert people by whining, licking the owner, and alerting others to an epileptic owner's impending seizure. They can open cabinets and drawers and pull wheelchairs. The use of service dogs is growing. They now assist persons with autism, post-traumatic stress disorder (PTSD) and traumatic brain injuries.

Social or therapy dogs provide emotional support in places such as elder-care facilities, day care, and schools and hospitals. These animals do not have the same legal status as a service dog and are not included in ADA legislation. Many visiting therapy dogs bring joy and comfort to trauma victims and people with illnesses or can help physically stimulate otherwise sedentary people by playing ball, being brushed or petted, and going for walks.

What Kind of Dog Is a Service Dog?

The most common service-dog breeds used are the German shepherd, Labrador retriever, and golden retriever. Depending on the training organization and the service dog's purpose, other breeds that are also used include the Doberman pinscher, boxer, smooth-coated collie, American white shepherd, and standard poodle.

Early efforts to provide service animals involved dogs from animal shelters; however, it became evident that a specific type of dog was usually necessary. Dogs needed not only excellent health, intelligence, and temperament, but also a willingness to work and thrive on praise. Today, most of the dogs used for service are bred by organizations for a specific purpose. There are many groups throughout the United States raising and training these dogs.

Guide Dogs

A guide dog is one type of service dog familiar to most people. Guide-dog use began in Germany in the 1920s for veterans of World War I who lost their sight. In 1929, the Seeing Eye became the first group in the United States to breed, raise, and train guide dogs. Although the formal training of guide dogs dates back seventy-five years, training only became widespread in the last thirty years.

Bill and Jeanne, puppy raisers

Jeanne and Bill are an active couple who golf, bowl, care for horses two days a week, and are passionate volunteer puppy raisers for the Fidelco Guide Dog Foundation in Bloomfield, Connecticut. Currently they are raising two German shepherds: Yogi, a male, who just turned eleven months and Zera, a ten-month-old female. All of the dogs bred by the Fidelco Guide Dog Foundation are German shepherds.

Bill: Back in 1991, I was supervising an outside construction job in a nearby town and every day I would help this guy walking across the street with his guide dog. Finally, after two weeks, he told me to stop trying to help him because he wasn't blind. He was just training a Fidelco dog. Nineteen years later, we got our first puppy to raise from the same Fidelco Guide Dog Foundation. We named him Victory.

How did you become interested in this pursuit?

Bill: I had been around German shepherd guard dogs in the military and later, in 1970, I lived next door to a blind woman. If she wanted to go somewhere, she would just tell the dog and off they would go. I was always fascinated with the way the dog took instruction.

Jeanne: Then our granddaughter, Katie, raised two dogs for the Fidelco Guide Dog Foundation, which is not far from our home. One of her dogs, Raja, was the breed dog and our first dog, Victory, came from her first litter. We got Victory when he was eight weeks old, and he is now a guide dog working well with his owner.

How did you get started?

Bill: We went to Fidelco to see all the puppies. I was hesitant to become a puppy raiser—afraid I might make mistakes. But my granddaughter told me, "Don't worry, Grandpa, whatever mistakes you make, the professional trainers will make everything right. That's how good they are."

Becoming a Puppy Raiser

Jeanne: First, we filled out an application, and then we took a tour of the facility. During the tour, we looked in the puppy house. When we were leaving, one of the staff picked up a puppy and waved its paw good-bye. I had tears in my eyes and I thought, I've got to get one of these dogs. And that was it for me. I was hooked.

Next, Bill and Jeanne attended an orientation that explained the program, and then observed three or four Saturday classes. Typically, a home visit is done, and there is lots of paperwork before you get started. There is no preferred type of family; single people, couples, or families with children raise puppies. Those chosen receive the puppies at eight weeks old and have the puppies until they are usually one and a half to two years old, at which point they return to the foundation for more advanced training.

Beginning Training

Puppy raisers are required to bring their dogs to a weekly class for the first twelve weeks at least; so for that reason, it's best to live fairly close to the organization. The class consists of all the puppies from the same litter and ranges from five to ten puppies. Puppies in litters tend to bond together and have great friendships with their siblings.

Bill: At the beginning of the class, we "recall" our dog [call the dog to come to you] and take it out for a walk. The walk is followed by a lesson that the trainers want us to work on that day. Trainers watch for signs that the puppy is progressing during the classes or that it needs additional training.

Puppy raisers teach their pup good manners and housebreaking. Car rides, frequent walks, and trips to public places are all part of the time spent together. A variety of situations, such as taking them to grocery stores, school, work, restaurants, shops and malls, trains, planes, and automobiles help to socialize the pup as it matures. When the dog returns to the organization, a professional with expertise in training dogs for specific disabilities then works with the dog for six to nine months.

Jeanne: German shepherds are known for their intelligence, stamina, and desire to please. One time I took Zera on an errand in my Jeep and parked the car in the lot. When we finished in the store, I said, "find the Jeep, Zera" and watched her sniff each bumper as she led me straight across the parking lot until she got to my Jeep and stopped. By using the same words, "find this, find that," she learns very quickly. These dogs are very smart and a pleasure to work with.

When the dogs are approximately four and a half months old, they get a jacket that identifies them as a guide dog, which allows you to go anywhere, such as stores, public transportation, and restaurants with the dog. Depending on the organization, red, orange, or blue vests are typically used to identify whether a dog is a guide dog or a hearing dog.

How much time do you spend on your passionate pursuit?

Jeanne: We spend a lot of time with our puppies. I'm kind of a hovering mom. We take them out for walks or running errands, and they play out in our fenced yard when we garden. If we are gone two or three hours playing golf, then I'll plan to spend the rest of the day near them.

Bill: If I run to the store, I always take a dog with me. The more I can socialize the dog, the easier it will make the trainer's job when the dog returns for more advanced training. Patience is the main attribute necessary for puppy raisers, and taking the time to give the puppies good instruction. Fidelco has certain rules you need to follow in raising the puppies, and I'm sure everyone makes some mistakes.

The biggest mistake I think we all make is letting the dogs on the furniture. These dogs are so incredible; it doesn't take long for them to learn what they should do or not do. You just have to keep working with the dogs, and that's so much fun. Also, you must be ready to walk. We often take lots of short walks, and you don't want the dog to run loose. When they're working with their ultimate owner, they must learn to stay and not go running off.

What expenses are involved?

Jeanne: We have very little expense because Fidelco supplies everything we need at no charge: all veterinary needs, immunizations, the crate the dog sleeps in, and a special training collar. If we go away, and the puppy is very young, they will find another home where the puppy can stay; older dogs can stay at the Fidelco facility. That's a huge benefit because boarding a dog can be a big expense. Our costs are only dog food, toys, and of course, marrow bones. I always give those as a special treat.

Naming a Puppy

Every time a litter is born, it is given a letter of the alphabet. They proceed through the alphabet until all the letters have been used. Then as the years go by, a number is added to show that it is the second, third, or twenty-fifth time that they have come around to that letter. For example, a litter of six pups is born and the puppy raiser can choose a name for their pup beginning only with the letter *J*. All of the pups in the litter have a name that starts with the same letter. The puppy raiser has the honor of naming their charge, as long they don't pick a name of another currently working dog.

Jeanne: Sometimes we have to get very creative with the letters Q or X. I use the dictionary and the Internet searching for names.

What is the most rewarding aspect of this activity?

Bill: One of my big joys is the social interaction; just taking the dogs out for a walk and seeing the smiles on people's faces. I have a routine of monthly visits. I go to certain stores and to the doctor's office monthly (even if I don't need to go) just so the nurses and staff can enjoy the puppies and see how much they've grown.

Jeanne: We take the dogs to a day care and the children get the opportunity to play with them. We bring them to fund-raiser walks and car washes, and we've gone to the high school. We've had very special visits. For example, after the Newtown tragedy, Zera was one of the puppies brought to Sandy Hook to visit the children for a "healing visit." It's wonderful to see the joy that people get seeing and petting the dogs.

Of course, the downside is when it's time for them to go back to the Fidelco Guide Dog Foundation for further training. We never forget that this is not our dog—he or she belongs to the organization, but it's always sad to see them go. It's just like sending your child off to college, and I cry. But we know they will be going on for more training to be the helper to someone in need. I know there is someone out there who needs that dog more than we do and that dog is destined for a special purpose, rather than just being a pet.

Bill: Having two dogs works out well. If you stagger the age, you have puppy overlap, and there's always one left. It's so much easier that way and helps solve the heartache of saying good-bye. Puppy overlap is great for the dogs, too, because the younger dog will learn from the older dog, or the older dog can put the younger one in his place if needed.

Have you experienced any unusual or funny situations?

Bill: Yes! I went to a supply store with Yogi one day. I parked the car and put his red jacket on to show that he is a service dog. I noticed a man parked right next to me was watching. A while later, I'm going through the checkout and the same man who was watching me is in the next checkout counter over. He asked the clerk, "What kind of a dog is that with the red vest on?" and the clerk tells him it was a guide dog for the blind. Surprised, the guy says: "But that guy was driving!" So I picked up the conversation as we both exited the store and said, yes, the dog and I have only been together two weeks—he bites me on the left ear so I steer to the left, on the right and I turn right. As we neared my car, I added, "As you can see we've had a few dents on the car."

Advanced Training

When the dog is between sixteen and twenty-four months, the puppy raiser's job is done, and the dog begins six to nine months with a professional trainer learning to be a guide dog. All of the dogs are trained to work in both rural and urban areas. The dogs are taught to believe they are six feet tall and three feet wide because that is the amount of space that the dog and owner will take up. They are trained to be cognizant of everything that happens within that space. Think of how many times you've been in a situation where you've had to duck to miss something. These dogs are trained to stop and wait for their owner to adjust to the circumstances.

Not every dog will become a guide dog. According to the Fidelco Guide Dog Foundation, approximately 60 percent of their dogs from birth will make it all the way through the program. Of those 40 percent who do not go on to become guide dogs, approximately 95 percent will go on to other working careers, such as in law enforcement, search and rescue, or avalanche rescue. The remaining 5 percent will become pets. The Fidelco Guide Dog Foundation representative assured me that every dog is placed and none are ever brought to a shelter.

Placement with an Owner

Service dogs are provided free of charge to the disabled. Owners are paired with the dog who best suits that person's personality, lifestyle, and physical needs. The organization that Jeanne and Bill work with pioneered the concept of "In-Community Placement" in the United States. This home-based training program makes it possible for a person who is blind to remain in his or her own home environment while training with the guide dog. Upon completion of training, the newly created team starts a new life together.

The Demand for Service Dogs

At any given time in the United States there is a waiting list of thirty people who have need of a service dog, and someone may wait three to six months for a dog who is the right match. Guide dogs are in demand because of many age-related degenerative eye problems, and an increase in military personnel returning from conflict with traumatic brain injuries and eye damage caused by an improvised explosive device (IED).

Some guide-dog owners live in urban areas, others in environments that are more rural. All of the guide dogs are personally matched, with prospective owners' unique needs taken into account. If the next dog that graduates is better suited to the city, that dog will go to an urban owner. Some people have very specific requests, such as a preference for a male or female dog. If a client is elderly, being paired with an older dog is more appropriate than being paired with a frisky two-year-old.

Retirement

A guide dog's working life can be six to ten years. When it's time to retire, the owner has the choice to keep the dog as a pet, give the dog to a family member, or return the dog to the Fidelco Guide Dog Foundation. Sometimes it is difficult for the retired guide dog to be just a pet; the dog may become jealous or depressed over the new guide dog partner. If the dog is returned to the Foundation, it is possible that the original puppy raiser will adopt the dog.

FASCINATING FACTS

- The dogs who become guide dogs for the deaf and blind are, in fact, technically born with the same affliction. *All* puppies are born deaf (with their ear canals closed) and blind (with their eyelids tightly closed) until they are 2 weeks old.
- The total cost for complete training of one service dog is estimated to be $45,000 to $50,000. This includes all expenses from breeding to raising, training, and matching the dog with a human companion.
- Roughly 10,000 people use guide dogs in the United States and Canada.
- Dogs have a huge advantage when it comes to finding things with their nose! While humans have only about 5 million cells for smelling things, the German shepherd has 220 million cells.
- A dog's wet nose helps him or her determine the direction that an odor is coming from.
- A dog can make out its owner's voice from up to half a mile away.
- A German shepherd guide dog named Orient, led her blind companion, Bill Irwin, over the 2,100-mile-long Appalachian Trail.

Resources

Websites

If you don't have a service-dog organization near you, don't despair. Most of these organizations have multiple locations, affiliates, and clubs, and recruit puppy raisers in neighboring states. Check each organization's website or call for updated information.

*Brigadoon Service Dogs—Bellingham, Washington: brigadoondogs.com.

*Canine Companions for Independence: cci.org, has many offices throughout the country:

The Northwest region office: Santa Rosa, California; North Central region: Delaware; Southeast region office: Orlando, Florida; Southwest region offices: Colorado Springs and Denver, Colorado; West campus: Oceanside, California; and an office in Los Angeles, California.

- Dogs for the Deaf—Central Point, Oregon: dogsforthedeaf.org.
- Fidelco Guide Dog Foundation—Bloomfield, Connecticut: fidelco.org.
- Freedom Guide Dogs for the Blind, Inc.—Cassville, New York: freedomguidedogs.org.
- Guide Dogs for the Blind—San Rafael, California, and Portland, Oregon: guidedogs.com.
- Guide Dogs of Texas, Inc.—San Antonio, Texas: guidedogsoftexas.org.
- Guiding Eyes for the Blind—Yorktown Heights, New York: guidingeyes.org.
- Guide Dog Foundation for the Blind, Inc.—Smithtown, New York: guidedog.org.
- Guide Dogs of the Desert—Palm Springs, California: guidedogsofthedesert.org.
- Kansas Specialty Dog Service—Washington, Kansas: ksds.org.
- Leader Dogs for the Blind—Rochester, Michigan: leaderdog.org.
- Mira Foundation—US and Canada; Quebec and Aberdeen, North Carolina: mira.ca/en.
- Next Step Service Dogs—Carlsbad, California, and Fort Dix, New Jersey: nextstepservicedogs.org.
- Pets For Patriots: petsforpatriots.org.
- Pilot Dogs, Inc.—Columbus, Ohio: http://bit.ly/WZz6ex.
- The Seeing Eye—Morristown, New Jersey: seeingeye.org.

- Southeastern Guide Dogs—Palmetto, Florida: guidedogs.org.

Videos

Fidelco—Share the Vision: http://bit.ly/1owS5rh.

Puppy Raising Video: http://bit.ly/1vBMfc7.

Reading

Mark Carlson, *Confessions Of A Guide Dog: The Blonde Leading the Blind* (Bloomington, IN: iUniverse, 2011).

Cesar Millan and Melissa Jo Peltier, *How to Raise the Perfect Dog: Through Puppyhood and Beyond* (New York, NY: Harmony Books, 2009).

Luis Carlos Montalván, Bret Witter, and Dan Dion. *Tuesday Tucks Me in: The Loyal Bond between a Soldier and His Service Dog*, (New York, NY:,Roaring Brook Press, 2014).

PART TWO

ARTS AND LETTERS

CHAPTER 7

Calligrapher

If I had never dropped out, I would have never dropped in on this calligraphy class, and personal computers might not have the wonderful typography that they do.
—Steve Jobs

Calligraphy comes from the Greek *kalli*, meaning beautiful and *graphia* meaning writing. It is a distinctive style of artistic handwriting that uses pen nibs, reeds, or brushes to vary the thickness of a letter's line elements. The practice takes patience, a willingness to learn, attention to detail, and appreciation for the art.

Thousands of years before the invention of printing, the only way to reproduce texts was by hand on parchment paper using a quill. Different parts of the world use different writing techniques. Today, the main styles of calligraphy are Asian (Oriental), Islamic, Indian, and Western. Each style artistically reflects a unique culture and way of life.

Calligraphic Styles

Asian calligraphy involves using reed pens as ink brushes instead of pens with special nibs. In China, where calligraphy was first used in the fifth century, it is considered equal to, or even superior to, painting. The Japanese began to practice the art in the seventh century with the introduction of Buddhist manuscripts from China. Kukai, a Japanese monk, invented the syllabic script in CE 800, and was based on Chinese characters.

Calligraphy is one of the highest forms of visual art in the Islamic world. Islamic calligraphy was first developed to write the Koran, the holy book of Islam, using letters of the Arabic alphabet. Because the Muslim faith discourages pictorial representation and reveres the word of the Koran, the Islamic people esteem calligraphy as highly as do the people of East Asia.

Indian calligraphy was first displayed on a stone surface, and the script was created by the angles of the chisel tip, as was Persian and Arabic script. Later writing surfaces included copper, birch bark, and palm leaves.

Western Calligraphy

Western calligraphy is recognizable by the use of the Roman alphabet, which evolved from the Phoenicians, Greeks, and Etruscans. The practice thrived during the medieval times when the Catholic Church trained monks in Latin reading and writing, which they used to create artistic copies of the Bible. The Gothic calligraphy style became dominant throughout Europe, and in 1454, when Johannes Gutenberg developed the first printing press, he adopted the Gothic style, making it the first typeface.

Pointed Pen Calligraphy

Two pointed pen styles of calligraphy that are part of a popular resurgence of the art form in America are Copperplate and Spencerian. Copperplate is a form of *roundhand script* used by master metal engravers in England several centuries ago. Americans are familiar with this script because the US Declaration of Independence is written in the Copperplate style of calligraphy. The second most popular script in the United States is Spencerian.

Spencerian Script

Platt Rogers Spencer (1800–1864), known as the Father of American Writing, developed a method of writing for the "common man" in America. He developed a unique oval-based writing style that could be written quickly and legibly. Before the widespread use of the typewriter, Spencer's penmanship was adopted as the American de facto standard writing style for business correspondence.

Dawn, the calligrapher

Dawn is a semi-retired Realtor who lives in a suburb of St. Paul, Minnesota. Her interest in calligraphy began when she was fresh out of high school and she worked as a receptionist at an awning factory in Ohio.

Dawn: It was the same awning company that many, many years before sold the fabric to the Wright Brothers for their plane. I worked with a woman named Marguerite, who was the bookkeeper. Back then, all of the ledger entries were done by hand. She used a simple ballpoint pen, but I always admired her beautiful, flowing handwriting. I told myself someday I would learn how to write like that.

How did you become interested in this pursuit?

Dawn: I kept Marguerite's beautiful writing in the back of my mind, and then many years later, I was looking through a catalog that sold small wooden boxes personalized with your name hand-lettered by a calligrapher. I hunted down the name of the artist and found out his name was Michael Sull. I never did buy that box, but eventually, Michael became my teacher, mentor, and good friend.

Master Penman Society

The International Association of Master Penmen, Engrossers and Teachers of Handwriting (IAMPETH) was created in 2001 to recognize members who have achieved a distinguished level of excellence in penmanship and the calligraphic arts. This includes business penmanship, ornamental and Spencerian script, and engrossing. (An engrosser is someone who is hired to hand-write formal text, such as legislative bills and proclamations). Penmanship and the calligraphic arts also includes illumination, offhand flourishing, and text lettering. A high degree of proficiency in two of the disciplines is required for consideration.

Michael Sull is a master penman and considered America's foremost living Spencerian penman, and is the author of several books on Spencerian Script. In 1987, Michael launched an annual weeklong seminar in Geneva, Ohio (Platt Rogers Spencer's hometown) wholly devoted to Spencerian script and ornamental penmanship. The seminar is known as the "Spencerian Saga."

Sull regularly teaches handwriting, calligraphy, and engrossing programs throughout the United States, Europe, and Asia. He was Ronald Reagan's calligrapher and is known worldwide for his skill and teaching ability.

How did you get started?

Dawn: First, I had a false start. Before I found Michael, I had decided to learn calligraphy, so I looked for instruction in my area. I found a woman who taught calligraphy in a small shop and asked her "Can you teach me Spencerian script?" She said, "Oh sure, but first you have to learn Italic (which is an Italian script)." So, I took her class. When I finished the Italic class, I asked her to teach me Spencerian script and she then told me she didn't know how to do it. Later, when I joined the Colleagues of Calligraphy Guild, I was told I had a lot to unlearn. My advice to those beginning is to join a local calligraphy guild and take classes that are taught by known and well-regarded teachers.

I read an advertisement for one of Michael Sull's classes in a calligraphy starter kit that I purchased. The kit included an invitation to the weeklong calligraphy workshop on Lake Erie called Saga. I attended the workshop and, since I have family in Ohio, I make it an annual trip. My husband joins me after the week's workshop and we continue driving on to visit the family relatives. I received an award for attending the most Sagas.

Ornamental Penmanship

Dawn: During the 1800s, writing was integral to a functioning society. Everything was handwritten before the typewriter. Men went to business writing schools so that all correspondence and official papers were legible. These students sitting across the table from each other would compete, trying to create the perfect letter, and writing became fancier and fancier. That's how they worked their way into ornamental penmanship.

Tell me about the calligraphy that you do.

Dawn: People follow probably five or six major letterforms. Spencerian script is based on an oval, and I like the beautiful flowing letters. Platt Rogers Spencer based his script on ovals because he felt it was much more appealing than "roundhand" or copperplate, the script used to write the Declaration of Independence. When you practice, you train your "muscle memory." As Michael instructs, "You want the script to gently flow across the page like an ice-skater going across the ice."

Palmer Method

Adoption of the Palmer method of cursive writing began around the 1900s in schools all across the Midwest and throughout the United States.

Dawn: Many of the letters of the Palmer method of writing are based on Spencerian, with minor adjustments in order to speed up the writing process. In the Palmer method, the "extenders," or part of the letter that stretches above the baseline, as in the "H," or "descenders," or part of the letter that stretches below the baseline, as in the letter "P" were shortened considerably. Letters were moved closer together.

What equipment do you use and what expenses are involved?

Dawn: First, you need a firm surface and a comfortable place to sit. Basic equipment needed for any calligraphy is paper, penholder, nibs (or pinheads), ink, and blotting paper.

You need a good-quality, smooth paper because you are going to move along the paper with an instrument like a pinhead, so you need a smooth paper or it will catch. You can't use paper with fibers. Many of us like to use a French paper that's expensive. You can get ruled or plain. It costs $15 for a tablet of 90 sheets. I also use another expensive paper for special projects that costs $18 for 25 sheets. However, to begin you can use a good, less-expensive bond paper. It is important to practice on good paper that doesn't smudge easily. A ream of 500 sheets of bond paper for practice is less than $10.

A calligrapher uses an oblique penholder and his or her preferred nib. The oblique holder attaches the nib to the side rather than the end. That helps force the slant when writing. Penholders are $50. They are all hand-made. It is possible to spend $200 or $300 on a penholder. Some are fancy, such as those made from ivory. Some of the best nibs are from Japan. Some calligraphers favor the same nibs that the Japanese cartoonists use. Pen nibs are $2.00 each.

There are many different kinds of ink. The ink that most calligraphers use is McCaffery's Penman's Ink. Michael Sull went back, found all of the old recipes for ink, and re-created them for optimum flow. The best ink choice depends on the type of calligraphy. A different texture ink is needed for pointed pen as opposed to broad-edge pens, which need a thicker ink. Ink is $7.00 for a one-ounce bottle. Ink comes in all the popular colors for use for all occasions, such as weddings.

It is necessary to use padding or blotting paper underneath. When writing thick and thin strokes, it is more effective to press down on the nib for the flat stroke. When pressure is applied, the nib opens up and more ink comes out. A pack of five sheets of padding or blotting paper is approximately $3.

The total budget for equipment and expenses to start with calligraphy is approximately $80. Additional money is needed for a book or a class.

Also, it is beneficial to join a calligraphy guild. They are all over the country. The guild I belong to offers a free two-hour class before the meetings every month. Quality teachers are affiliated with each guild.

How much time do you spend on this pursuit?

Dawn: I'm lucky to have a separate place in my house that I call my studio. I try to practice at least two hours a week. Sometimes I have something specific I'm working on, such as writing a letter to a friend, or I'll do Christmas cards. I make my own cards for all of the holidays.

If I don't have a specific project, I watch television shows and write what they are saying. This prevents me from only practicing letters that I like doing. By watching TV and writing what they say, I practice writing all the letters, not just the ones that come easily.

Is there an organization connected to your hobby?

Dawn: I discovered a local calligraphy guild called Colleagues of Calligraphy in St. Paul. I found the group when they were creating and selling bookmarks as a fund-raiser at a local store, and I joined the guild. Like most organizations, members have to step up for the leadership, so my second year I became president of the guild. With my Realtor background, I'm not afraid to speak in front of people and I like to organize speakers and workshops. Part of the guild's mission is teaching calligraphy, so I arranged to have Michael Sull present Spencerian classes.

I also belong to the International Association of Master Penmen, Engrossers and Teachers of Handwriting. They have an annual conference that includes workshops.

The St. John's Bible

The art of illumination took hold in the thirteenth through sixteenth centuries in Europe. The process is ancient and involves illustration on calfskin using quills, hand-ground pigments, natural inks, and gold-leaf gild. Religious parchment was decorated with colorful and detailed borders, floral patterns, imaginary animal and human forms, and often a single extremely ornamented letter. The body of the document is usually in a heavy-bodied Gothic, Celtic, or Uncial text, and not as elaborate as the border treatment.

In 1998, St. John's Abbey and University commissioned renowned calligrapher named Donald Jackson to produce a handwritten Bible with borders also decorated by hand (hand-illuminated). The St. John's Bible is the first handcrafted Bible commissioned by a Benedictine abbey in more than five hundred years.

The St. John's Bible contains more than 160 illuminations in distinct books: Pentateuch, Historical Books, Psalms, Wisdom Books, Prophets, Gospels and Acts, Letters, and Revelation. The work was completed in May 2011 and touch-up work completed in December 2011. The project is exhibited at the Hill Museum & Manuscript Library on the Saint John's University campus in Collegeville, Minnesota.

What is the most rewarding aspect of this activity?

Dawn: I like the relaxation and the enjoyment. I also enjoy the friendships I've developed over the years from going to the Saga and attending workshops. Since calligraphy is a solitary thing to do, connections with other members of the guild are enriching. There's this whole other world of people who love letters too. Most calligraphers are hobbyists, creating simply for the enjoyment. I make every greeting card I send. If I sent my dad a card I bought at the drugstore, he would be surprised.

Do you have any advice for beginners?

Dawn: First, many people think you have to have good handwriting to do calligraphy, but you don't. It's more drawing letters rather than writing. You can do it. Many of my guild members have terrible handwriting but their calligraphy is beautiful.

FASCINATING FACTS

- The term *Master Penman* (applies to both men and women) is used to describe individuals who have attained mastery of the writing arts.
- The *Book of Kells* is a famous and beautiful manuscript produced in the 800s by monks and shows complex illustrations, such as Celtic Knots and Christian symbols. It was written in Latin and includes the texts from the Gospels and some other passages from the Bible.
- Many of America's colonists could read—including women and people of color. However, not everyone could write. In New England, there were a high number of men who could sign their name rather than mark an *X*. In urban locales in 1670 in New England, 75 percent of men could sign their names, and by 1790, 95 percent could.
- Jamyang Dorjee Chakrisah, a Tibetan master calligrapher from India, created the longest calligraphy scroll, measuring over 500 feet and containing long-life prayers composed for the Dalai Lama.
- When designing the first Macintosh computer, Steve Jobs remembered his calligraphy course at Reed College and built in a variety of calligraphic fonts in the Mac.

Resources

Websites

The Calligraphy Pen, blog covering how-to information for illumination and more by A. Lucas, including a comparison of various calligraphy inks: calligraphypen.wordpress.com.

Cynscribe Directory's list of USA calligraphers: http://bit.ly/WIUWTD.

The Flourish Forum, a community for calligraphers of every skill level and every style to learn and share: theflourishforum.com.

International Association of Master Penmen, Engrossers and Teachers of Handwriting IAMPETH: iampeth.com.

John Neal Books (Calligraphy supplies): https://www.johnnealbooks.com.

Yahoo! groups Ornamental Penmanship: http://yhoo.it/1k2pkm7.

Apps

Calligraphy Art by Nguyen Tan Hon-Hu: http://bit.ly/1lK0VwU.

Calligraphy Practice on an iPad: calligraphypractice.com.

Calligraphy Teacher Pro by Team Greenfire: http://bit.ly/1qGkCgT.

Videos

Discover a Hobby, How-to Videos: http://bit.ly/1AmGoIq.

IAMPETH: a variety of videos and tutorials: www.iampeth.com.

Spencerian Calligraphy on YouTube: http://bit.ly/1khHhxt.

Reading

William E. Henning, *An Elegant Hand: The Golden Age of American Penmanship and Calligraphy,* (Newcastle, DE, Oak Knoll Press, 2002).

Michael Sull, *Spencerian Script and Ornamental Penmanship*, *Learning to Write Spencerian Script*, and *American Cursive Handwriting* (Prairie Ville, KS: Lettering Design Group, 1991).

Molly Suber Thorpe, *Modern Calligraphy: Everything You Need to Know to Get Started in Script Calligraphy*. New York, NY, St. Martin's Griffin, 2013).

Eleanor Winters, *Mastering Copperplate Calligraphy: A Step-by-Step Manual* (Mineola, NY, Dover Publications, 2000).

Famous Calligraphy Museums

Hill Museum & Manuscript Library, Collegeville, Minnesota

Karpeles Manuscript Library Museum, Buffalo, New York

Contemporary Museum of Calligraphy, Moscow, Russia

Ditchling Museum, East Sussex, England

Schrift-und Heimatmuseum, Pettenbach, Austria

Manuscript Museum of the Library of Alexandria, Egypt

The Modern Calligraphy Collection of the National Art Library at the Victoria and Albert Museum, London, England

CHAPTER 8

Crossword-Puzzle Constructor

I love words. Sudoku I don't get into, I'm not into numbers that much. But crossword puzzles. . . if I get a puppy and I paper train him and I open the paper and there's a crossword puzzle – "No, no, you can't go on that, honey. I'll take it."
—Betty White

What's a fourteen-letter word for a crossword-puzzle creator? The answer is *cruciverbalist*. An estimated 50 million Americans do crossword puzzles every week. Are you skillful at solving crossword puzzles? Want to try creating them?

December 2013 marked the hundredth birthday of the crossword puzzle and the love affair is going strong. A journalist named Arthur Wynne from Liverpool created the first known published crossword puzzle. It appeared in a Sunday newspaper, the *New York World* on December 21, 1913. During the early 1920s, other newspapers picked up the newly discovered pastime, and within a decade crossword puzzles were featured in almost all American newspapers.

The *New York Times* Crossword

Considered the gold standard by most puzzle aficionados, the *New York Times* crossword puzzle is syndicated to over 200 newspapers around the country and is available online as well. The puzzle starts relatively easy on Monday, and gets progressively harder through the week until Saturday, which features the most difficult puzzle. The Sunday puzzle varies in difficulty. To a crossword puzzle constructor, having your creation published in the *New York Times* Saturday edition is a thrill.

Celebrated in the 2006 documentary *Wordplay*, the American Crossword Puzzle Tournament is held every March in Stamford, Connecticut. Directed by *New York Times* crossword puzzle editor Will Shortz, this is the nation's oldest and largest crossword competition.

David, cruciverbalist and New York Times contributor

David is seventy-two years old and a retired actuary living in New York City. At the time of my interview with him, he has had 157 crossword puzzles published in the *New York Times* and is the author of several crossword puzzle books on such themes as baseball and opera.

David: I've been a crossword solver since I was eleven years old. I started solving the New York Times crossword puzzles, or trying to, after watching an uncle complete the Sunday puzzle in ink and in under twenty minutes. He showed me how and that got me started. This was in the 1950s, when the crossword puzzles weren't as creative as they are now. Over the years, I got very good at it.

The Crossword Personality

Researchers from the University of Buckingham, England, studied what contributes to the crossword puzzle solver's ability. Dr. Philip Fine, who led the study, proposed that experience alone didn't fully explain the differences between expert and nonexpert performance. He concluded that having higher problem-solving ability plays a role as well.

In the documentary *Wordplay*, it is noted that the champions usually have a math-related, computer-science, or music background. David is a prime example, having attended the High School of Music and Art and then minoring in math in college. In his career as an actuary, David used mathematics, statistics, and financial theory to analyze the financial consequences of risk.

How did you get started?

David: Prior to 1993, I had sent a couple of puzzles to the editor, but he wasn't very receptive in terms of encouragement and didn't give much feedback. When Will Shortz became the New York Times crossword editor in 1993, things changed. I decided to give constructing a shot. Will was very encouraging and even if he didn't accept a puzzle initially, he was a good teacher and mentor. With lots of advice from Will, I began to understand what constitutes a good puzzle. I developed my own style because of that. Since 1995, my puzzles have appeared regularly in the New York Times and other places.

Most people want to solve puzzles for fun; they like the idea of completing something, so they to spend an hour or half hour doing that. I also agree that psychologically, people like the idea of putting things in boxes or gaining a sense of control.

One of the problems people have when they first begin to create puzzles is they really don't understand what constitutes good construction. Most puzzles (with the exception of the Friday and Saturday New York Times puzzle) have a theme, and it is important to make sure that your theme is consistent.

Basic Construction Guidelines

Margaret Farrar was the first crossword editor of the *New York Times*, and a crossword genius, according to Stanley Newman, editor of the *Newsday* crossword. He credits Ms. Farrar with the creation of many, if not all, of the rules that guide modern crossword design.

David: The two most important things in the construction of a crossword puzzle are coming up with a good theme and writing good clues. There are people who can just sit down to write a puzzle and think of a theme. I don't do that. I need a word or a phrase to remind me of something good. I'll be watching TV or in a museum and something will hit me that would make a good theme for a puzzle.

Back in 1997, my wife and I went to an event at the Metropolitan Museum of Art in celebration of its 125th anniversary. Tom Brokaw was giving a talk about computers and the Internet, and at one point he said, "A lot of people don't understand this new Internet lingo." In 1997, computers hadn't become mainstream, and he said, "A lot of people think 'hard drive' means a difficult commute into Manhattan." I turned to my wife and said, "Bingo, there is an idea for a puzzle." I wrote a puzzle that was published in the Sunday Times called "Technophobe's Delight." The clues were computer-related words or phrases and the answers had nothing to do with computers. For example, if the clue is "floppy disk," the answer is "Frisbee"; with the clue "digital monitor," the answer is "manicurist"; and for the clue "hard drive," the answer is "Tiger's tee shot."

A couple days after my puzzle appeared, President Clinton gave a news conference in the White House on technology and the Internet. He said that his daughter was attending Stanford University and was sending him e-mails. He said he was trying to communicate back but wasn't sure how to do it. He didn't know how. He then pulled out my crossword puzzle, "Technophobe's Delight," and started reading the clues and answers. He wanted to show how he was totally confused about it amid laughter in the news conference.

More on Theme

When creating a puzzle, you must develop at least three theme answers that all have something in common, and they should be the longest answers in the puzzle. The theme should be consistent throughout the puzzle and the title should give a hint to the theme without using any of the words in the answers.

Making the Grid with Computer Software

David: After you decide on your theme, you then decide where you're going to put the themed answers in the grid. After that, you fill in the rest of the grid with common words and phrases that are popular today. There are a number of crossword-writing programs to help you fill in the grid. I use Cross Lite for the Mac.

If you're using crossword-puzzle-making software, you may be restricted to a certain range of available sizes. If you're making your puzzle by hand, you can make it any size you want. The general rule for grid construction is 15 blocks high by 15 blocks wide and containing approximately 78 words.

Not all of the grid's squares are white; some are black. No more than one-sixth of the grid should be black squares. The black squares must be placed symmetrically, meaning that if you took the crossword puzzle and flipped it 180 degrees, the pattern of black squares would stay the same. The crossword creator fills the words into the blank squares. Once he or she lays the words out, the next step is to black out any unused squares. Many crossword-creation programs automatically lay the words out; it is only necessary to specify puzzle size and input the list of words and clues.

Clues

The crossword creator must create a clue for every word that is included in the puzzle. He or she numbers the clues according to the corresponding words' places in the puzzle (for example, 7-*Across*, 23-*Down*) and lists all of the *Across* clues together in numerical order, followed by all the *Down* clues.

Crossword clues should be short and consistent in difficulty throughout the puzzle. Easy puzzles have clues that are straightforward, such as a fill-in-the-blank or a common definition. A crossword creator always checks the dictionary to be precise. Puzzles that are more difficult might use a clever play on words, anagrams, modern idioms, or a lesser-known definition for a word.

Don'ts

Cruciverb.com, a resource center for crossword-puzzle constructors, suggests some things to avoid are overly exotic themes; references to death, disease, drugs, or sex; and unusual or obscure words in clues or theme answers. Most guidelines stipulate no two-letter words and no repeated words, even in the clues.

What are the elements of a good puzzle?

David: I think the answers have to be words or phrases that people have heard of—words the average person has a chance at solving. In the old days, there were a lot of answers a solver would only know if he or she read the dictionary. There were very esoteric words people don't ordinarily use. You don't see that anymore in any publications, and that's good because it gives everybody a shot at completing the puzzle.

What expenses are involved?

David: If you already have a computer, the software is the only cost. (The cost is approximately $50.)

How much are crosswords worth?

David: The going rate for any weekday puzzle in the New York Times is $300, paid when the puzzle is published. When I first started out, I received $62.50 for a weekday puzzle (a 15 x 15 puzzle) and $300 for a Sunday puzzle (a 21 x 21 puzzle). Now they pay $300 for a daily puzzle and $1,000 for a Sunday puzzle. Typically, a daily puzzle will take three to five hours to produce, from creating the grid to writing the clues. A Sunday puzzle could take fifteen hours or more.

The prices at other newspapers or magazines vary from $50 to $200 for 15 x 15 puzzles and from $150 to $300 for 21 x 21 puzzles. Check the guidelines of specific newspapers and magazine for information.

How much time do you spend on this pursuit?

David: Some days I don't spend any time constructing puzzles. I'll only spend time when I get a good idea for a theme. I don't have the urgency or the need to work all the time, but if I have a great puzzle idea in my head, I won't even take a break until I've completed it.

I host a crossword-puzzle program for all ages a couple times a year at the 92nd Street YMCA in New York City. I talk about some of the fun things that have happened to me and it's a lot of fun. I write private puzzles for some companies as well.

What is the most rewarding aspect of this activity?

David: To me the most rewarding aspect is the feedback I get, and I've had some very interesting experiences. Celebrities have gotten in touch with me. When Rita Moreno turned seventy-five years old, I did a tribute puzzle for the Monday New York Times. When she was in town, she called me to thank me for the puzzle and invited my wife and me to come to her show.

Because of the Clinton "Technophobe" puzzle, when his library opened in Little Rock, they invited me to write a puzzle for the event that also appeared in the Sunday Times. My wife and I attended the library opening. That was a lot of fun. The best time for me is when I complete a puzzle that I think is great. But I am always prepared that the editor might not think it's great.

Is there a negative side to this pursuit?

David: The negative side is when I think I have a great puzzle, I've spent a lot of time on it, and I submit it and they say no. I might submit it to other places and, for one reason or another; they don't care for it either. But rejection didn't stop me. Once I finally started seeing puzzles published and seeing my byline, it became very appealing.

What do you consider your finest puzzle?

David: One of my favorite Sunday puzzles I wrote a long time ago was called "To Make a Long Story Short." It was a puzzle based on the book The Prince and the Pauper by Mark Twain. I had the title of the book as a "Down" answer in the middle of the grid. Then in six

"Across" answers, I had the beginning and end of the story intersecting the title. I liked that puzzle a lot.

Another one I liked was one I created when Obama was first elected president. It was called "Making History," and there were politically related answers in the puzzle, such as "American flag," and "Hail to the Chief." Within those answers were the letters of the states that he won. For example, the word "American flag" contained the letters "ME," the 2-letter abbreviation for Maine, "RI" for Rhode Island, and "CA" for California. That was one of my favorites.

Is there anything else that you think is important for readers to know?

David: I started this as a hobby twenty years ago when I was still working. I think it's always better if you have something on the side to do while you're working and love it enough to continue doing it after retiring. That's what happened with me.

Also, if you start constructing puzzles and you receive rejection letters from the publishers, don't take it personally. Just be persistent, because if you have talent and you really want to do this, it will work out. It did for me. When my first Sunday Times puzzle was accepted, I was so excited I threw a party for myself. I invited the New York Times crossword editor, Will Shortz, and he came!

FASCINATING FACTS

- Jon Stewart of *The Daily Show* proposed to his wife with a custom crossword puzzle designed with the help of Will Shortz, the crossword-puzzle editor of the *New York Times*.
- What's an *enigmatologist*? It's Will Shortz, the world's only academically accredited puzzle master.
- During World War II, Britain's main decryption establishment, Bletchley Park, asked its cryptologists to solve a *Daily Telegraph* crossword in under twelve minutes as part of its recruitment process.
- *Forty* is the only number in English that has its letters in alphabetical order. *One* is the only number whose letters are in reverse alphabetical order.
- *Rhythm* is the longest English word without any of the normal vowels, a, e, i, o, or u.
- In Japan, the corner squares of a crossword must be white.

Resources

Websites

Cruciverb, a resource center for crossword puzzle constructors: cruciverb.com.

Crossword puzzle markets:

Cricket Magazine Group: *Calliope, Cobblestone, Cricket, Dig,* and *Faces*: cricketmag.com.

Games Magazine: http://bit.ly/1tdsfvc.

Los Angeles Times: http://abt.cm/1pktRPY.

New York Times: http://abt.cm/1AmIIze.

US Kids (3 children's magazines): *Turtle* (for ages 3–5), *Humpty Dumpty's Magazine* (5–7), and *Jack and Jill* (8–12): http://bit.ly/1nw2Jyi.

USA Today: http://abt.cm/1wYu2Hs.

Apps

Crossword Maker for Cruciverbalists by Xiang Wei: cmfcapp.com or http://bit.ly/1lK3yyK.

New York Times Crossword: http://bit.ly/1rNb3e9.

Software

Across Lite for Windows, Mac and iPad: litsoft.com.

Crossdown for Windows by Sam Bellotto Jr.: crossdown.com.

Crossfire (for multiple platforms) by Robert Stockton: beekeeper-labs.com/crossfire.

Crossword Compiler (for Windows) by Antony Lewis: crossword-compiler.com.

Crossword Forge 7 (Windows and Mac): http://bit.ly/1rr60hi.

Video

How to Make a Crossword for the New York Times: http://bit.ly/1mSpbww.

Wordplay (2006), Will Shortz (Actor), Ken Burns (Actor), Patrick Creadon (Director)

Reading

Patrick Berry, *Crossword Puzzle Challenges for Dummies* (Hoboken, NJ: Wiley, 2004). Reviews say the name is misleading, that the book is more for constructors than puzzle solvers.

Matt Gaffney, *Gridlock: Crossword Puzzles and the Mad Geniuses Who Create Them* (New York, NY: Thunder's Mouth Press, 2006).

Stanley Newman and Mark Lasswell, *Cruciverbalism: A Crossword Fanatic's Guide to Life in the Grid* (New York, NY: Harper, 2006).

Mel Rosen, *Random House Puzzlemaker's Handbook* (New York, NY: Times Books, 1995).

CHAPTER 9

Magician

The real point of magic is telling a beautiful lie.
—Teller

Wow! How'd he do that? Even with all of the twenty-first-century technology we use every day, a good magician can still create awe and wonder. When Teller, of the famous magician duo Penn & Teller, talked about magic in an interview with Chris Jones of *Esquire* magazine he said, "It lets you see what the world would be like if cause and effect weren't bound by physics. It's the collision between what you know and what you see that provides magic's greatest spark."

Bill, the magician

Bill is sixty-two years old and lives in Northern California. After serving in the Marine Corps, he worked for a major oil company as a process operator, mixing chemicals. After working at that for ten years, he moved to the laboratory for twenty years. After he retired, his passionate pursuit of magic became a second career.

Bill: During my time at the oil company, I was sent to a High Performance Work Team seminar in Florida. The very first presenter, Ed Rose, stood up and did a couple of magic tricks as part of his instruction on good presentations. I thought, Wow, that's pretty cool. I had never done magic before. I was required to give a presentation back in the office, so I decided to perform a couple of magic tricks as part of my presentation. I bought Ed Rose's book and had some fun with it.

I started my presentation by doing the exact two tricks Ed Rose did at the seminar. One of the tricks was used to demonstrate trust—trusting your teammates to have good relationships. I put water into a cup. I had someone come up and I asked him if he trusted me to invert the cup of water over his head. I promised him no water would come out. First, I tilted the cup then totally inverted it. No water came out. Everybody was amazed.

For my second trick, I tied three separate pieces of rope together. Then I tossed them up into the air. Instantly, all of the pieces were all connected—it was a single piece of rope. That seemed to get everyone's attention and I decided that magic was really powerful stuff.

I think most office presentations can be boring. A lot of people just go so they can take a nap. After my presentation, if a department meeting was announced, people would ask, "Bill, are you going to do some magic?" If I said no, they'd say, "Oh, then we're not going." Every time there was a retirement party at work, they would ask me to do a show. And that forced me to learn new tricks and perfect my performance.

What's the best way to learn magic?

Bill: Magic is like everything else. If a person has an interest in something, there's going to be a way that person can learn it. In the first book I bought, Ed Rose explained how he did every trick. He exposed all of the secrets for learning the trick and included a list of magic shops. The library is a great source of books on magic. I recommend that a beginner check out a book of basic magic tricks and learn "sleight of hand" tricks. Another good way to learn magic is to join a magic club. That puts the beginner into the circle of others who share that interest. I attend lectures and meetings that help a lot.

There are also many DVDs available. People seem to prefer a video to a book these days. A good way to learn is to watch the video all the way through and then start piecing it out, learning a little bit at a time. If it's a good video, it will be easy for a beginner to pick it up quickly. Most magic tricks for sale today come with a teaching video. There's also a lot of video available for streaming off the Internet, as in YouTube. It's not worthwhile to spend a lot of money on gimmicks or props sold in magic shops. It's best to learn solid tricks that don't rely on special props.

I also took a formal two-week magic class, which was a Christmas present, but I feel I learn more on my own. However, I learned about psychology in that magic class. Magic is all about psychology—reading people and trying to interpret them.

Psychology and Magic

In 2007, psychologists attended a symposium entitled "The Magic of Consciousness" in Las Vegas. The psychologists were at the conference to hear the magicians' insights into perception and awareness. They wanted to learn the neuroscience behind techniques used to successfully manipulate people's expectations, misdirect their attention, and subtly influence decision-making.

Five well-known magicians shared their expertise on critical psychological techniques to help psychologists in their research. In his presentation, Teller explained how magicians use some psychological principles to create magic. For example, in a coin trick that he performed, Teller pointed out that the magician expects the audience to look for the *wrong* pattern, and every time the audience thinks they've figured out the method, the magician will change the process. The trick is happening too fast for the audience to realize that the magician is shifting methods. He explained that a person will be deceived when he or she takes for granted that a repetition will continue and it doesn't.

Do you belong to an organization connected to your hobby?

Bill: I belong to the Society of American Magicians and the International Brotherhood of Magicians. Both have local chapters, and I go to those meetings. A local club can have anywhere from ten to forty people show up for a chapter meeting.

The SAM club meets once a month and has a typical meeting structure and announcements. After the meeting, different members will teach a magic trick, sometimes on a theme. For example, all of the tricks may have a money theme, or a comedy theme, or a holiday theme such as Halloween magic. There are also swap meets in which members can purchase various tricks, props, and equipment.

The club puts on one or two public shows a year to raise money for the organization, and both organizations conduct workshops and conferences. Since the IBM is international, people come to the conference from all over the world. People come to sell, to lecture, and to perform in competitions.

Who becomes a magician?

Bill: The majority of magicians are men, but the women magicians do very well. The Society of American Magicians has a youth program that attracts elementary school–age youth. A person must be eighteen years old to attend the monthly chapter meetings. A meeting may have people eighteen, nineteen, and twenty years old all the way up to people in their eighties and nineties. One fellow in our club is ninety-three; another, who recently passed away, was a hundred and one. One woman in our club started magic at age seventy-five.

What qualities make a good magician?

Bill: A magician must like to practice a lot. If I'm preparing for a show at a county fair in my area, I'll practice a couple of hours a day for two weeks. A county fair is a venue for all ages and an opportunity to show the variety of work that I can do. I always practice my sleight-of-hand tricks before a show, even if I know them well. It's like a sports player stretching before the game.

Dexterity is important. If I'm learning coin tricks, for example, I'll use muscles in my hands I never knew were there. I found out that my hands can do a lot more than I thought and I look at them differently. When I was first learning coin tricks, my hands would ache!

A magician must like to perform in front of people. The more he or she does it, the more comfortable the magician becomes. Also, diet and exercise are really important. A magician must have good physical stamina, watch his or her weight, and eat healthy to stay in good physical shape. Magicians like David Copperfield are in good shape. When they're performing, they use a lot of energy.

How do you learn a trick?

Bill: I use books and videos. I think it's important to pick tricks that appeal to me. Some tricks are very difficult to learn and can take weeks to perfect. Many of the tricks that I do, I've perfected over time, and then I'll add to them. Some of my rope tricks have evolved that way. I don't expect to learn an entire routine right away; I just learn pieces of it. If a coin routine is five minutes long, I may just use one piece of that in my show. I think the Magic Café is probably the best website to go to if you're having trouble learning a trick. It's an online forum where magicians help each other.

Magicians evaluate other magicians by their technical ability and presentation skills, whereas the audience looks more at the personality of the performer. It's hard to fool another magician. When you can get another magician to say, "Wow, I don't even know how he did that," that's a good performance.

The Magician's Oath

Bill: The motto is "A Good Magician Never Tells a Secret." When they join one of the societies and their local club, they take an oath that they won't disclose the secrets of magic to non-magicians. (Magicians, who reveal secrets, either purposely or through insufficient practice, may find that other magicians are unwilling to teach them any more secrets. They are then no longer eligible to join the IBM and are banned from magic society.)

Tell me about your magic shows.

Bill: Anyone can learn magic tricks. But what do I do with it? How do I present it? I like a combination of elements in my show. I like to use music with my presentation. A simple component adds to the magic. I use some props. For example, I use a live bunny. The kids especially like that trick. I try to use a little comedy. Even if people don't particularly like magic, everyone likes to laugh.

I like to do sleight-of-hand tricks. That appeals to sophisticated audiences. I do a wide variety of tricks and a lot of rope and coin tricks. The only ones I don't do are big illusions where I need an assistant. I don't do a lot of card tricks because I find them a little boring.

I do children's shows for birthday parties or visit the schools and libraries. I find the best ages for children's shows are from age four to ten. I incorporate lots of fun and funny props. I'll have one of the children wear a funny hat, and another help me with a trick in which I pull a live rabbit from my hat.

The adult shows are different from the children's shows in that adults appreciate the magic part rather than comedy. Favorites are rope tricks and an escape act I do also with a rope. I perform at resorts, food and wine festivals, county fairs, and for Rotary and other social clubs.

What expenses are involved?

Bill: I would suggest to use the many free books available at the library to begin to learn about magic. A magician can do great magic with everyday things he or she can find around the house. I did a trick the other day at the bank for some of the tellers with a dollar bill, a paper clip, and a rubber band. They were blown away.

It's important to join a local magicians' club. I think it's a requirement to join the national organization at the same time as the local chapter. The national organization membership is currently $65 and the local club dues are currently $25 a year. Membership includes a magazine and notifications of upcoming conventions.

When I first started out, I didn't have a mentor, so I went to commercial lectures where everyone's trying to sell you something. I bought a lot of props and spent a lot of money. I have some tricks that are still in unopened packages. I know now that's not necessary. It's hard to resist, because you get very enthused about it.

What special clothes and equipment do you use?

Bill: Since I'm a performer, I want to wear something flashy, so I shop at stores that cater to performers. I wear pants that are comfortable and have lots of pockets that are easy to get my hands in and out of. I'm not going to wear jeans.

One thing that's important to know is that at one time or another everything I've worn except my shoes has been a magic prop—coat, shirt, pants, and hat. The coat is very important as far as making magic happen. I've spent a lot of money having my jackets altered so they fit well and it's easy to get my hands in and out quickly. I want to be comfortable in my clothes and since I'm on my feet for the entire show, I need comfortable shoes.

For performances, magicians need some basic equipment that is invisible to the audience but necessary for a seamless experience. This includes a wireless microphone that can cost between $150 and $600. A sound system is important, even if it's only something to play background music. I use an amplifier and plug in an iPod. Some magicians just use their iPhone with an amplifier. I try to use upbeat music without words that is familiar to the audience. One time I forgot to bring the music to a small gathering and it really threw my rhythm off not having music in the background. I use a Crate sound system that I bought at a music shop for about $200. It puts out good, clear sound that has worked out really well for me.

I have a professional magic carrying case that folds out into a table. I transport all of my tricks and props in that. A box can cost anywhere from $500 to $1,000. A total budget range including clothes: $1,000 to $2,400.

How much time do you spend on magic?

Bill: If I'm learning a new trick, I'll spend two to three hours a day on my magic. I also have a website that I keep up so that people can contact me and book shows. Occasionally, I'll take a whole week off and do nothing connected with magic.

A typical show is one hour long. Before I leave the house, I will spend a couple of hours going over some routines, laying out the clothes I will wear, and packing up the car with all of the equipment I use. Then it will take fifteen to thirty minutes to unload and to set up before a simple performance. If it's a more elaborate show at a community center, for example, I bring my sound system and set that up. I never depend on the venue to supply a sound system. If it doesn't work or if I'm not familiar with how to operate it, I'll have a big problem.

What is the most rewarding aspect of this activity?

Bill: Like most entertainers, I like the applause. Just recently, I performed at an after-school program. After the show, I was packing up and a little boy came up to me and gave me his drawing of some of the magic tricks I did. He wrote on it, "Thank you to the best magician I've ever seen." Little things like that are very rewarding.

30 Seconds of Fame

Bill: It was 2003, four years after I started magic and one year after I started performing shows. I was brand-new to the trade, really green. I hadn't watched too many magicians, but I knew that I really enjoyed doing magic. I was in a magic shop, and the shop owner tells me that a television crew for 30 Seconds of Fame was coming the next week to interview for talent. This was a program very similar to America's Got Talent. He encouraged me, saying, "Sure, you can do it!" So I called the telephone number and was told I needed to perform two tricks. They had to be short, thirty seconds or less. So I practiced a couple of tricks.

I showed up for the audition and was surprised to see a lot of magicians, many who had been performing for thirty years! They were presenting tricks with live doves and accomplishing other complicated feats. I did two simple tricks to music. In the first trick, I showed a small, empty paper bag. I dropped a regular drinking straw into the bag. I reached in and produced an eight-foot straw, two inches in diameter and then, a second eight-foot straw from the same bag; thus changing one regular drinking straw into two eight-foot giant straws from a small empty paper bag.

For the second trick, I took a red silk handkerchief from my coat pocket and produced a bottle of strawberry soda from the empty handkerchief. Then I poured some of the soda into a glass and when I turned the glass over the liquid turned into a red silk handkerchief.

The audition crew said, "OK, thank you," and that was that. A week later, they called me and told me that I had been chosen to perform. I asked incredulously, "Me? Why did you pick me?" They told me they were tired of seeing the doves and all the old tricks and said my tricks were so different!

They flew me to Hollywood, picked me up with a limousine, and provided a hotel, all expenses paid. I performed live on national television. I received a payment for the performance. I think it was $250 and a per diem amount. When the people at the magic shop found out that I was chosen to perform, they couldn't believe it.

Any advice to someone who wants to start?

Bill: Wander in a magic shop if one is available where you live and look around. Tell them you're brand-new and they will start you off with the right tools and give advice. There are lots of websites available, but it's hard to know exactly what you're getting when you order online unless you have some experience. Conventions can be overwhelming. I wouldn't suggest that to someone just starting because you might get too discouraged. Start out slowly; learn one magic trick at a time. Become very accomplished at what tricks you perform.

If you want to be a good magician, the more shows you do, the better you will be. You can practice forever, but until you perform in front of people, you won't excel. Get out there in front of your family, your friends, then work up to small groups and then larger audiences. It builds up your confidence and encourages you to learn more tricks.

FASCINATING FACTS

- Charles Dickens was an enthusiastic amateur magician.
- Harry Houdini could pick up pins with his eyelashes and thread a needle with his toes.
- Famous celebrities who are (or were) also magicians: Johnny Carson, Don Johnson, Woody Allen, Dick Cavett, Dick Van Dyke, Milton Berle, Cary Grant, Bill Bixby, Jimmy Stewart, Steve Martin, Muhammad Ali, Bob Barker, and Jerry Lewis.
- The great film director Orson Welles had a lifelong interest in magic. During World War II he had his own magic show that he presented for members of the US armed forces. His assistants at times included such stars as Rita Hayworth and Marlene Dietrich.
- Teller, of the duo Penn & Teller, owns a rare copy of the book *Discovery of Witchcraft*, from 1584. It's extremely rare, because, as the story has it, King James ordered every copy burned.
- David Copperfield is the first living magician to have a star on the Hollywood Walk of Fame. The only other magician so honored is Harry Houdini, who received a star after his death.

Resources

Websites

Find a magician in your area: magicsam.com.

Find a magicians' club in your area: http://bit.ly/1l5lcNj.

International Brotherhood of Magicians (IBM): magician.org.

International Magicians Society: imsmagic.com.

Magic by Bill: magicbybill.com.

The Magic Café is a forum for magicians helping fellow magicians and also contains reviews of magic shows: themagiccafe.com/forums.

The Society of American Magicians (SAM) website has links to find a local assembly http://bit.ly/1l5lcNj.

Videos

Magic Instructional videos: magician.org/resources/videos-and-magic; http://bit.ly/1tdwt5W; and http://bit.ly/1zjkoNb.

Teller Speaks (at the 2007 Magic of Consciousness Symposium): http://bit.ly/1nJenoO.

Reading

Ed Rose, *Presenting & Training With Magic: 53 Simple Magic Tricks You Can Use to Energize Any Audience* (New York, NY: McGraw-Hill, 1997).

Jim Steinmeyer, *Hiding the Elephant: How Magicians Invented the Impossible and Learned to Disappear* (Clermont, FL: Paw Prints, 2010).

Mark Anthony Wilson, *Mark Wilson's Complete Course in Magic* (Philadelphia, PA: Courage Books, 1988).

CHAPTER 10

Performing-Arts Usher

The theatre is a spiritual and social X-ray of its time.
—Stella Adler

If you enjoy the arts and want to help other people enjoy them as well, consider becoming a volunteer usher. Performing arts include dance, music, opera, theatre, musicals, magic, circus acts, and festivals. As a goodwill ambassador on behalf of the performing-arts venue, you assist patrons to their seats, answer questions, and create a pleasant and welcoming environment. Volunteers meet many people and also have the opportunity to see quality performances.

Multiple Venues

There are many types of performances to choose from, depending on what is available in your location. Whether it is a metropolitan opera or ballet, a rock or country music concert, or your local amateur theatre troupe, volunteers are usually the backbone of the usher program at each performance.

The number and variety of usher opportunities depend, of course, on where you live and how far you are willing to travel to the venue. Any location with a college or university that includes programs for dance, music, and theatre usually need ushers. Most community theaters need volunteers to usher for stage productions. Larger metropolitan areas have a greater array of performing-arts offerings. There are also niche events that have a need for volunteers at unique times and special occasions, such as Christmas holiday shows, state fairs, summer Shakespeare theater, and Off-Broadway shows in New York City.

Harlan at the San Francisco Opera

Harlan, a sixty-eight-year-old retired chief title officer, told me that becoming an usher was a fluke.

Harlan: While attending a rock concert, I ran into a woman I had worked with and was now retired and a volunteer usher at the music pavilion. I thought the idea of attending free music concerts would be fun, so I signed up.

Music Concerts

Harlan: I attended a two-hour orientation program, which detailed what the organization expected. Ushers are responsible for greeting the people, checking their ticket, and showing them to the correct seat. The music pavilion was a relaxed venue offering a variety of concerts from jazz combos, hip-hop, heavy metal, and classic rock groups. The uniform is simple dark pants and a white shirt. The ushers are easy to spot and accessible to answer questions or to contact management in case of lost children or other emergencies.

My schedule was very flexible. I chose the concerts I wanted to work and heard first-rate bands. Volunteers receive extra points if they sign up for less popular music. For my tastes, that was heavy metal or rap. Extra points move us up on the list to choose our schedule first. Of course, all of the ushers want the more popular concerts, so accumulating points to move up on the schedule is strategic.

The atmosphere is relaxed and the customers, looking forward to a lively concert, are always cheerful and friendly. I enjoyed my volunteer usher role for six years, and then after thirty-one years of having volunteer ushers, the pavilion decided to change to paid-only ushers. The schedule was less flexible, so I decided not to continue there.

The Opera

Harlan: One evening when I was flipping through channels with the TV remote, I began watching La Bohème, sung by the New York Metropolitan Opera. I didn't know a thing about opera, but I decided to learn about it. I live in the suburbs of San Francisco, so when I saw that the city opera company was presenting La Bohème, I took my family to see it.

I learned that every performance features "supertitles," which are the English translations of each song, projected above the stage and visible from every seat. A printed program is issued at each opera, which explains what the opera is about. Additionally, prior to each performance, a twenty-five-minute lecture is available. It covers when the opera was composed, who created the music, and who wrote the libretto, or written story, of the opera. The lecturer discusses how long it took to compose the opera and the story behind it; little tidbits of information that you would not ordinarily find out just by reading the story. Sometimes the opera is written and composed due to some particular happening in history or the life of the composer. One of the reasons I started ushering is so I can get to know and understand opera better and not have the expense. I really enjoyed that performance, so I signed up to become an usher.

What is required to be an usher?

Harlan: As with the music concerts, there was a two-hour orientation. My group toured the San Francisco Opera House and learned all of the seating sections. My uniform for this venue is more formal than at the music pavilion: a dark suit, white shirt, and tie. Women wear a dark skirt and white blouse.

As an usher, I must be able to read ticket seat numbers in dim light. My job is to ensure that each guest is seated properly, receives a program, and has a wonderful experience. I may be assigned to work the entrance doors, opening them and greeting patrons. Or I may direct patrons to the correct door to use when going to their seats, where to get refreshments, or the location of the restrooms. Ushers must be reliable and arrive promptly at the required time. I assist the staff with the enforcement of the camera/recording policy, answer questions, and offer attentive service. An usher must be alert and think quickly in an emergency.

There are different levels of ushering. I usually sign up as a "regular usher," which means that I do not have to stay for the entire opera if I can't or don't want to. There is also a "house usher." As a house usher, you are required to stay for the entire performance and help tend the doors and empty the theatre. Regular ushers and house ushers are volunteers. Additionally, there is paid staff that coordinates and oversees the regular and house ushers.

Time Commitment

Harlan: For an eight p.m. performance, an usher is required to arrive by six thirty p.m. The opera story is explained, and we receive our assigned places and a briefing of any special group seating arrangements or special programs happening. We are at the doors to greet the patrons or in position at seven p.m. to start seating. Each usher is responsible for bringing his own flashlight; otherwise the organization would be constantly buying replacements when volunteers drop out or forget them.

How much time do you spend on your passionate pursuit?

Harlan: I have the flexibility of choosing which operas to work. The opera season begins in September and goes through December; then there are more performances again in June and July. I usually work five to six operas each year. As a regular usher, I can leave after the first intermission, but I usually stay to watch the entire performance. If an aisle seat is vacant, I can sit there, sit in an empty row in the rear, or stand in the back. Performances are usually three hours, unless it is a Wagner opera, which runs longer.

The Ballet

Harlan's volunteer usher job at the opera rolls into ballet season, with *The Nutcracker* performed in December.

Harlan: This is a very popular Christmas program with thirty or more performances. In order to get my first choice of operas, I am required to work a certain number of Nutcracker performances. The San Francisco Ballet performs from December until May. I usually work two to three ballets per season. My volunteer usher job consumes a lot of my time for each performance. I take public transit to the city, so the commute adds to the time spent. It's an eight- or nine-hour commitment when I stay for the entire performance.

Any downsides to being an usher?

Harlan: Late-seating policies are strictly enforced, so if someone arrives after the lights dim, they must remain in the back until intermission. This can be a touchy situation, since some seats cost upwards of $350. I've experienced an irate couple who arrived late and therefore were not allowed to disturb the others already seated. I was happy to hand the problem over to the floor manager, who found them seats in the back until intermission.

As an usher, you are on your feet a long time and walking up and down stairs a lot. Another drawback for me is that the travel into the city is tiring. In order to catch the last train home, I often miss a culminating aria or blockbuster ending. This is unfortunate.

There's a difference between ushering and enjoying the opera as a spectator. When you attend the opera as a patron, you can just sit and enjoy the opera without interruptions. Whereas when you work as an usher, you are always looking around to make sure there are no problems or complaints; or maybe patrons arriving late and wanting to be seated. Though the opera does not allow late seating, you still need to deal with the late arrivals. You sometimes miss what's happening onstage due to dealing with an ushering matter. But that doesn't spoil the opera for me.

Diversity

Performing arts, and opera in particular, gets a bad rap, with people assuming the programs are only for the elite, dressed in tiaras and furs. But that's not true. Performing-arts companies draw attendance from a wide range of the community. Audiences of all ages, including families with children, attend, and there is no dress code.

Harlan: The clothing worn at the San Francisco Opera ranges from haute couture to Levi's. Ushers, too, are a variety of ages, and have different backgrounds and lifestyles. Many of the ushers I work with have been volunteering for eighteen, thirty-five, and fifty years! Personalities vary as well. Some ushers are reserved, while others are very open and friendly.

What are the most rewarding aspects?

Harlan: The opera building is beautiful and a great place to work. I enjoy the ambiance and the entire atmosphere of the opera. I also enjoy meeting the variety of people who come to the performances. The difference between the opera and the music pavilion is like day and night. Some people come to the opera dressed up in tuxedos and gowns, others in blue jeans and sneakers. Some are aloof; other people are very friendly. There is a great variety. I also like to see the small children who come at Christmas to see The Nutcracker. They look darling in their beautiful dresses and little suits and bow ties. They're mesmerized by the opulent stage sets.

I've experienced wonderful operas. One of my favorites is The Marriage of Figaro. It is a lively, fun, and uplifting performance. I appreciate the beautiful singing and lavish sets. I am seeing the most famous talents of our generation performing in opera and ballet classics, and it's free!

The creativity of set design, coupled with the technology, is impressive. The stage for the performance of Madame Butterfly rotated like a merry-go-round. La Traviata, written in the nineteenth century, was updated to the 1920s and the staring diva was dressed in furs and a diamond tiara. She was transported onto the stage in a vintage car, a magnificent white convertible Cord. The set designers used video and electronics to make the Moby-Dick stage undulate with rise and fall of the ocean waves. Each opera is an experience.

FASCINATING FACTS

- New York's Lincoln Center for the Performing Arts is the largest performing-arts venue in the United States. Lincoln Center has 29 indoor and outdoor performance facilities.
- Total attendance at all US live-theater events in 2010 was 45.26 million people.
- In 2010, nonprofit arts and culture organizations pumped an estimated $61.1 billion into the US economy.
- The longest-running show on Broadway is *The Phantom of the Opera*, which opened January 26, 1988.
- The longest opera is Richard Wagner's *Ring Cycle*, which clocks in at 18 hours (including intermission). It is made up of 4 parts, *Das Rheingold, Die Walküre, Siegfried,* and *Götterdämmerung*.
- The San Francisco Ballet is America's first and oldest professional ballet company, founded in 1933.
- The "Ode to Joy" hymn is the official anthem of the European Union. Beethoven wrote the best-known musical setting for the ode as the final movement of his Ninth Symphony. He wrote it in 1824, when he was almost completely deaf.

Resources

Websites

List of ballet companies in the United States: http://bit.ly/1qGoi26.

List of orchestra and opera houses in the United States: http://bit.ly/1sTKy4Z.

The Performing Arts Encyclopedia from the Library of Congress: http://1.usa.gov/1l5qh8j.

Theater Mania (for theater everywhere): theatermania.com.

Volunteer Match lists performing arts centers that are looking for volunteers: http://bit.ly/1nMIQm4.

Yahoo! Directory of Performing Arts: http://bit.ly/1tdL9lR.

Apps

The Internet Broadway Database of shows produced on Broadway over the last three centuries, historical information about theaters, and various statistics: ibdb.com, and app for iPhone, iPad, and iPod Touch: http://bit.ly/UvFBUH.

Video

First Position (2012), starring Aran Bell, Gaya Bommer, Yemini; directed by Bess Krugman.

The Italian Opera Collection (2008), starring Luciano Pavarotti and the Metropolitan Opera.

Magic Moments of Opera (2011), starring Placido Domingo, Joyce DiDonato.

Place to Dance—Royal Ballet School Documentary: http://bit.ly/1psLU3O.

Reading

The Guide to Performing Arts Resources provides information on collections and other resources at the Library of Congress pertaining to music, theatre, and dance: http://1.usa.gov/1o4ukSe.

Gustav Kobbé, *The Complete Opera Book: The Stories of the Operas, together with 400 of the Leading Airs and Motives in Musical Notation* (Charleston, SC: Nabu Press, 2012).

Henry W. Simon, *100 Great Operas And Their Stories: Act-By-Act Synopses* (New York, NY: Anchor Books, 2013).

CHAPTER 11

Fiction Writer

Writing is easy.
All you have to do is cross out the wrong words. —Mark Twain

Fiction writing includes a wide variety of genres with different characters, settings, and conflicts. Popular fiction, also known as commercial fiction, includes genres such as mystery/thriller, romance, horror, adventure, science fiction, and fantasy, among others. Literary fiction can touch on some of these genres as well, but focuses on complex issues and the style of the prose is emphasized. Fiction appeals to all ages, and there are separate categories within the genres for adults, children, and young-adult readers.

The Business of Writing Books

Americans buy billions of books each year. Most are in print format, but e-books continue to grow in popularity. In 2012, e-book sales represented 22 percent of the market. Of all titles on the Amazon bestseller list, 70 percent are fiction. Amazon sold 822,585,334 fiction books worldwide in 2009. Mystery, YA (young-adult), and romance are the most popular and make up nearly 40 percent of sales. Readers sixty years old and older purchased 52 percent of all mystery/detective books. When that boomer demographic is combined with Gen-Xers (those age forty-two to fifty-nine years old) that statistic jumps to 83 percent. This same percentage (83 percent) holds true for romance novels for the same combined age groups.

The book-publishing business is changing significantly, and authors have many more options to publish their work than in the past. The large traditional publishing houses have consolidated and independent publishers, known as indies, are proliferating. Independent publishers include small presses, midsize independent publishers, university presses, e-book publishers, and self-published authors.

Phyllis, author of The Gold Banded Box

Phyllis is sixty-seven years old, lives in Fresno, California, and is a retired teacher. She credits the many students she's taught through the years as her greatest incentive for writing.

Phyllis: I began my career teaching elementary school and then left for thirteen years to raise a family. When my children were older, I returned to college, earned a secondary-school teaching credential, and taught high school English for twenty-five years. I started writing by creating skits for the students to use in the classroom. The skits gradually became plays with scenes and dialogue. My writing intertwined with creating curriculum to teach my classes.

Every February, our school would commemorate Black History Month. One summer, a parent helped me write a kindergarten-through-third-grade Black History curriculum unit. It was so successful, we were asked to create a curriculum unit for grades four through six. Our goal was to teach our black students how to understand their heritage without being ashamed of it. All of the research I did to prepare that curriculum was the springboard for my future writing.

What genre of fiction do you write?

Phyllis: I write historical fiction, stories that take place in the past. My stories have fictional characters living in real places and participating in true events. *Readers can learn a great deal of factual historical information from historical fiction.*

How did you become interested in writing historical fiction?

Phyllis: Years ago, I attended a concert featuring a hundred-boy choir. They sang gospel music, songs once referred to as the "old Negro spirituals of the South." I was raised in California, not the Deep South, and I knew some of the songs, but not many. One of the songs was "Lift Every Voice." I didn't know it. My California education didn't include the same music that is treasured in the South. The performance was a very moving experience for me.

On the ride home, a story began to develop in my head as I wondered what it must have been like for an African to come to this country as a slave. What was it like to experience traveling that Middle Passage that brought slaves from West Africa to the New

World? I thought about the journey taking weeks or longer, depending on weather conditions. I was so moved by the music that I wanted to develop a story with it in mind.

The Journey

Phyllis: I wrote a play called Oh Freedom based on that music. I spent many months doing the background research to present a historically accurate picture, and presented the play in many churches all over California. People told me that I should turn this play into a book. I kept telling myself, "I don't know how to write a book." For years, I dismissed the idea. One woman in particular kept telling me, "It must be a book; it must be a book." The play became the backbone of what would eventually become a trilogy.

What is the story?

Phyllis: The story is a saga that traces the heritage of Dignity Fairchild's family. She discovers the proud heritage of generations fractured by one fateful choice. In 1801, her ancestor, sixteen-year old, pregnant Folayan, is plunged into a shocking journey from Africa to America. Folayan's faith, fortitude, and determination show Dignity the path to true freedom.

"We Want the Book"

Phyllis: I wrote the book and sent it off to a publisher and the publisher said, "We want the book." They told me that they wanted more and asked if I could develop it into a trilogy. I spent years working on it, dividing the book into two with the goal of adding a third book.

I called the trilogy The Gold Banded Box. Book 1: Folayan's Journey; Book 2: Secrets of Erin Lane; and Book 3: Redemption Song. The golden box is a music box that was purchased by the mistress on the same day that Folayan was purchased as a slave. She uses the box as a jewelry box and it has a parallel adventure through the story.

Ultimately, the publisher did not accept the manuscript. The review board consisted of twenty-one people. Three of the members felt that the book wouldn't have the audience needed to make the book a success.

Writing Workshops

Phyllis: After that experience, I joined a writing workshop. I learned step-by-step how to write a novel; I learned how to structure the story, develop characters, create imagery, and generate emotion. Our instructor always reminded us that sometimes truth is stranger than fiction. We should make our stories include truth whenever possible.

I learned to write so that when people read the words they feel like they're there, that it's believable. The workshop turned into a writing group that met every week for three hours each session. People would come and go—I stayed. The instructor became my mentor. I continued writing for three years while I was earning a master's degree.

This writing workshop was the beginning and the kick-start that brought the writing process all together for me. Every writer needs other eyes and ears to read his or her work. We used to say each one of the other writers in the group represented twenty to thirty thousand other readers. When the other writers in the group comment on your work, it's important to listen. Their opinions are valuable to the writing process. If they were confused with a passage, then many others will be confused as well. It might be your experience, but as a writer, you must make sure that the reader is experiencing the same feelings that you have.

Travel

Phyllis: I've traveled to twenty-nine countries, sixteen in Africa. I've traveled to Ghana twice. This is where the story in my book begins. Before I arrived, I made a list of twenty things that I wanted to see and do. When I visited places, I wanted to make sure I could describe the settings in detail. I wanted to see and experience the many places that I had researched.

I met with a historian who was the curator of a museum in Ghana. He gave me three hours of his time. I read to him what I had written from my research and he filled in the blanks with full, true detail. He knew the area that I studied that became the setting for the dungeon where my character was taken. I wanted to describe the hilltop where she lived and the markets that she frequented. It adds to the richness of the story.

My First Writers' Conference

Phyllis: Writers' conferences are very important because I gain a great deal of information all in one place and the prospect of a completely new set of eyes and ears reviewing my work. It is an opportunity to meet with editors, agents, and representatives of publishing houses. The Southern California Writers' Conference included a program in which professional editors critique writers' manuscripts. I submitted the twenty pages required for review. Since I keep my chapters short, between nine and twelve pages, the twenty-page submission included most of the first two chapters. Each chapter is a mini story of its own. It has its own dramatic structure that hooks the reader to continue on to the next chapter. The dramatic structure includes the exposition (or introduction), the rising action, climax, falling action, and dénouement (or resolution).

Several people read my submission and I received very good feedback. At the end of the conference, at the farewell banquet, they announced that I was the winner of the Southern California Writers' Conference Outstanding Fiction Award. I was flabbergasted.

Critique Is Important

Phyllis: I think writing groups are very necessary, and I belong to two groups. One I go to every week, and the other maybe once a month. You have to have something prepared to present to the group each time. A writer needs to hear feedback. Even if it's just one other person. Join meet-up groups in your area or meet groups online. It is very important to have people critique. The more ears listening to your words, the better. Is the writing believable? Are listeners confused? What do they not understand?

An effective group doesn't only give compliments; it must be a working group. A good working group might include individuals that show different strengths; for example, it may include someone to comment on grammar, and another who is good in character development. Rather than comments like "This is great," it is more helpful to hear ones like "But does it track chronologically? Does it track emotionally? Is it vivid with good imagery—sight, sounds, taste, and touch? Can you pare down the words to produce crisp, clear writing? Are you saying things repetitively?" I learned that the same word shouldn't be used twice on the same page. I also try to replace the "to be" verbs such as "am," "are," and "is," with words that are more powerful. Sometimes everyone will catch the same problem or inconsistency. Feedback is valuable.

My writing teacher also belongs to a critique group for her own benefit. They call themselves the "Fang and Claw" group, which suggests you should be open to constructive criticism and not be thin-skinned if you want your writing to improve.

A Contest a Week

Phyllis: Creating a credible writing portfolio or "platform" is important. "Something in the mail every Friday" is the motto of one of my colleagues in the writing group. She enters lots of writing contests. All of this builds her platform. Many different writing groups and conferences sponsor contests all of the time. The motto encourages writers to write something and get into the habit of submitting their work regularly.

Any other writing tips?

Phyllis: Many of my colleagues use storyboards, but since my story is over a long period of time, I use extensive timelines. I also color code each of the characters' dialogues. I use different-color highlighters for each character to see how it's tracking or I use the highlight function on the computer.

What expenses are involved?

Phyllis: A computer is a must and MS Word software or a compatible program is the standard. You need a printer and you'll go through lots of ink and paper. I print on two sides of paper to save money. Budget $600 to get started if you don't have that equipment.

Add to the budget the cost of writing workshops. Writing is not something done quickly, so our writing instructor tries to keep monthly tuition low. She told us it takes just as long for someone to learn to write well as to become a physician. I pay $35 a month for writing-workshop tuition. Look into what your local communities offer in terms of adult education programs and local writers' groups. You can always purchase instructional writing books and do the exercises if you don't have a class nearby.

Prospective writers need Strunk & White's Elements of Style, one grammar book, and a good dictionary to look up the meaning, spelling, or etymology of a word. Etymology is especially important to me, writing historical fiction. I need to know what words meant at a certain time in history.

How much time do you spend on this pursuit?

Phyllis: I'm trying to be healthy, so I make myself go to bed during sleeping hours. Now, I spend between five and seven hours a day writing. When I first started writing, I would spend twelve hours a day at it. It becomes an obsession. It's an isolating pursuit with lots of time away from the family. Even though I'm in the house, I'm not available. If I could spend more time I would, but my family beckons.

What is the most rewarding aspect of this activity?

Phyllis: When I sit down to write I don't know where the story is going. It's very exciting to me when the story starts developing. I don't have it planned, nor do I know what to do next; it just evolves. I feel that I'm receiving spiritual direction.

I find it rewarding to write historical fiction. It's a form of story that appeals to both adults and youth. When I would read my stories to my high school students, the boys would be just as engrossed as the girls were. I loved it when students said, "I didn't know that" and were learning through a story.

Self-Publishing

Phyllis: I went to another writers' conference and submitted my work for critique. One editor took me by the hand and introduced me to a professional literary agent, who wanted me to send her the entire manuscript. However, I feel that if I bring my book to a traditional publisher, it will be put in line with a long list of others. Maybe it will be accepted, maybe not. It's a long process. I'm going to self-publish the story. I've decided it will give me the control I want.

I have many stories in my head. I want to do a book a year. I think my next book will be a children's book. I'll combine my kindergarten-through-twelfth-grade teaching experience and lean in that direction.

Is there anything I haven't asked you that you think is important for readers to know?

Phyllis: My writing has been a journey of twenty years. I have a supportive group of writing friends that have bonded together and watched my progress. The story has morphed from song to play to novel to trilogy. My friends have witnessed the trauma, drama, and stresses of a writer and I still keep going. It's not an activity for the faint of heart. It that's what passion looks like—methinks it probably is.

FASCINATING FACTS

- In 2014, the Harris Poll reported that the Bible remains America's favorite book. *Gone with the Wind* and the Harry Potter series are second and third favorites.
- J.K. Rowling's *Harry Potter and the Deathly Hallows* had an initial print run of 12 million copies, making it the largest initial print run ever.
- John Grisham has not missed a year in the top-fifteen bestseller list since his first appearance with *The Firm* in 1991.
- According to a survey conducted by *The New York Times*, 81 percent of Americans feel they have a book in them. However, most haven't written it.
- Authors Virginia Woolf, Walt Whitman, Emily Dickinson, Jane Austen, e.e. cummings and Mark Twain self-published their early works.
- Several different authors under the pseudonym Carolyn Keene wrote the old Nancy Drew mysteries. Every writer of a Nancy Drew book earned $125.

Resources

Websites

Agent Query: agentquery.com.

International Thriller Writers: thrillerwriters.org.

A list of free fiction-writing courses: http://bit.ly/1khMAgc.

A list of writers' conferences and contests by date: http://bit.ly/1o4uVDy.

National Novel Writing Month (NaNoWriMo): Write a novel in a month! nanowrimo.org.

Resources for Children's Writers: resourcesforchildrenswriters.com.

Script magazine is a great online resource for scriptwriters: scriptmag.com.

Science Fiction & Fantasy Writers of America: sfwa.org.

Writers Café: writerscafe.org.

Writer's Digest. Their website is a resource for competitions, conferences, and online writing classes: WritersDigest.com.

Apps

Dragon Dictation: Not Being Near a Keyboard Is No Excuse: nuancemobilelife.com.

Spice Mobile by The Writer's Muse, LLC, a helpful creative-writing app: http://bit.ly/1rVvQv5.

Write or Die 2 by Dr. Wicked eliminates writer's block by providing consequences for procrastination and rewards for accomplishment: writeordie.com.

Video

90 Inspiring Author Videos for Aspiring Writers: http://bit.ly/1l5rrAO.

Video interviews with top children's book authors and illustrators: http://bit.ly/1nLBUXP.

Writing by Writers: http://bit.ly/1oxfSXZ.

Reading

Sherrilyn Kenyon, *The Writer's Digest Character Naming Sourcebook* (Cincinnati, Ohio: Writer's Digest Books, 2005).

Carla King, *Self-Publishing Boot Camp Guide for Authors: Step-by-Step to Self-Publishing Success* (Misadventures Media, 2013).

Stephen King, *On Writing: A Memoir of the Craft* by (New York, NY: Scribner, 2000).

William Strunk Jr. and E. B. White, *The Elements of Style* (New York, NY: Penguin Press, 2005).

Ronald B. Tobias, 20 Master Plots and How to Build Them (Cincinnati, Ohio: Writer's Digest Books, 1993).

CHAPTER 12

Stone Sculptor

Art washes away from the soul
the dust of everyday life.
—Pablo Picasso

Sculpture is three-dimensional art; it has height, weight, and depth. It can be viewed from all perspectives, or as a "relief," raised to stand out from a background. Sculpture includes any form of art that involves shaping a medium—for example, molding clay, carving wood, welding metal, or chiseling stone.

Cultures of every era incorporate the art of stone sculpture to express their human spirit. Early examples include China's Terracotta Warriors; the Greek statute of *Venus de Milo*; the monolithic statues of Easter Island; and Michelangelo's *David* and the *Pieta*. Examples that are more modern include Mount Rushmore and Christ the Redeemer in Brazil and the Martin Luther King Memorial erected on the National Mall in Washington, DC, in 2011.

The History and Evolution of Sculpture

The earliest known works of sculpture date from around BCE 32,000. Early peoples created small animals and human figures carved in bone, ivory, or stone. In the fifteenth century, monuments to biblical heroes lined the streets of Italian cities. Neoclassical sculpture in the eighteenth century used white marble to imitate the great art of the ancient Greeks and Romans.

In the latter half of the nineteenth and the early twentieth century, sculptors paid more attention to design, form, and contrasting qualities of the surface of the material. In the later twentieth century, artists explored abstraction or simplified forms and eliminated realistic details. Some artists removed their sculptures from traditional pedestals and instead hung the work on wires or cables to allow movement and created kinetic sculptures. Recently, some are mixing sculptures with sound, light, and video images to create three-dimensional environments, producing a multisensory experience.

Carolyn in her studio

Carolyn: I was born seventy years ago and raised in San Francisco at a time when the city was family-friendly, and my neighborhood included two famous museums: the Legion of Honor and the De

Young. As a child, I would run and play in the parks surrounding those museums all the time. I would wander throughout the grand halls whenever I wanted and explored all the famous collections.

The Legion of Honor was built to commemorate the Californian soldiers who died in World War I, and is a replica of the eighteenth-century Palais de la Légion d'Honneur in Paris and was built by the French for the San Francisco International Exposition of 1915. It is recognized for its European decorative arts, sculpture, and painting. The de Young Museum first opened in 1895 and displays American art from the seventeenth through the twentieth centuries, textile arts, and art of the ancient Americas, Oceania, and Africa.

Carolyn: Back when I was a young girl, there was no cost to get into the museums, and so I would go there all the time. It was relaxed and you could stay as long as you wanted and no one thought a thing about an unaccompanied child wandering around. I think viewing wonderful art is what inspired me. I also had a father who was interested in the arts. Those days of my exposure to the museums, that's what caught me.

How did you become interested in this pursuit?

Carolyn: It started just from being interested in the arts from childhood, but I never pursued it. Years later, I went back to school to finish my degree. I needed another class, so I took Sculpture 101 at my local community college, and my teacher told me, "You know, you're a sculptor."

But it really wasn't until my husband, Don, was diagnosed with Alzheimer's disease that I discovered I could sculpt. He was the artist. He had the classical art training that I never had. Don was twenty-two years older than I was, and after World War II, he used the GI Bill to attend Kansas City Art Institute for two years. From there he studied in Paris for one year and another year in Florence.

His intention was to become a portrait artist but that didn't work out. He moved out west and became a drafter. He took other jobs using his art to make a living, but it was never fine art. I married him with a fantasy that I was marrying an artist, but he never brought it to real fulfillment. So I said, "I'm tired of trying to get him to do art that I want, so I'll have to do it myself." And that's where it led. When Don was diagnosed with Alzheimer's, sculpting was my anchor. But it was also helpful for him because I could ask him for advice and he became my mentor as much as he could and was engaged in something that was fascinating to him, too.

How did you get started?

Carolyn: My sculpture class at the community college was limited to what materials the budget allowed, and that was clay and wood. Don and I attended an art festival and got into a conversation with a stone sculptor. He gave me a piece of soapstone and I took it to class and worked on it. I would sculpt, and both the teacher and Don would give me pointers. I also learned a lot by just doing it myself and talking to others. Sometime after that first class, I joined with a group that continued sculpting at a nearby town that had a class at a community recreation center.

As my husband's illness progressed, I did what sculpting I could. I stopped for a while because it became too solitary. After my husband died, I reconnected with students from that sculpture class. We now rent a garage that serves as our collective studio.

Describe the setting where your activity takes place.

Carolyn: I sculpt in a residential garage on a large parcel of land nestled in the green, rolling foothills of Mt. Diablo in Northern California. Eight sculptors share the space and divide the rent. It's filled with everyone's projects in various stages of completion. Sculpting is a solitary hobby, but I'm often with the group in the studio. I think this improves my output. For me it's the social connection. There are times when the chatter interferes, but I get advice, motivation, and inspiration from the group as well. I spend about twelve hours a week sculpting. I don't usually keep track of how many hours I spend on each piece.

What special clothes and equipment do you use?

Carolyn: I have my own tools, which I bring back and forth with me because I sculpt at home as well as in the studio. I wear safety glasses and a dust mask and work with a variety of tools. You have to take care of your health. There is this problem with stone dust. Granite dust is toxic, as are others. When I worked on a piece of Baja onyx, I had to use a wet grinder to keep the dust down because that dust is like slivers of glass and you don't want that getting in your lungs. I have a special mask that I use. When I'm working with some stone, I use rubber boots and a rubber apron as well.

Tools Used in the Sculpting Process

Carolyn: I use the subtractive process when sculpting stone, which is removing material that doesn't belong. I start with a hammer and a point chisel to get the rough shape. Then I start to refine the form using a variety of chisels. Sculpting chisels come in different widths and numbers of teeth. I also use flat chisels and rondelles, which are rounded chisels, and different files, which are crosshatched flat blades.

You can buy inexpensive tools for $12 to $15 each that work fine with soapstone. Harder stone requires better tools—for example, those made in the UK or Italy. I have three different electric tools that are costly. When working with marble, which is very hard, you need a grinder. When I worked on a 350-pound piece of travertine marble, I needed pneumatic tools, so I had to buy a compressor and tools for that. I've spent hundreds of dollars on equipment.

When I am happy with the shape, I stop chiseling and start to sand. You may begin with a sixty or eighty-grit sandpaper and graduate to finer and finer sanding. I used Picasso marble to create one piece and worked up to two-thousand-grit sandpaper. You can choose to keep some texture, or if you want your piece perfectly smooth, you don't stop until stone no longer comes off while sanding. It varies with the individual artist and stone.

What kind of stone does a sculptor use?

Carolyn: The first stone I used was soapstone.

With a Mohs hardness of 2, soapstone is an easily worked stone, commonly used by beginning students of stone carving. In 1812, the German mineralogist Friedrich Mohs (1773–1839), who selected the ten minerals that were commonly used during that time, devised the Mohs scale of mineral hardness. The Mohs scale of hardness ranges from 1 (talcum powder) to 10 (diamond).

Alabaster (3 on the Mohs scale) is more durable than soapstone and is cherished for its translucence. Limestone and sandstone, at about 4 on the Mohs scale, are the only sedimentary stones commonly carved. Marble, travertine, and onyx are at 6 on the Mohs scale. Marble, especially Carrara marble from Tuscany, is the preferred stone for sculptors in the European tradition and has been used since the time of Ancient Rome. For Michelangelo, at least, Carrara marble was valued above all other stone. It's said that he would spend months in the Carrara mines looking for the right stone. The hardest stone frequently carved is granite, at about 8 on the Mohs scale. Mount Rushmore and the Crazy Horse Memorial are massive examples of this extremely hard stone to work.

What comes first, the stone or the idea? How do you decide what to carve?

Carolyn: Every one of us at the studio decides differently. I find a stone I like and then I develop my design around the lines of that stone. That's called direct carving. One of my colleagues is a painter and she sketches out her designs of what she wants to sculpt. Others create a mock-up in clay, known as a maquettte.

For me, I see a stone that I like—the color, shape, feel. On my last piece, I found a stone that wasn't very big, but on the front of it was this wonderful round, rust-colored skin. I wasn't fond of the shape, but I really liked the rust color. I worked with it and it evolved into a nice artistic piece. Another time, I chose a piece of soapstone and immediately saw a bird in the shape. I had no idea how the final piece would look, but in the end, it turned into a pretty bird.

I'm an abstractionist, an organic abstract sculptor, actually. As my work evolves, my original concept doesn't change. It remains constant. It might be something like creative writing: the writer starts with an idea and the creative impulse reveals hidden expressions as the writer progresses. I work on stones that have some natural shape to them, not angular blocks of cut stone. I study the stone for its rhythms and special characteristics and work with those qualities. The shape, the color, and texture evoke an emotional response that represents the challenges and pleasure I like to work with. I like to honor the stone and in some way let the stone speak for itself.

I once worked with a 350-pound piece of travertine marble that was a project commissioned by a friend. I studied it for a long time, agonized over it, until it revealed itself. It's an ongoing process. Uncertainty doesn't bother me, and as I work, the sculpture evolves. It's an instinctive process; you allow yourself to connect with the stone and the piece develops.

What expenses are involved?

Carolyn: One ongoing cost is my share of the rent for the studio. There are start-up costs for tools. You buy the kind and size stone that you can afford. I'm always looking for good deals. I know a fellow who is downsizing his supply, so I bought a stone from him for

$1.20 a pound. The last piece I did was from Japanese Wonderstone and that was $2 a pound. I've also worked with Baja onyx, Carrara marble, gold travertine, and Utah, Raspberry, and Colorado alabaster. The gold travertine was for the 350-pound commissioned project that I mentioned, and I spent over $500 on that. My favorite stone that I've worked with so far is the Carrara marble because of the wonderful texture and smooth finish when it's polished, and the emotional connection with Michelangelo.

For someone just starting, you can take it slow and limit your expenses. Take a class, view videos on YouTube, and there are many books in the library or online. You can buy a beginning stone-sculpting kit for $25 to $40 that includes soapstone and some tools. Additional costs include the many workshops all over the US and Europe that are available.

What is the most rewarding aspect of this activity?

Carolyn: The final job. My piece is finished! But it's also the pleasure sculpting gives to me and those I share it with. There's a satisfaction about that. Sculpting gives a stone a different life. It brings out the life that a piece of stone wouldn't have had otherwise. There's pleasure in that.

I don't think we pay enough interest in the arts, and those of us who ignore our artistic skills do so at our own peril. I think it's important to our well-being to create with art. I think this applies to everyone, but especially young people meandering through life. It's important that we allow our kids to develop rather than suppress artistic expression. When you find an artistic outlet—wow, it's a wonderful experience. I feel I would have done so much more if I had known that earlier.

Any interesting stories connected with your passionate pursuit?

Carolyn: Learning how to move a 350-pound piece of stone onto a sculpting table was a first for me. A friend helped me and we used a plank of wood about eight inches wide and two inches thick. We set up a fulcrum point and used the plank as leverage. Of course, the fulcrum and lever is one of the six simple machines identified by Renaissance scientists. I know a woman in her eighties who is still sculpting and moving large stones.

My Biggest Financial Success So Far

Carolyn: I began working with a Japanese Wonderstone, and I wasn't happy with it. In fact, I hated that stone. At first, the stone kept crumbling, but after I lopped off a piece and conferred with an associate, I started sanding it and continued to work with it. A man I had worked with wanted one of my sculptures. He had no idea what I was working on; he just said he wanted to buy one of my pieces. So I brought him that piece when it was finished.

I was worried as to how to price the piece, but I felt $2,000 was the minimum amount I wanted to receive for all of my work. My colleagues gave me some negotiation pointers, telling me not to go more than $200 below what I thought was a fair price. So I went to see him and I figured if he didn't want it that would be OK. He and his family looked at the piece and after an hour of visiting, he said to me, "Carolyn, I'll write you a check, and you fill in the amount." I left with a check for $2,500!

Do you have any plans that may evolve within this hobby?

Carolyn: I want to increase the number of pieces I sell. I've only done twelve pieces so far and sold five of them. Of the pieces I've sold, the prices range from $50 to $2,500. I think I would enjoy doing that instead of getting a part-time job to supplement my income. Also, maybe I'd like to have a small show, but I will need more pieces for that. And I know I need to get a website and network with more people who may want to buy my work.

FASCINATING FACTS

- Michelangelo's father and uncles often beat him when he first began to draw. They worried that an artist in the family would bring disgrace.
- The Spring Temple Buddha, depicting the Vairocana Buddha, was built in 2002 in China and, at 420 feet, is the tallest statue in the world.
- The Renaissance masterpiece *The Pieta* is the only work that Michelangelo ever signed.
- Mr. John Gutzon Borglum began sculpting Mount Rushmore on October 3, 1927. His son, Lincoln Borglum, completed it on October 3, 1941.
- Actress Gina Lollobrigida sculpted over 60 pieces, many of them graceful dancers and some in marble.
- Michelangelo, Raphael, and Leonardo da Vinci were all left-handed.
- *L'Homme Qui Marche I* (Walking Man I), a life-size bronze sculpture by Alberto Giacometti, sold at auction in 2011 for $104 million. Bidding for the most expensive work of art ever took just 8 minutes.

Resources

Websites

The International Sculpture Center lists universities that offer graduate and undergraduate classes in stone sculpting: http://bit.ly/X00xVt.

US local and regional sculptors' societies: http://bit.ly/1xla3O7.

For classes, check your local town or city art museums, recreation departments, adult education programs, community colleges, and nearby universities.

Apps

iMuseum is a web tracker, and searches via GPS for the nearest museums in your immediate area: http://bit.ly/1xla98j.

Videos

YouTube has many tutorial videos of various media: YouTube.com.

Introduction to Stone Carving Tools and Techniques, Minneapolis Institute of Art: http://bit.ly/1psPScJ.

Stone Sculpture Tutorial: Limestone carving by French artist Frederic Chevarin: http://bit.ly/WIYndb.

Reading

Milt Liebson, *Direct Stone Sculpture: A Guide to Technique and Creativity* (Atglen, PA: Schiffer Pub, 2001).

Dona Z. Meilach, *Contemporary Stone Sculpture: Aesthetics Methods Appreciation* (New York, NY: Crown Publishers, 1970).

Stephen C. Norton, *Shaping Stone Volume One: The Art of Carving Soapstone* (Victoria, BC: NorthwindInk, 2011).

Josepmaria Texido and Jacinto Santamera, *Sculpture in Stone* (Hauppauge, New York: Barron's Educational Series, 2001).

Sculpture Magazine: http://bit.ly/1rrA8Ju.

PART 3

CIVIC AND SOCIAL PARTICIPATION

CHAPTER 13

Disaster-Response Worker

On every battlefield, a flag of mercy flies.
Its white field bears a Red Cross-the universal
symbol of human compassion.
Under that flag, there are no enemies,
no racial or religious animosities.
There are only brothers.
—President Lyndon B. Johnson

Americans help one another during disasters. Neighbors from down the street, across town, and across the country respond to one another in emergencies. In natural and man-made disasters, citizens step forward to provide relief, recovery, and rebuilding. Disaster-response volunteers respond to the emergencies of bombings, fires, floods, tornadoes, hurricanes, earthquakes, heat waves, and blizzards. They provide food, shelter, clothing, medical attention, and emotional support.

Working Together

The National Voluntary Organizations Active in Disasters (NVOAD) includes 110 organizations throughout the nation. Members represent a diverse group of established emergency-service organizations providing a wide range of skills when a disaster strikes. Faith-based and community-based groups work together with government entities to coordinate their unique skills to serve the needs of disaster victims. Some well-known groups are the American Red Cross, Community Emergency Response Teams (CERT), Catholic Charities, Convoy of Hope, Habitat for Humanity, Lutheran Disaster Response, and the Salvation Army. The Resource section gives information on these and other emergency responders.

American Red Cross

The American Red Cross has a special relationship with the US government. In 1905, the independent organization received a congressional charter that delegates specific responsibilities to the organization. The Red Cross provides disaster relief, supports America's military families, gathers and provides life-saving blood and blood products, and offers health and safety training. It is not a federal agency and does not receive federal funding. The nonprofit organization depends on charitable contributions and cost-recovery charges for providing blood for all medical needs and teaching safety training courses. Chapters are organized in communities all over the country and are staffed primarily (96 percent) by volunteers.

The American Red Cross responds to more than 70,000 disasters and emergencies every year, supporting first responders as well as victims of disasters. Emergency assistance is available daily in communities throughout the country, coming to the aid of those displaced by single-residence fires in local neighborhoods, as well as large-scale efforts during a national disaster.

Disaster Services

Every eight minutes the American Red Cross responds to a disaster in a US community. Most often, these disasters are home fires. Red Cross volunteers work with firefighters and other emergency personnel attending to the victims' immediate needs—food, lodging, clothing, medication replacement, and mental-health counseling. In the days following a disaster, Red Cross caseworkers continue to work with families while they find ways to rebuild their lives.

Peter, American Red Cross disaster services leader

Peter is sixty-four years old and lives near Berkeley, California. He retired from a varied background, including nineteen years working in the high technology sector involved in the design of integrated circuits. He's also done consulting and contracting work in the high-tech and biotech fields.

Peter: I fell into volunteering. I became involved in Experience Unlimited, a volunteer network of business professionals who support each other with job-search marketing skills and by sharing job leads. I really enjoyed it and wound up running it for two years. I tend to jump into things with both feet.

My brother-in-law told me about the Red Cross. I joined in 2010, but had previously committed to working on a temporary assignment for the US Census. So when that was completed, I became involved with the Red Cross Disaster Action Team.

What is your involvement with the Red Cross locally?

Peter: I'm the chairperson for the Red Cross Disaster Services Team for my local county. I work with a dedicated group of volunteers who respond to disasters by providing a variety of services to clients in need. Disaster Services includes emergency response vehicles, mass-care shelter and feeding, logistical and technology support for response teams, client caseworkers, health and mental-health support, and the Disaster Action Team.

Disaster Action Team

The Disaster Action Team (DAT) responds twenty-four hours a day, 365 days per year. Volunteers sign up for a twelve-hour on-call day or night shift and respond immediately when called by emergency dispatch. A team lead, technician, and trainee provide emergency relief to clients who have suffered a loss, such as a house fire. Red Cross assistance may include temporary emergency shelter, emotional support, replacement medication and eyeglasses, and financial assistance for items such as immediate food and clothing needs.

Peter: I serve as a DAT lead. The fire department calls us to help those in need. Most of our calls involve helping individuals, a single family, or multiple families affected by disaster. The DAT team also responds to bigger calamities. My team worked on a large gas-line explosion and fire in San Bruno. We prepared a safe place for those evacuated, opening a shelter where multiple families could regroup, rest, eat, and sleep.

How much time do you spend on this activity?

Peter: How much time a volunteer spends depends on the volunteer job. DAT volunteers sign up for shifts. They can choose to be on-call days or nights, and they choose how many shifts they want to cover. As chair of the entire Disaster Services Team, I've spent a lot of time this past year on special projects. A client caseworker might be a better example of how much time a typical volunteer spends. If it's busy and the area has had a lot of fires, caseworkers might spend six- to eight-hour days for one week per month helping clients with their recovery plans. The more caseworker volunteers there are, the lighter the individual load.

Tell me about your Red Cross deployments to disasters away from home.

Peter: So far, I've been deployed three times. In the summer of 2011, I spent three weeks at a flood disaster in North Dakota. All available motel rooms were taken because of the huge economic oil boom in the area. So over a hundred relief workers were housed in a mass-care shelter and we slept on cots. It was July, with no air conditioning. Four huge fans, five feet in diameter, ran all night to move air and cool the facility.

I deployed as a Disaster Services Team technology worker, which is a position on the team that provides information technology and communications to support the disaster headquarters or satellite offices. The Red Cross will typically set up offices to perform client casework in different towns to help those affected. Caseworkers provide financial assistance and referrals to local resources and help the family organize its recovery plan.

The Disaster Technology Team will go in and set up computers, printer, and telephones so that caseworkers can meet with those who need assistance. If there is no phone service, we set up satellite terminals. When the disaster has subsided and the caseworkers are finished, we pack all equipment up and ship it back to a large depot in Austin, Texas, to prepare for the next disaster.

The Disaster Technology Team assesses needs, orders the equipment, and then sends it back when no longer needed. We're always installing equipment, taking it down, or moving it. We help people with software applications and troubleshoot any operational problems. We also supply simple, inexpensive cell phones for the Red Cross workers so they can communicate with the rest of the team, shelters, and satellite offices. Multiple workers may use one phone that is passed on as people come to and leave the disaster scene. We might have one hundred phones and surprisingly enough, we generally get them all back. Relief workers are a very conscientious group.

Hurricane Sandy

Peter: For my second and third deployments, I responded to Hurricane Sandy. The first time, I deployed for three weeks and arrived on the first plane allowed to land at JFK Airport after the storm. I made my way to New Jersey and helped set up one of the relief headquarters in North Brunswick. The Andersen Corporation loaned an empty office building for the relief effort. There was no power, so we ran all electrical needs off a small portable generator. Soon, the governor sent in a huge generator that arrived on a flatbed truck. We set up networks, computers, printers, and telephones for all of the support functions.

Unfortunately, we only had the fuel that was delivered in the generator, and we had to shut down because we ran out of fuel. The company owner instructed all of the diesel fuel siphoned out of any trucks that weren't needed, and we used it to run the generators. The logistics team, scouring to find more fuel, found out we were twentieth in line, behind police, fire, hospitals, and other emergency services and received the fuel we needed.

After three weeks, I returned home. I was home for two weeks, and then got the opportunity to deploy back, this time to New York. I did a variety of tasks, such as working in a warehouse helping the effort to load fifty or sixty box trucks with two-way radios for a huge bulk distribution.

I also had the job of delivering phones to ten shelters all over northern New Jersey, and I saw what the hurricane had done. It wasn't total destruction everywhere. Instead, there were large areas here and there where the high winds had touched down and it looked like a giant had stepped down and destroyed everything in its path. There was one footprint of destruction and then way far away, another total-loss footprint. In between, areas were untouched. Even if the residents were spared destruction, everyone was without electrical power.

What are the living and working conditions like during a deployment?

Peter: It varies by location. When you work in a shelter, you eat and sleep at the shelter. Often, the workers will have a separate area within the shelter to sleep, but the cots are just the same as what the clients get. When I was in North Dakota, we had to be careful not to drink the water that was polluted due to the massive flooding. We took quick showers in water that was available and used bottled water for drinking and brushing our teeth.

During Hurricane Sandy, I stayed in a hotel room and had a series of roommates. We all come, go, and don't see much of each other. I was advised ahead of time to bring eyeshades and earplugs, and they came in handy in both situations.

Working in a disaster-relief effort is very busy. During my first New Jersey deployment when I helped set up offices, we worked twelve- to sixteen-hour days. Generally, you'll work twelve-hour days, then taper back to eight- or nine-hour shifts when things calm down. It's long hours in the beginning and it stabilizes after a while. The relief effort is always gaining and shedding workers in response to needs. It's like an inverted "V," scaling up, scaling, up; then scaling down, scaling down.

Who are Red Cross disaster workers?

Peter: I've met people of all ages and from all walks of life and 99.9 percent of them are really nice. Most are easy to work with and very friendly. Most volunteers are retirees. One of my hotel roommates was an eighty-one-year old Emergency Response Vehicle driver from Texas. His name was Carroll, and he was having a difficult time because they kept giving him female roommates because of his name. I've also worked with young AmeriCorps volunteers. Young adults are very helpful, especially in the IT world, because they're so comfortable with technology.

If you have people skills, or office skills and mobility, you can do this work. You don't have to have an educational degree in anything. It depends on the activity that you sign up to do. If you work in a mass-care shelter, you have to like people and be easy to get along with; logistics workers have to be detail-oriented. There's something for everybody.

Occasionally you'll work with someone with a quirky personality, and it's best to work around the situation as best you can. If people are there for the wrong reasons, not medically able to perform tasks, or unable to contribute for other reasons, they are sent home.

Coping with tragedy and devastation is hard. First responders, front-line relief personnel, and caseworkers work under difficult conditions. I was very moved in North Dakota, where houses were flooded with water up to the roofline. I saw saturated furniture and clothes in huge piles of trash outside on the street. Homeowners had started to rebuild by opening up the walls to stop the growing mold. The houses consisted of a floor and vertical studs holding up the roofs. You could look through the studs and see house after house with just the skeleton left. It was very emotional for me.

During Sandy, I saw houses washed out into the ocean and hundreds of people in shelters. The widespread loss of electrical power caused many people to seek refuge in the shelters. An army of power-line workers came from all over the country with hundreds of trucks and worked day and night to restore power.

What special clothes do you pack for a deployment?

Peter: I bring comfortable clothes that wash and dry easily. Synthetics are good because they dry quickly. I come prepared for weather. It's best to "layer up" in cold weather. Workers don't bring their own electronics and don't wear jewelry or bring anything personal that can be lost.

What expenses are involved?

Peter: There are very little out-of-pocket expenses. Red Cross orientation is free, as are most of the training classes. When a Disaster Action Team trainee learns the procedures, and graduates to a technician level, he or she is given a Red Cross vest, identification card on a lanyard, and a hard hat for protection at the disaster site. Most volunteers do buy their own Red Cross T-shirts, hats, or jackets. Volunteers who use their own car will incur the cost for gas. The federal government allows an income-tax credit for volunteering for charitable work, but it's not much. Sometimes a Red Cross chapter vehicle is available for certain assignments.

The Red Cross will cover the cost of travel for deployment assignments, and workers receive a small per diem amount for meals and necessities. The Red Cross supplies workers with phones and computers needed to accomplish an assignment.

What is the most rewarding aspect of this activity?

Peter: The feeling that I'm lending a hand and helping people when they need it. Most people don't ask for help very much; they just work harder to overcome their loss. Occasionally events overwhelm an individual's ability to cope, and it's a chance to go and help someone out. That's why I like being on the DAT team. I get the chance to help in our local community. Sometimes, I'll meet people who are not as needy as they say they are, or those who expect more than a nonprofit organization can afford to give. However, most times people are extremely grateful for us just being there.

Since I'm working in a disaster support function, I get to go everywhere and meet many people throughout the Red Cross effort. I enjoy talking to people and having interesting conversations, finding out where they're from, learning why they're there and what they get out of the experience.

Is there anything I haven't asked you that you'd like to add or think is important for readers to know?

Peter: Not enough people ask themselves, "What if the volunteer work gets to be too much? What if I feel overloaded?" It is very important that you decide how much you want to volunteer. The organization will accommodate that. Don't be afraid to manage your own time. If you want to go on vacation or even try something else for a while, please tell the organization. You can come and go as you wish and do as much as you please. That's not a problem, and many volunteers do that. But you have to tell the organization. Just don't disappear.

FASCINATING FACTS

- Clara Barton risked her life to bring supplies and support to soldiers in the field during the Civil War. At age 60, she founded the American Red Cross in 1881 and led it for the next 23 years.
- The Red Cross has won more Nobel Peace Prizes than anyone.
- September is National Preparedness Month.
- The National Oceanic and Atmosphere Administration (NOAA) organized a list of the most expensive disasters in US history. The top 3:
    1. Hurricane Katrina (August 2005): $148.8 Billion. (Dead: 1,833), Mississippi and Louisiana.
    2. Drought and Heat Wave (1988): $78.8 Billion (Dead: 7,500), central United States
    3. Superstorm Sandy (October 2012): $65.7 Billion (Dead: 159), New York, New Jersey, and other parts of the East Coast.
- On March 4, 2012, President Barack Obama declared March Red Cross Month. This has been a presidential tradition that has been carried out since Franklin Roosevelt's original declaration in 1943.

Resources

Websites

Many of these organizations offer orientation programs, free training, monthly meetings, and practice drills:

American Red Cross: redcross.org.

Catholic Charities: catholiccharitiesusa.org.

Charity Navigator: www.charitynavigator.org.

Community Emergency Response Teams (CERT): http://1.usa.gov/UvMl59.

Convoy of Hope: convoyofhope.org.

Habitat for Humanity: habitat.org.

Lutheran Disaster Response: lutheranchurchcharities.org.

Members of the National Voluntary Organizations Active in Disasters (NVOAD): nvoad.org.

Ready/Get Involved: ready.gov/get-involved.

Salvation Army: salvationarmyusa.org.

Apps

American Red Cross Safe and Well: http://rdcrss.org/1uw9ncA.

Hurricane Tracker: http://rdcrss.org/1owMdKd.

Tornado Warning & Alert: http://rdcrss.org/1rNQiPl.

Videos

American Red Cross: http://bit.ly/1rVFDkV.

Disaster Relief Training videos: http://bit.ly/1xlriPg.

Habitat for Humanity: http://bit.ly/1rrQh1s.

Search on YouTube for "disaster preparedness videos": http://bit.ly/1nLQBtV.

Reading

American Red Cross, KST Productions, and Inc. *First aid for dogs and cats.* (Los Angeles, CA: KST Productions, 2000.

Arthur T. Bradley, *Handbook to Practical Disaster Preparedness for the Family*, 2nd Edition (Lexington, KY: Arthur T. Bradley, 2011).

Bernie Carr, *The Prepper's Pocket Guide: 101 Easy Things You Can Do to Ready Your Home for a Disaster* (Berkeley, CA: Ulysses Press, 2011).

CHAPTER 14

Medicare Counselor

I think that age as a number is not nearly as important as health. You can be in poor health and be pretty miserable at forty or fifty. If you're in good health, you can enjoy things into your eighties.
— Bob Barker

In 1945, President Truman called for a national health insurance program for everyone, but it had no support in Congress. He asked again in 1947 and again in 1949. Any bills introduced were always defeated. Twenty years later, on July 30, 1965, at a public ceremony in Independence, Missouri, President Lyndon Baines Johnson signed Medicare into law. He presented former President Harry S. Truman, then eighty-one years old, with the nation's first Medicare card.

Understanding the ABCs (and Ds) of Medicare

At its creation, Medicare consisted of two parts: Medicare Part A and Medicare Part B. Medicare Part A is hospital insurance coverage, which is financed by payroll deductions and charges no premiums to those who have contributed. Medicare Part B is an optional medical insurance program for which enrollees pay a monthly premium. If the participant is collecting Social Security benefits, the Medicare premium is automatically deducted from the monthly benefit payment.

In 1997, private insurance plans, or Part C, later renamed

Medicare Advantage, gave beneficiaries the option of choosing an HMO-style Medicare plan instead of the traditional fee-for-service Medicare program.

In 2003, President George W. Bush expanded Medicare by signing the Medicare Modernization Act, which established a prescription-drug benefit. This optional drug coverage, for which beneficiaries pay an additional premium, is known as Medicare Part D.

Patient Protection and the Affordable Care Act

The health-care law signed by President Barack Obama in 2010 mandates that Medicare beneficiaries receive certain preventive care services and health screenings, such as yearly physicals and mammograms, free of charge, and reduces the out-of-pocket expenses of Part D enrollees.

Dave, a Medicare counselor

Dave, a sixty-two-year-old retired chemical engineer, moved back to the Detroit, Michigan, area to be closer to his elderly parents. He works part-time in an after-school tutoring program and volunteers as a Medicare Counselor for the Michigan Medicare Medicaid Assistance Program (MMAP), which is part of the State Health Insurance Program (SHIP).

The SHIP Volunteer Program

The State Health Insurance Program (SHIP) is a national program that provides free, local, one-on-one counseling and assistance to Medicare beneficiaries who have questions or issues with their health insurance. The SHIP program is not affiliated with the insurance industry, and major funding comes from the federal Medicare agency.

Most states refer to their Medicare counseling programs as SHIP; however, some states call the same program by a different name. For example California, New York, and Texas call the program HICAP (Health Insurance Counseling & Advocacy Program). Florida's program, called SHINE, is the acronym for Serving Health Insurance Needs of Elders, while the Massachusetts SHINE program stands for Serving Health Insurance Needs of Everyone. The goal remains the same for all state programs: to provide free health-benefit-counseling services to those aged sixty-five and older.

Dave: When I moved back to the Detroit area, I wanted to become involved in volunteer work, which I've done most of my adult life. I heard about a program called RSVP, and spoke with an advisor about volunteer opportunities in my community. The counselor mentioned a dozen organizations and suggested six that might be a good fit. I investigated several of them, and chose to work with the Medicare counselor program.

The RSVP Program

The Retired & Senior Volunteer Program (RSVP) is one of the three Senior Corps programs sponsored by the Corporation for National and Community Service (CNCS), a federal agency that engages millions of Americans in volunteer community service. Another one of the programs is the Foster Grandparents Program, and is featured in Chapter 18 of this book. A third program called the Senior Companion Program provides assistance and friendship to elder adults.

Dave: What made the Medicare counselor assignment appealing to me was that I spent a number of years helping my parents in their transition from handling everything by themselves to where they needed help figuring things out. The first time I got involved with my dad's Medicare summary notices, I asked him, "How do you understand this?" I educated myself and had the feeling at the time that it would be nice if somebody would explain all this stuff to people like me who are helping their folks, and those on Medicare as well. When the RSVP counselor suggested the MMAP/SHIP assignment, that rang a bell right away. I had been through the learning curve already, and I thought that this volunteer opportunity would be a good fit for me at this time in my life.

Transitions

Dave: I learned firsthand how, as we age, things become more difficult. My dad was a very sharp person. He died a month short of his ninety-ninth birthday and still had all of his faculties. He was a little more forgetful, but very capable of independent living. The one thing that became difficult for him was to understand complex things. Complex thinking tasks become difficult as we age. By the time he passed, I was taking care of all the Medicare paperwork and reading notices to help him understand those.

The Training Program

Dave: First, I met with the regional coordinator for the program and helped with some general, non-counseling tasks. Then, I took the counselor training, which was six days long. It is a significant training program. The first day covers, "What is Medicare?" and thoroughly explains all the different parts: A, B, C (Medicare Advantage), and D. Another day covers when people are eligible to sign up for Medicare, different plans, what makes them eligible, when they can change plans, and all the details you will need for counseling. Training also covers Medicaid, and one half day on fraud prevention. There are quizzes at the end of each session to make sure there is complete understanding and that everything was covered adequately.

We attend monthly training updates, which consists of finding out what policy has changed, and preparing for open enrollment. In addition, our coordinator sits in at our first meetings to make sure we are comfortable and offers suggestions if needed.

What makes a good SHIP volunteer?

Dave: I think you need to be able to relate to the senior population. You are going to meet people who are at all stages of the aging process. You must learn to recognize when people are having difficulty making decisions so you know how you go about assisting them without making the decision for them. We are counselors. We are there to educate the Medicare beneficiary so that they understand the system. We are very careful to provide the information without favoring one insurer over another. We empower people to make their own informed decision.

You need to be able to understand all of the rules and regulations of the federal Medicare program. You need to be articulate enough to explain the information, yet be a good listener in order to catch cues that the person is confused. The volunteers come from diverse backgrounds; our group includes a former social worker, market analyst, pharmacy technician, nurse, and a business manager. One former client who called looking for help became a counselor. The volunteers in our office are in that retirement-age range from sixty to eighty years old. One fellow is eighty-five years old and helps by greeting people who come in during busy times such as open enrollment.

I think another important part of the training process is once you learn all of the mechanics of the program, you must learn to structure what you tell people to remain within the bounds of what is impartial.

Where does your activity take place?

Dave: Our group is located with another local program on aging called the Senior Alliance. They provide many services for seniors, such as calling to check in on the welfare of the elderly living alone, home visiting by social workers, and arranging transportation needs for the elderly.

The volunteer will use whatever cubicle is available to counsel by phone. We have an 800 number that allows callers to leave questions and we call them back with answers and consultations. When some subjects are complicated, we may ask the client to come into the office and we will meet with them in a comfortable meeting room.

At open-enrollment time, held annually October 15 through December 7, we go to senior centers, libraries, and churches to reach as many people as we can. We will set up an information area. We bring laptop computers and printers and have four to ten counselors there to answer questions one-on-one. We help them review their prescription drug plan or their Medicare Advantage plan because open enrollment is the time they can change those.

Another area is outreach. We go out into the community to health fairs and senior centers and set up an information table. We also give presentations throughout the year. Some of the topics are Medicare 101, fraud prevention, or an update on what is new in the Medicare program. When the Affordable Care Act became law, many seniors wondered how that would affect Medicare, so we give presentations to reassure those concerned recipients and answer questions.

Medicare Fraud

The FBI works closely with federal, state, and local law enforcement partners to address fraud and abuse. All health-care programs are subject to fraud; however, Medicare and Medicaid programs are the most visible. Estimates show that between 3 and 10 percent of total health-care expenditures are fraudulent billings. Fraud schemes are not specific to any area, but affect the entire country. The schemes target large health-care programs as well as beneficiaries. The fraud schemes are becoming more sophisticated and are now increasingly being used by organized crime groups.

Dave: Fraud is a huge problem. I took some additional training in fraud prevention and became a Senior Medical Patrol specialist. As a counselor, I am the eyes and ears of what's going on in the community. If we suspect something suspicious, we will pass that information to our local contact for the Inspector General's Office, who is in charge of the investigations.

Our office uncovered a ring of twelve to fifteen people, who were arrested and charged for fraud in cases involving millions of dollars. In one instance, a doctor who collected $3 million worth of suspicious Medicare claims was charged with fraud. We listen for instances of people collecting Medicare information when they shouldn't be. For example, you might go to a health fair and someone offers a "free" diagnostic service and then asks you for your Medicare number. If it's a free service, they don't need the Medicare number.

If the Medicare beneficiary doesn't read his or her summary notice, he or she might not realize if an unwarranted claim has been made without their knowledge. Sometimes we receive a call from a person who says, "I just got called from someone claiming to be from Medicare and they wanted my information," and we tell them that Medicare will never call you on the phone unless you initiated a call and they are responding back to you. One time we received a call from a whistleblower who worked in the office that was committing fraud.

What is the biggest issue or most common question?

Dave: First, we answer many questions from the people who are new to Medicare and don't understand the program. Prescription drugs are a big issue. Someone may be prescribed a new medication that his or her current plan doesn't cover, so we help with a plan comparison looking for a plan that might save him or her money on the medication that is needed. Some people have low incomes and need help because they can't afford their medicine. We can also counsel on Medicaid help. We get many calls from adult children of Medicare recipients. They need assistance trying to figure out what is the best plan for their mom or dad's situation.

What expenses are involved?

Dave: We receive a mileage reimbursement when we use our car in our volunteer work. All laptops and other equipment are supplied by the office.

How much time do you spend on this pursuit?

Dave: Since I have a part-time job tutoring, I volunteer one to two days a week. I will spend more time during the open-enrollment period because that is the busy time. During that time, I may give three or four presentations a week.

What is the most rewarding aspect of this activity?

Dave: When the person says, "Thank you, you've made this much clearer for me." Most of the time, older people need assurance that they are doing the correct thing. One of the great satisfactions is taking a load off their mind by just saying, "Yes you're pursuing the right thing and you understand what you're doing, and you're making a good decision." Helping people by giving them new information about a program that will cover their medication and saving people money are also rewarding.

Also, I saw the impact that anxiety can have on my own parents. It's rewarding to me that Medicare issues aren't a source of angst or uncertainty for them because I know how much that means to them.

Any advice for future volunteers?

Dave: You need to pick something you enjoy. If you are volunteering, the experience needs to have that "fun factor." I enjoy helping people and solving problems. If I can save someone some money or make his or her life easier, then it's fun for me.

FASCINATING FACTS

- When Medicare services began on July 1, 1966, more than 19 million Americans age 65 and older enrolled in the program. Over 1 million people enrolled the first week.
- In 2012, more than 50 million Americans depended on Medicare for their health insurance coverage.
- With increasing life expectancies and more people turning 65 every day, the number of people in Medicare is expected to double between the years 2000 and 2030.
- Just like with Social Security, you must accumulate 40 credits (worked for approximately 10 full years) to qualify for Medicare Part A.
- Medicare fraud accounts for $30 billion a year in losses to the program.
- Nationwide, over 12,000 SHIP counselors provide free, personalized counseling assistance to Medicare beneficiaries.

Resources

Websites

AARP's "Ask Ms. Medicare" archive, a collection of answers to questions from people with Medicare: http://bit.ly/1nwumXX.

The State Health Insurance Assistance Program, or SHIP, is a national program that offers one-on-one counseling and assistance to people with Medicare and their families: http://bit.ly/1rVGO3R or call 800-677-1116.

Michigan Medicare Assistance Program (MMAP): mmapinc.org.

The National Association of States United for Aging and Disabilities: http://bit.ly/UvN3PP.

The Official US Government Site for Medicare: medicare.gov.

Senior Corps Programs and RSVP website: http://1.usa.gov/1pt6dhs.

Videos

Medicare Fraud: Commonsense Solutions by AARP Advocates: http://bit.ly/1khRzxw.

The Story of Medicare: A Timeline by the Kaiser Foundation: http://bit.ly/1lKsW7n.

What Is Medicare? by Bloomberg News: http://bit.ly/1rJCCXd.

Reading

Patricia Barry, *Medicare for Dummies* (Hoboken, NJ: John Wiley & Sons, 2014).

US Department of Health And Human Services, *Medicare and You.* Download free:

http://1.usa.gov/1lKt6f1.

CHAPTER 15

National Park Volunteer

National parks are the best idea we ever had.
Absolutely American, absolutely democratic,
they reflect us at our best rather than our worst.
—Wallace Stegner

The US National Park System (NPS) began with establishment of Yellowstone National Park in 1872. That was the beginning of the creation of one of our nation's finest treasures and the ongoing effort to protect our natural, historical, and cultural heritage. The NPS encompasses more than four hundred sites and includes national parks, monuments, battlefields, military parks, historical parks, historic sites, lakeshores, seashores, recreation areas, scenic rivers and trails, and the White House.

VIP Program

The National Park Service actively recruits volunteers every year, to work side by side with National Park Service employees. The NPS Volunteers-in-Parks (VIP) Program was implemented in 1970 to provide a way for the public and the NPS to engage in mutually beneficial relationships. More than 221,000 people volunteer each year. Volunteers of every age, background, and ability level log millions of hours every year.

Ann, Rocky Mountain National Park volunteer

After a thirty-year career as the recreation director at a major Illinois university, Ann retired and spent time relaxing, traveling, and enjoying many outdoor activities. Three years ago, she moved to Colorado to volunteer at Rocky Mountain National Park. Ann, who is sixty-six years old, volunteers for a variety of positions interacting with some of the thousands of visitors who come to appreciate the spectacular vistas and wildlife each year.

Ann: My professional career included arranging programs and taking students from the Midwest and showing them the splendor of our national parks. One of the trips was hiking to the bottom of the Grand Canyon. Some of these students had never traveled west of the Mississippi River. It was gratifying to open their eyes to the wonders of the world. It was such a delight to be able to teach them how to become physically fit and independent and enjoy nature. I learned that a national park was such a teacher of people and we need to preserve all this land and all these wonders.

When I retired, I knew I wanted to move out west and asked myself, "Why don't you go where you always love to go?" And that is Rocky Mountain National Park. It's a park filled with natural pine, spruce, and fir trees. It is a very rich land with ecosystems that stretch from the prairies and climb to 14,000 feet elevation.

How did you get started?

Ann: I came to the park and signed up to become a volunteer. Two weeks later I started an assignment. There wasn't too much available. My first volunteer job was three years ago at Sheep Lakes. This park is known for its bighorn sheep and three million people come to experience the wildlife each year. We have a lot of visitors come who have never seen this land and its wildlife before and there's always a teachable moment talking about the park and how it relates to their lives.

You can sign up online or you can apply to the individual park. The volunteer coordinator interviews you and finds out what your interests are. If I came in with a biology degree or another particular skill, they would suggest specific opportunities.

Orientation

Ann: There is an orientation program for all volunteers. At the beginning of the season we will meet for four hours to learn of any news or changes at the park. For example, we had raging floodwaters this winter, so some bridges are closed for rebuilding.

Depending on the position, individual rangers that run a specific program will give an orientation. For example, one of our visitors' centers is at 12,000 feet elevation. This can pose a health problem for an unsuspecting visitor. That center has a full-time EMT staff, and any volunteers that work there must go through one week of entry-level EMT training so they can help the EMT staff.

Schedules and Accommodations

Ann: I relocated to a small town of 7,000 just outside of the park. I live five minutes away, so it's easy for me to volunteer for daily shifts. Some people who live farther away drive fifty miles or more and work one day a week. Some stay in hotel rooms in town and pay monthly rates so they can work more hours. The park does have an RV campground for seasonal employees and volunteers and they can stay in the RV park free. There are twelve to twenty spots available. There is a handful of modest housing available, and that is usually for those who work forty hours a week in the summer. The park struggles to find housing for their seasonal employees.

In February, I received my schedule for the coming summer. The park administration schedules the regulars ahead of time because they know our skill levels and our capacity. The more time you spend and prove yourself dependable, you will get the positions and the shift hours you want.

What volunteer positions are you involved with at the park?

Ann: I'm at the front desk of the visitors' center and explain all the available features of the park. Rocky Mountain National Park is one of the few parks where visitors can call in directly to the park and volunteers answer the phone. We help with a lot of vacation planning and answering lots of questions, such as what can they see and where they can camp.

I've also been a Tundra Guardian up at the 10,000-foot level. "Tundra" means land with no trees and Rocky Mountain National Park has the longest continuous highway in the US above the tree line. Tourists can drive the forty-eight-mile highway and stop at vista points manned by volunteers. This allows many people who would not able to hike the opportunity of enjoying the scenery. Volunteers talk to visitors about the wildlife hibernation, species of birds, resource management, and the herd of eighty elk that inhabit the surroundings.

Not all volunteer jobs involve assisting visitors. Some are grunt work. Volunteers called "road hogs" go around in trucks and move rocks off the roads. There's trail maintenance. Others are involved with resource management. They may collect data for an annual inventory of the bristlecone pine trees. They log whether the trees are tolerating the wind and growing. Others help conduct research with frogs. The rangers will teach you what to do. A lot of the volunteer jobs are "counts." I've been involved with elk counts. Three days a month, we go out and count females and calves to help keep track of the population.

Variety of Jobs

Each national park may have specific needs, but in general, volunteer positions include these categories:

1. Working directly with people: These positions include visitor center staff, docents, leading tours, staffing education centers, and distributing information. Historical interpreters may wear period clothing and perform jobs that represent the era, such as cooking over an open fire or demonstrating candle making.
2. Maintenance work: Volunteers do general cleanup, landscaping, and gardening. They build fences, paint buildings, and make cabinets. Many of our national parks have outdoor facilities and miles of trails. Volunteers restore picnic areas; maintain hiking paths, and clear away winter damage from fallen trees and rockslides.
3. Conservation and resource management. Volunteers are used to monitor wildlife populations. For example, they count bighorn sheep in Rocky Mountain National Park. Volunteers also gather data, such as map coordinates of parklands, and record areas of damage from beetle blight or invasive species.

Ann: Volunteers are also there to keep people safe and in proper places. Some visitors need to be reminded not to stray off walkways. They don't realize that some of the flowers up in the tundra are unique to the park and have hundreds of years of history. Some people have no concept of how many people come to the park and the dangers that trampling on vegetation causes. We try hard to assist them with their experience.

How did you learn so much about the park?

Ann: I've been in teaching all my life and I had to be a wealth of knowledge to my students. I attended many interpretative centers and I read a lot. Whenever I had a vacation, I would go to the national parks, so I knew a lot before I started. I'm also involved in photography of the park flowers and birds on my own time, and I've learned through that as well.

There's no better place to go and be with nature. There are no fences. You have to respect the wildlife space. A lot of it is self-taught. The Park Service and the rangers take the volunteers under their wing and teach us what to point out and how to interpret what is going on before visitors' eyes. Take the flowers alone. There are hundreds up on the tundra that you will never view anywhere else. People will ask, "What kind of flower is that?" and you have to be able to tell them. You need to at least have some understanding. I carry a pocket flower book with me, but after a while, you learn what's growing where and at what time.

What expenses and special clothing are involved?

Ann: If you don't live in or near the park, then gas and transportation costs must be figured in the budget. You need to pack a lunch or buy one if you are near facilities. The national park provides our shirts. The rangers wear a gray shirt and green pants. All the volunteers wear brown. We have to buy our own pants. So a budget for pants might be $60. The Park Service gives us baseball caps with the volunteer logo on it. These must be worn only while working inside the park. I bought my own wide-brim hat and put the volunteer logo on it. We receive brown-colored raingear and a fleece jacket. You need to wear good sturdy shoes or hiking boots. All equipment and tools you need to perform your job are provided.

How much time do you spend on this pursuit?

Ann: I work every Thursday from 8 a.m. to 12:30 p.m. in the information office and I do that year-round. In the summer, I work Saturday as a Tundra Guardian from 8:30 a.m. to 4:40 p.m. It takes forty minutes to get up to the 10,000- to 12,000-foot elevation.

That high elevation level doesn't always work out for some people. There is a level of fitness to this volunteer job. I'm sixty-six years old and I know I have to do something to maintain my health. Many of our volunteers understand the value of good health. You need to consider the environment. There certain things that you have to be aware of before you commit yourself.

I work out every day. In the winter, if it's too muddy for hiking, I exercise on an elliptical trainer. I do cardio exercises, some weight-lifting and Pilates. In good weather, I do a lot of hiking. I like to go out and be part of the park. Rocky Mountain National Park has over three hundred miles of trails.

What is the most rewarding aspect of this activity?

Ann: My favorite part is talking to visitors outdoors in the summertime and inside in the winter. It's all about giving the people of the United States and all over the world an opportunity to appreciate what they're viewing. It's very different from what they are familiar with and they are so grateful to have someone to talk to about understanding the depth and magnitude of the park.

We have many foreign visitors to our park, often in September. Tourists come from all over the world, especially from China and Europe. Billions of dollars are contributed to our economy because of our national parks. But they are so underfunded; the fact that we're here makes a big difference. The National Park Service couldn't possibly afford to employ the number of park rangers needed to interface with all of the visitors. Without volunteer help, park rangers would be spread too thin and many tourists wouldn't get the interaction that is so important to learning. If you figured out how much you could pay a volunteer and how many collective hours we give, all of us together save the national parks millions of dollars.

The Pine Beetle Epidemic

Rocky Mountain National Park is only one part of a larger area throughout the West where trees are dying from the mountain pine beetle epidemic. Because the task is enormous, the park's priorities for mitigation of the effects of the beetles are focused on removing trees affected by the beetles for the protection of life and property.

Ann: People were asking, "Why isn't the park combatting the beetle?" The volunteers are there to explain to visitors why not. We tell them that it's impossible to try to eliminate the beetles, because we would have to spray everything in the park, polluting everything else, to save the trees. We want them to understand the scope of what is going on and have them take away the knowledge of our environment, and how it affects them and all of the wildlife.

Any interesting stories connected with your volunteer time?

Ann: I am always surprised by our visitors' scope of knowledge. Rocky Mountain National Park is known for its wildlife, especially the bighorn sheep. The sheep come down from the upper elevations at random times throughout the day on their way to the mineral lakes. (They graze and eat soil to obtain minerals not found in their high mountain habitat. The minerals are essential in restoring nutrient levels, depleted by the stresses of lambing and the poor quality winter diet.)

Ann: These are wild bighorn sheep and they cross the highway on their way to where they're going. The volunteers in the area stop the traffic to accommodate the sheep and protect drivers. The visitors come up to us religiously and ask, "What time do the sheep come?" or "When do you open the pens to let the sheep out?" We have to explain patiently that these are wild animals. We are also asked, "When do the deer turn into elk?" People are so out of their element, they don't realize the things they ask.

The tundra at the park is at 10,000- to 12,000-foot elevation and has snow year round. You would have to travel to Alaska to discover the tundra that we have. It makes our park so unique. In August, visitors will ask, "What is that white stuff?"

FASCINATING FACTS

- In 2011, the total recreational visitors to the national parks: 278,939,216
- The National Park System is comprised of 401 areas covering more than 84 million acres in every state, the District of Columbia, American Samoa, Guam, Puerto Rico, and the Virgin Islands.
- The largest national park is Wrangell–St. Elias National Park and Preserve in Alaska: 13.2 million acres; the smallest is Thaddeus Kosciuszko National Memorial in Pennsylvania: 0.02 acres.
- The top 3 national parks visited in 2012 were (1) Great Smoky Mountains National Park (9,685,829 visitors); (2) Grand Canyon (4,421,352); and (3) Yosemite (3,853,404).
- Just 1/14th of 1 percent of the federal budget funds our national parks ($2.98 billion in 2012), which generated $31 billion from tourism and recreation.

Resources

Websites

Find a national park: http://bit.ly/1q5MTbJ.

Find volunteer opportunities in the national parks: nps.gov/volunteer; or volunteer.gov; or contact the park of your choice directly.

National Park Service VIP program brochure: http://1.usa.gov/WJ1jq9.

National Park Service Volunteers Facebook page: facebook.com/npsvolunteers.

Apps

Canyon Country National Parks app by Utah.com includes Arches, Bryce Canyon, Canyonlands, Capitol Reef, Zion, Grand Canyon, Mesa Verde, and Great Basin: http://bit.ly/1lKu4b8.

Chimani National Parks Series App: http://bit.ly/1nwvZ84.

Doh-Ray Media's National Parks Explorer: http://bit.ly/1uwdx4f.

National Park App by National Geographic: http://on.natgeo.com/1tefmRy.

Oh, Ranger ParkFinder by American Park Network: http://bit.ly/1pt8oBF.

Passport to Your National Parks App by Eastern National: http://bit.ly/WJ1lOC.

Sierra Club Trail Explorer by Sierra Club: http://bit.ly/1qGsEpX.

Videos

America's National Parks: A Video Tour of All 55 National Parks (2001), produced by Questar.

The National Parks: America's Best Idea (2013), directed by Ken Burns.

Several videos on YouTube. Search "National Parks."

Reading

Dayton Duncan and Ken Burns, *The National Parks: America's Best Idea* (New York, NY: Alfred A. Knopf, 2009).

National Geographic, *National Geographic Guide to National Parks of the United States, 7th Edition* (National Geographic, 2012).

Danny Palmerlee, Adam Karlin, Brendan Sainsbury, and Ned Friary, *Lonely Planet Discover USA's Best National Parks* (Footscray, Vic: Lonely Planet, 2012).

CHAPTER 16

Nonprofit Board Director

I've learned that you shouldn't go through life with a catcher's mitt on both hands; you need to be able to throw something back.
—Maya Angelou

Nonprofit organizations have always played a significant role in American society. People of all ages, in all communities throughout America, give their "time, talent, and treasure" helping those in need. The Bureau of Labor Statistics reports 25.4 percent or 62.6 million Americans volunteered through or for an organization at least once between September 2012 and September 2013. In 2011, Americans gave $298.3 billion to approximately 1,080,130 charitable nonprofit organizations in the United States, according to the National Philanthropic Trust.

Board of Directors

Because American nonprofits are corporations, they are required by law to have a board of directors. Just as for-profit corporations answer to its owners or shareholders, nonprofits answer to the public they serve and those who contribute to them financially. Nonprofit organizations are diverse in size and purpose; universities are very different from day-care centers. Large nonprofits, such as the American Red Cross, differ from local food banks. Each nonprofit has its own board members, policies, and resources.

Duties of a Board Member

Boards are responsible for the overall health and effectiveness of the organization and nonprofits need committed volunteers. BoardSource reported in 2012 that 77 percent of boards of directors were actively recruiting one or more members. Here is a list of the "Ten Basic Responsibilities of Nonprofit Boards" from BoardSource:

1. Determine the organization's mission and purposes
2. Select the executive staff through an appropriate process
3. Provide ongoing support and guidance for the executive; review his/her performance
4. Ensure effective organizational planning
5. Ensure adequate resources
6. Manage resources effectively (the buck stops with them, ultimately)
7. Determine and monitor the organization's programs and services
8. Enhance the organization's public image
9. Serve as a court of appeal for unresolved issues or complaints
10. Assess its own performance

Ida, current president of a board of directors

Ida is sixty-two years old and lives in Birmingham, Alabama. She retired after having dual status working for the Department of the Army for twenty-six years and a member of the Army Federal Reserves for thirty-four years. She's been told, "You don't know how to retire." She is an attorney in a practice she shares with her daughter. Ida is also a small-business entrepreneur and an author.

Ida: I like to say I'm semi-retired and enjoying it. I don't consider myself working really hard, because I love it. I'll probably do this for another ten years and then I'll be fully retired. I have a different feeling about the work I do now. I feel the need to help others more than the need to make money.

Ida is currently the president (chairperson) of the board of directors of Christian Service Charities, which partners with more than 100 like-minded charities to help them become eligible to receive funds through a federal worker deduction program called the Combined Federal Campaign (CFC). The US Office of Personnel Management explains the purpose of the CFC is to receive pledges made by federal civilian, postal, and military donors during the donation campaign season (September 1 to December 15) and support eligible nonprofit organizations that provide health and human service benefits throughout the world.

How did you become a nonprofit board member?

Ida: I didn't know about the group. They found me. They contacted me and asked me if I was interested in applying to join the board of directors. The former president of the organization who knew of my previous volunteer work for other organizations recommended me. I was a former federal employee and familiar with the CFC.

I went online and researched the organization, and I liked what I found out. So in 2010, I became a member of the board. After a year, I became secretary of the board, then vice president for four years. In 2014, I began my role as president.

Board Makeup

BoardSource reports that the average size of a US nonprofit board is sixteen voting members, compared to eleven voting members for-profit boards. Board size tends to increase along with a nonprofit group's income. Women represent 43 percent of nonprofit board members, which contrasts sharply with corporate boards, of which only 6 percent are women. Eighty six percent of nonprofit board members are white, compared with 92.7 percent of corporate board members, and 14 percent are minorities, including 7 percent African American and 7 percent Hispanic/Latino. Thirty-six percent are between the ages of thirty and forty-nine and 49 percent between fifty and sixty-four.

Ida: We have eleven people on our board. You always want an odd number for voting reasons. People stay on the board for a specific term according to the rules, and then they have to rotate out for at least a year. The board has to reflect the mission of the organization. Our board of directors is comprised of representatives from our partner organizations and our rules say they should also be represented by the demographics of our donors who are federal civilian and military employees. In choosing board members, we look for representatives of the working community, persons with military connections, youth, and people who will provide diversity. We want a board that reflects our group.

It is essential to have some board members who have accounting and legal expertise. It helps to have some who are members of the younger generation with social-media acumen. Taking a contribution out of a paycheck used to work in older generations, but today younger employees like to use PayPal and other ways to give.

Qualities that Make a Good Board Member

Ida: First, show up. Make the meetings. Quarterly meetings are in-person; other meetings are teleconferenced. Always respond to e-mails. We use e-mail to complete much of the business. In the past, we sent agendas in packets of printed information. Now everything is e-mailed. We sometimes vote by e-mail.

Good board members volunteer for committees, participate, provide feedback, and help with fund-raising. It's all part of the job. Raising funds is something that everyone looks to board members to do. The organization needs people to be a part of the team, *and it is vital for the board to work together toward achieving the organization's mission.*

Orientation

Ida: When my organization has new board members, an orientation program is conducted the day before the annual meeting, and new members come a day early. Orientation usually lasts three hours. Each department will give a presentation and we discuss policy. The president of the board will go over what our mission is, how we operate, all aspects of policy; what is left up to management is what the board does, and how we stay within those lines. The CFO will go over the process of how the funds are raised and paid out and will go over the budget.

A Typical Board Meeting

In this technological age, board meetings may take place via conference call or webcasts as well as in-person, depending on the business conducted and the rules of the state. The average number of board meetings per year according to BoardSource is 6.9, with 79 percent of boards averaging above 75 percent attendance. The average board meeting lasts 3.3 hours.

Ida: We conduct quarterly in-person meetings. Everyone receives an e-mail with the agenda no less than forty-five days ahead of time because travel arrangements must be made. Our board meetings are held in Virginia, and people are coming from all over the country. I am coming from Alabama; other board members come from Colorado, Tennessee, North Carolina, Washington, and other states. Many of the organizations that we work with are doing their work globally, so some attendees may be coming from out of the country and need to plan ahead of time.

Formerly, when we did not have our own facility to meet in, we had our board meetings at a different organization's location each time. This provided us the opportunity to learn more about many of the organizations. Sometime during the meeting, we might take a tour or hear a presentation about what that organization does. Now we are fortunate to have our own facility where we meet, but I do miss that connecting opportunity with multiple nonprofits.

Depending on the agenda, a meeting may take four hours or a full day, and most people bring their laptops. We use Robert's Rules of Order, which is standard. We start with the "CEO chat." The staff comes and talks about what going on. It's not a formal presentation and not part of the board meeting. The actual board meeting begins after that get-together.

We start with a devotion, then a roll call and approval of the minutes. The CEO (or executive director) will go over the monetary reports. Board members get these reports a month in advance. We are responsible for going to a private screen on the website, and making sure we read and understand them. Our job is to monitor. We will review the reports under policy governance, for example affirming an issue complies with the law. Certain committees, such as Audit, Policy/Governance, and Nominating committees, know when they are responsible to present at board meetings.

Did you take any wrong turns or false starts on other pursuits?

Ida: The board of directors I currently chair is a board from heaven. But there are boards from hell, too. I've been a member of a dysfunctional board in the past. Members are not on the same page and have different agendas. There's lots of politics. It's much easier when you have a board that works together and speaks with one voice.

You really have to look at what the nonprofit stands for and make sure that it mirrors your views. Are you interested in serving on this board? Before you say yes, think about it. You have to walk the walk because you are representing them, and their policies reflect on you. You are the face of this organization.

Ten Questions to Ask Before Joining a Board

In his article posted August 23, 2013, for the *Huffington Post*, Greg Vermeulen lists ten important questions to ask before joining a board:

1. Is a Strategic Plan in place?
2. What are the fund-raising requirements?
3. How often does the board meet?
4. How many board members are there, and what are their responsibilities?
5. What roles does the board need to fill?
6. Is there an orientation package of current organization business available?
7. Do they have board-member liability insurance?
8. What is the relationship between the board, the staff, and supporters?
9. Is the organization in good standing with governmental authorities?
10. What are the performance criteria?

How much time do you spend on this pursuit?

Ida: On average, I spend two hours a month. Of course, it depends on the time of the year because we have a specific time for the federal-worker donation campaign. A lot of work is done through e-mail, so we're always watching our e-mails. We have teleconference meetings and preparation for orientation and quarterly meetings. Some times are busy and other times are quiet. Quarterly board meetings can be one, two, or four days. The meeting usually will start at noon to give people time to arrive.

What expenses are involved?

Ida: None of the directors receives any compensation, but the organization pays all travel costs to board meetings. The organization pays for lodging and transportation from the airport or they *reimburse any costs incurred. We try to get a more reasonable rate by organizing the group at the same time. We schedule group lunches and dinners together.*

Are Board of Directors expected to donate to the organization?

According to Cisco Corporation's free "Guide to Nonprofit Board Basics," donation expectation depends on the specific organization you're joining. Some nonprofits ask their board members to make substantial personal donations. Many community-based nonprofits ask that each board member make a personal contribution—but at an amount that's comfortable. That might mean $10,000 for some board members and $25 from others. Ask the nonprofit what is expected. It's a legitimate question when you're considering joining a board.

In a 2007, BoardSource reported that the inability to raise money is the major weakness of many charities' boards of directors, and only 5 percent listed fund-raising as a board strength. Fund-raising ranks number one among board areas needing improvement. The report also stated that 68 percent of nonprofit groups required board members to make annual personal donations. The average minimum donation requested was $150. Arts and cultural groups also received the greatest number of donations from board members. Those groups reported that 80 percent of their trustees made donations, compared with 63 percent for human-services groups, 58 percent for health organizations, and 57 percent for educational institutions.

What is the most rewarding aspect of this activity?

Ida: To be in the presence of and work with all of our dedicated nonprofit member organizations. Our organization brings together many organizations in a collective effort to acquire funds. This diverse group of charities presents exciting approaches to offering health and human services to different people. We have over 100 organizations; some large, some small, all doing wonderful work. I want to understand fully what they do and how they do it.

Every June, member charities come and meet with the board. We get acquainted, they ask questions and give us feedback. At the luncheon, board members are encouraged to sit at different tables. We get the opportunity to mingle with all of the different charities. I've learned so much about all of their organizations. The ones that started in the basement of the founder's home to fulfill a need. I hear how they share their faith with others in Third World countries. I hear how they are solving problems and helping people. For example, the awesome responsibilities of getting water to those who have none.

FASCINATING FACTS

- Religious institutions receive the most charitable contributions, 33% of all donations, followed by the educational sector (13%).
- In 2012, nonprofits' share of Gross Domestic Product was 5.5%.
- The largest public charity by total assets (2011) is the President and Fellows of Harvard College, with $59,837,950,000.
- Mark Zuckerberg and Priscilla Chan were the most generous philanthropists in 2013, giving $992.2 million to the Silicon Valley Community Foundation in San Mateo, California.
- In 2006, Warren Buffett, billionaire investor and founder of Berkshire Hathaway, announced he was donating much of his fortune to charity. Over time, most of Buffett's $44 billion in stock holdings will be given to the Bill and Melinda Gates Foundation.
- The top 3 states with the most generous population in 2012 were Utah, where the Mormon tradition of tithing requires one to contribute 10.6% of discretionary income to charity. Mississippi was second, with 7.2%; and Alabama placed third, allocating 7.1% of discretionary income for charitable donations. *New Hampshire ranks last, as the* typical household reported charitable contributions totaling 2.5% of discretionary income.

Any advice for future members of a board of directors?

Ida: As a retired person, you have a world of knowledge that you can give to any nonprofit. You have a lot that you can bring to the table and have what that nonprofit needs. We may tell ourselves that we don't have the time, but it can be a very rewarding thing to do. You will be surprised at the person you can become. You can give so much more, and that will make you feel good. It's a very satisfying feeling.

Resources

General Information Websites

Blue Avocado is the online magazine for people who work and volunteer in the nonprofit sector: blueavocado.org.

BoardSource: https://www.boardsource.org.

Cisco Corporation's "NonProfit Board Basics": http://bit.ly/VZV6oK.

Compass Point provides support for nonprofits and leadership: compasspoint.org.

Giving USA reports annual trends and important data about the health of nonprofits in the United States: givingusareports.org.

GuideStar gathers and disseminates information about each nonprofit's mission, impact, reputation, finances, and programs: guidestar.org.

The National Council of Nonprofits is a network of more than 25,000 nonprofit organizations in the United States: councilofnonprofits.org.

Websites Linking Nonprofits and Board Volunteers

BoardnetUSA: boardnetusa.org.

LinkedIn Board Connect: nonprofits.linkedin.com/.

Volunteer Match: volunteermatch.org.

Volunteerpath: http://bit.ly/WJ1MIK.

Videos

Nonprofit Board Governance: http://bit.ly/1zjOSP2.

Policies That Every Non Profit Organization Should Consider Having: http://bit.ly/1rrZnvp.

Ten Basic Responsibilities of Non Profit Boards: http://bit.ly/1nNbmnu.

Reading

BoardSource, *The Nonprofit Board Answer Book: A Practical Guide for Board Members and Chief Executives* (San Francisco, CA: Jossey-Bass, 2012).

John Carver, Boards *That Make a Difference A New Design for Leadership in Nonprofit and Public Organizations* (San Francisco, CA: Jossey-Bass, 1997).

Laurence Scot, *The Simplified Guide to Not-for-Profit Accounting, Formation and Reporting* (Hoboken, NJ: John Wiley & Sons, 2010).

CHAPTER 17

Ombudsman for Elder Care

No act of kindness, no matter how small, is ever wasted. —Aesop

Ombudsman is a Swedish word that means *one who cares for another*, *a citizen representative* or *advocate*. The Swedish Parliament established the first independent ombudsman in 1809 to respond to public complaints against the government and to protect citizens against bureaucratic abuses and excesses. The creation of ombudsman offices became popular in the United States in the mid-1960s, motivated in part by revelations of government secrecy and concern for vulnerable populations.

The Ombudsman Program

Begun in 1972 as a demonstration program, the program today exists in all states, the District of Columbia, Puerto Rico, and Guam, under the authorization of the Older Americans Act. Each state has an Office of the State Long-Term Care Ombudsman, headed by a full-time state ombudsman. Thousands of local ombudsman staff and volunteers work in hundreds of communities throughout the country as part of the statewide ombudsman programs, assisting residents and their families and providing a voice for those unable to speak for themselves.

Ombudsman programs are designed to help ensure quality of life and quality of care for residents of nursing homes, board and care homes, assisted-living facilities, and similar adult-care facilities. Most states have created additional companion legislation to the federal law.

Volunteer Program

More than three-fourths of states use volunteer ombudsmen to visit facilities and handle grievances. Their primary responsibility is to protect vulnerable individuals from abuse and neglect. They investigate and try to resolve complaints made by residents in long-term care facilities, including nursing homes, assisted-living facilities, and residential care homes. Through regular visits to facilities, these specially trained volunteers investigate and mediate complaints, monitor residents' care and quality of life, and provide public education for clients and families. Ombudsman services are free and confidential to all long-term care residents.

Bonnie, ombudsman

Bonnie: After twenty-five years as general counsel for a large, nationwide staffing company, I was laid off, along with all the other department heads when the public company transitioned and was acquired by investors. I was getting close to the end of my career, but the timing was still a surprise. So when I found myself retired, I was kind of at a loss initially about what I was going to do.

How did you become interested in this pursuit?

Bonnie: It took me a while, maybe over a year of just chilling out, before I started thinking about what I wanted to do next. I was winding down from the demanding process of the company's transition. My son had left home; he had graduated from West Point and was preparing to be deployed to Afghanistan. I was facing all those unknowns and fears and I really needed some downtime.

A Planned Approach

Bonnie: I wrote down objectives I had when thinking about volunteering. I wanted to learn something new, I wanted to use my skills that I already had as an attorney, I wanted to contribute to a good cause, and I wanted to feel that I was appreciated. I definitely wanted a program that had training. I didn't want to be thrown into something that I didn't know anything about.

I read about a free placement program in town that focused on finding volunteer opportunities for people over fifty. I didn't want to do legal work, but at the same time wanted to use the skills that I had developed over the years. Part of my career job was to interview managers throughout the company's national network and help them strategize and work through problems. I did it from the standpoint of avoiding potential lawsuits and I enjoyed the aspect of being a problem-solver.

I spoke with the volunteer advisor and filled out a questionnaire about my interests. After considering my answers, the advisor suggested a number of volunteer programs. One choice was an elder-care advocate—an ombudsman. I had never even heard the term before and I didn't know anything about it. I had never set foot in a nursing home or an assisted-living center. I got the name of the nearest ombudsman program contact and I went from there.

What type of person makes a good ombudsman?

Bonnie: Someone who is concerned about seniors and wants to make a difference for a group that doesn't get a lot of attention. It's a good activity for people with a background in the medical and legal fields and others who are objective and problem-solvers. Your goal is to try to make things better for the resident.

Training and Commitment

Bonnie: After an interview and background check, volunteers undergo between twelve and forty hours of training, depending on their state's requirement to receive certification. My ombudsman-training program required thirty-six hours, attending class twice a week. The instructor talked about conditions that develop as we age (especially Alzheimer's disease and dementia), interviewing skills, and residents' rights. They discussed many hypothetical situations in class; what you would do in this or that situation, and how to investigate, resolve, and report complaints. The instructor reviewed federal and state rules that pertain to the different facilities. Skilled nursing facilities receive Medicare and therefore answer to the federal government mandates; assisted-living facilities are regulated by the state.

Keeping Current

Bonnie: Due to the heavy turnover rate, volunteer training is offered four times a year. There were two men and six women in my training class. Most of the volunteers are retired from professional jobs; however, one of the volunteers was a retired truck driver. Some of the volunteers had a bad experience with care of a loved one or are currently caregivers themselves. All of the volunteers in the class were over fifty years old; one was in his eighties. Of the eight people in my class, only two of us are left as ombudsmen.

There are new rules all the time. Most are clarifications on the state level. If it weren't for the training, I probably would have felt that this role was way past my comfort zone. As part of the guidance, I did "job shadowing," following experienced advocates to the various facilities—assisted-living, skilled-nursing, and residential-care homes. I chose to spend my volunteer time at one assisted-living facility.

During training, it was stressed that my role is not to step in and do things that are not in the purview of the ombudsman. For example, ombudsmen don't give legal advice, and they don't fix wheelchairs. They should not foster an adversarial role with administration.

Is there a support group connected to your pursuit?

Bonnie: We have to keep up our certification current by attending nine to ten meetings a year. The meetings last approximately three hours and we hear speakers on helpful topics. It's an opportunity to meet with other ombudsmen. That's critical, because I feel I need to interact with the other advocates. We talk about common problems and get good feedback. It is helpful and I feel I'm not alone.

Describe your visits.

Bonnie: I visit one assisted-living facility once a week for one or two hours. Assisted living is a private-pay system, meaning the residents must have the assets to pay the bill. Medicare or Medicaid pays only for skilled-nursing facilities, not assisted living. I chose to visit one facility in my town that has fifty-five residents. Some ombudsmen take on two facilities. Those who choose to visit board-and-care homes, which usually have only six beds, visit a number of facilities.

I wear a name tag when I visit so everyone knows my name. When I enter the facility, I go directly to the lounge area and say hello to all who are there. Most of the residents in the facility are quite elderly. Very few are under seventy-five years old. Two women are a hundred years old. This is an assisted-living environment, so most of the residents are able and dressed. Some may be sitting in wheelchairs and some may appear to have other limiting physical or mental ailments.

After visiting the lounge, I go to the front desk and ask if there are any new people. I also knock on doors. The hardest part of the job for me is knocking on doors, because you never know what you're going to get. Some residents are delighted to have someone to talk to, others not so much. However, my job is not to just chat. Another group of volunteers called "friendly visitors," who walk around and visit, does that. I do this to some degree in order to find out what's going on, but I have to remind myself that is not why I'm there. I have to find out if the residents are getting good care and if they have any complaints. The talkative people can be helpful, telling me what's going on. I want to talk with the more lucid residents to find out if things are changing, such as staff turnover, residents' attitudes, or individual problems.

Maintaining privacy and confidentially of a resident's information is very important. Ombudsmen must get permission to look at medical records or to delve into residents' personal lives. Many times residents are reluctant to bring things up because they are afraid of retaliation or to be labeled a complainer.

Visits are intense. Every time I visit, I'm dealing with a problem. Usually new people have a hard time adjusting, so they're upset. You might see people who are bruised, because they've taken an innocent fall. But you have to make sure that is the case.

In the facility I visit, there are single people as well as couples. I have seen a large influx of men; almost one-third of the facility residents are male. One of the biggest complaints I get from the residents is that there aren't enough activities. A varying population changes the dynamic and creates challenges of what activities to offer. I make suggestions to the administration in response to the residents' concerns.

The Advocate Works with Both Sides

Bonnie: My goal is to make things better for the resident. To achieve this goal, it's important to work within the system and remember that the facility is the resident's home. Sometimes I bring the concerns of the resident to the facility and sometimes the facility wants me to talk to the resident for them. Communication goes both ways.

Solving Problems

Bonnie: We often hear stories about elderly abuse and neglect and of course, when suspected, an ombudsman will report that immediately. I haven't had that experience, but there are other problems, such as when a resident needs to move.

In an assisted-living facility residents have their own room, and they can leave to go out to lunch or shopping. Skilled-nursing facilities are more like a hospital—residents are sicker or frailer and rooms are often shared. It's a problem when residents do not want to leave the assisted-living environment and move to a skilled-nursing facility because it's not as nice. Sometimes they really need to make that move to a place where more care is offered. This is a two-sided problem because the facility doesn't want to say, "We can't care for you anymore," and some residents who have been there for a long time don't want to leave. However, they aren't getting enough help and that can be a difficult challenge. In this case, the ombudsman can offer suggestions to the family to ease the transition.

Family Matters

Bonnie: Family situations and conflicts can be challenging. A common problem I have encountered is conflicts between the resident and his or her family. There are issues with siblings in disagreement over their parents' care. Sometimes bills to the facility are paid too slowly—or not at all. In an assisted-living facility if the resident can't pay, they have to leave, and the administrator has to give them notice. If such an issue comes to my attention, I look into the cause of the problem. Often the resident doesn't even know because they have delegated payment of their expenses to the family. I tell the resident that he or she has a right to his or her money.

I experienced a family situation where the siblings hadn't spoken to each other for fifteen years. On occasion, one relative will complain and accuse another of upsetting the resident and the facility will ask me to intervene. Regardless of who makes the complaint, the ombudsman's client remains the resident, and the goal is what the resident wants and/or needs.

Good Transition to the Facility

Bonnie: Helping the family and the resident transition to the facility is important, and the process does vary. I think a key ingredient in a smooth transition is that the resident is involved in the selection of the facility. It's good when they have had a chance to visit and tour a variety of places. This is the ideal situation because the resident feels they have some input and are part of the decision. It helps them to acknowledge to themselves that they are not going to be able to live at home alone. When they do this, they buy into the whole idea.

What is the most rewarding aspect of this activity?

Bonnie: The residents are very happy to see someone and have a conversation, and I feel like I'm making a difference. Although many of the residents have families, they still don't get many visitors, even if the family lives close to the facility.

I feel that it is the little things that make a big difference. If the resident has a small problem sometimes, I can help it get resolved right away. Other times just listening is what's needed. It feels good to let them know there is someone they can talk to and trust. I'm preventing small problems from becoming big problems.

The families also feel relieved that they have someone to call. It works for the staff as well. I'm an outside person who has more objectivity and can offer a fresh look at the issue. Through my visits as an ombudsman, I get the opportunity to advocate for quality of life and quality of care of residents, respond to concerns, promote self-advocacy and educate both providers and the residents.

FASCINATING FACTS

- Most people who study Alzheimer's disease strongly believe that the reason aerobic exercise delays the onset of dementia is that it increases heart health, and it increases blood flow to the brain.
- The 85-and-older population is projected to double from 5.7 million in 2010, to 11.4 million in 2035, and nearly double again to 19 million in 2050.
- The most popular names of people who are currently in their eighties and nineties are Robert and Mary.
- In 2013, the Academy Awards named its oldest nominee ever in the Best Actress category, 85-year-old Emmanuelle Riva for her role in *Amour*. Also, that same year, Christopher Plummer, at age 82, became the oldest winner in any acting category for his performance in *Beginners*.
- In a 2012–2013 survey of people 65 and older, 45% identified themselves as Facebook users. That's up from 35% a year ago.
- In the federal fiscal year 2011, ombudsmen investigated and worked to resolve 204,044 complaints made by 134,775 individuals.

Resources

Websites

The Administration on Aging's Eldercare Locator: http://1.usa.gov/1tel5Xz.

Department of Elder Affairs: eldercare.gov.

Locate an Ombudsman, State Agencies and Citizen Advocacy Groups: theconsumervoice.org/ombudsman.

The National Long-Term-Care Ombudsman Resource Center: ltcombudsman.org.

Videos

Day in the Life of an Ombudsman: http://bit.ly/1rO0c3r.

Reading

J. Kevin Eckert, *Inside Assisted Living: The Search for Home* (Baltimore, MD: Johns Hopkins University Press, 2009).

L E Green, *The Nursing Home Survival Guide: An Insider's Perspective on Everything from Admission to Discharge* (Charleston, SC: L E Green, 2013).

Joseph Matthews, *Long-Term Care: How to Plan & Pay for It* (Berkeley, CA: NOLO, 2004).

Bette Ann Moskowitz, *The Room at the End of the Hall: An Ombudsman's Notebook* (Rotterdam, NL: Sense Publishers, 2012).

CHAPTER 18

Youth Mentor

What counts in life is not the mere fact that we have lived. It is what difference we have made to the lives of others that will determine the significance of the life we lead.
—Nelson Mandela

Caring, healthy relationships, and generational support are the cornerstones of the many youth mentoring programs throughout the country. The mentor relationship is a key strategy for improving the lives of youth. Role models provide academic support, friendship, and encouragement, and a sympathetic ear through challenging life transitions.

The National Mentoring Partnership advises that mentoring basically guarantees a young person there is someone who cares about them. Mentors help young people learn to believe in themselves and tackle challenging goals, helping them to increase graduation rates, make healthier lifestyle choices, and become productive citizens.

Foster Grandparent Program

The Corporation for National and Community Service (CNCS) is a federal agency that engages millions of Americans in volunteer community service. The CNCS's Senior Corps consists of three programs: the Foster Grandparent Program, the Senior Companion Program, and the Retired & Senior Volunteer

Program (RSVP). Some of the programs pay a small stipend to qualified low-income participants; others are strictly volunteer programs.

The Foster Grandparent Program started in 1965 as part of President Johnson's War on Poverty. The majority of participants are placed in elementary schools, day-care facilities, or Head Start centers. Others serve in hospitals or juvenile correctional institutions. Foster grandparents spend fifteen to forty hours per week as role models, mentors, listeners, and friends. They help care for young children with disabilities, provide one-on-one tutoring, and help improve reading skills. They mentor troubled teenagers and young mothers or help children who have been abused or neglected. Qualified low-income participants receive a small stipend, which is tax-exempt.

The program works. In his 2008 book, *Prime Time: How Baby Boomers Will Revolutionize Retirement*, author Marc Freedman reported that thirty-one studies have been conducted directly on the three-decade-old Foster Grandparent Program, validating the benefits to both the older volunteers as well as the youth they serve. In a seven-year Detroit-area study, university investigators found that the strong bonds formed between the children and their elder mentors in the Foster Grandparent Program had a very positive impact on the children's intellectual and social development.

Burneil, a foster grandparent

During her fourteen years with the program, Burneil has worked in two schools, offering continuity and a caring presence to elementary school students. The director of the Foster Grandparent Program describes Burneil as having a passion for life and children. In bad economic times, many budget-crunched districts must deal with teacher layoffs and service reductions. The continuity of the Foster Grandparent Program is a valuable asset. Currently, there are 100 participants in the Sacramento Foster Grandparent Program; 89 are women and 11 are men. Nationwide, in fiscal year 2012, there were 28,250 volunteers in the program serving 215,700 children.

Burneil: I have participated in the Foster Grandparent Program in Sacramento, California, for fourteen years. I worked many years in the retail industry and raised three children on my own. I retired twice, once in 1987 and then again in 1995. I'm eighty-four years old, but people look at me and think I'm in my seventies. They say at my age I should stay home, but no way! I live in a senior-living apartment, but I feel it's very important to socialize with multiple generations. I keep my distance from cranky old folks.

How did you get started in this pursuit?

Burneil: I had been retired for about a year and a friend in my senior apartment building invited me to go with her to a meeting of the Foster Grandparent Program. My two friends talked about it so much, I decided to look into it. I liked the program and signed up for training.

The in-service meeting I attended was what got me hooked. I chose to work in a school rather than juvenile hall or another location. I was assigned to the first and second grade. It's funny, my grandmother always tried to talk me into becoming a teacher and now, years later, here I am in the schools. Each foster grandparent receives forty hours of training prior to placement, five additional hours of in-service training monthly, and ongoing supportive informal training from program staff.

Tell me what you do as a foster grandparent.

Burneil: For the first six years, I was assigned to help first-graders in one elementary school. That school became a school with unique programs for the disabled, so I moved over to the school where I am now working, helping with two first-grade classes and two second-grade classes. The teachers are wonderful, but have so many children. Sometimes there are twenty-eight to thirty students in a class. I'm there to be the teacher's extra arm. I help with group reading and spend one-on-one time with students who need a little extra help with reading, spelling, and vocabulary. I'm an avid reader, so I especially like working with the children on reading.

The Foster Grandparent Relationship

Burneil: Some days, I'll read a story to the whole class. Other days, I'll work individually with four or five children through the course of the school day. We work on reading, phonics, and spelling. One day, I was working on "o" words with a student and she was having trouble with a word. I said to her, "What am I?" and she answered, "You're old," and I said, 'That's right, and that's the word!"

Years of experience and patience are valuable connectors with children. Sometimes a child just needs to talk or get a little help with his or her self-confidence. I once worked with a little boy who sat under my desk and wouldn't come out every time the teacher sent him to work with me. So I told him when he was willing to talk to me, I'd listen. I was very patient with him.

Then one day, for no apparent reason, he didn't do it anymore. He sat down at the desk and told me how unhappy he was. So I gave him some paper and a pencil told him to write down everything that was wrong—and he did. Oh, it was quite a list. I asked him if he minded if I gave the list to the principal and he told me to go ahead. Astounded, the principal asked me, "How did you get him to open up like that?"

Another time a boy told me that the other children make fun of him. We talked and I told him, "You are your own person; don't worry about those other kids." That helped and we got down to the business of learning.

How much time do you spend on your passionate pursuit?

Burneil: I go to school Monday through Thursday and spend four hours there every day. The last half hour is for lunch. I never take a break before lunch—I'm too busy with the children. Of course, foster grandparents work when school is in session and have time off when the school is closed for holidays and seasonal vacations. If the school is on a year-round schedule, the schedule will be different from those schools that do not have a summer session.

What expenses are involved?

Burneil: Right now, I ride with another person, because I don't drive, or I take the bus that brings me right to the school. The Foster Grandparent Program pays each qualified person a small stipend, which is not counted as income and does not affect other benefits or other assistance the volunteer may receive. All volunteers receive a daily meal, an annual physical, transportation allowance, and accident insurance.

What are the most rewarding aspects?

Burneil: I love being with the children. I have nine grandchildren of my own, but they're all grown-up now. Some of the children at school are full of mischief, but I settle them down and we get right to work. I feel I'm fulfilling a real need. For example, I worked with a little boy who speaks some English, but primarily Spanish. He was so attached to me that if I took a day off, he wanted to know why.

There are certain children whose memory sticks with you and makes you feel the rewards of your work. Years ago, I worked with a little second-grade girl who was suffering with an autoimmune disease. Oh, I love that little girl. She let me know from the beginning that she wanted to learn so badly. She was hospitalized in intensive care for three months. I made her dolls and gave her a dictionary. Later, when she was able to return to school, she put her arms around me. Now, tell me that's not gold! We are still in touch and she's now in middle school. I carry a picture of her with me all the time. I guess experiences like that attract me to the program.

I bring a camera to school and have pictures taken with each child, then use them to decorate the area where we work together. I save the pictures year after year—and all the letters I get from the children. I was hospitalized a few months ago, and received the dearest letters full of pictures they drew, wishing me a speedy recovery.

Research on Mentor Participation

The Foster Grandparent Program is rewarding socially and psychologically for the mentor as well as the child. Marc Freedman also reported on one study regarding the satisfaction of the mentors in the program. Those participating in the Foster Grandparent Program were overwhelmingly more satisfied with their life compared to those waiting to become mentors in the program (83 percent vs. 52 percent). Additional studies, specifically on the benefits to older adults who participated in the Foster Grandparent Program, showed participants had more complex brain activity, better memory, and better sleep patterns than before they became involved in the program.

How to Get Involved

Foster grandparents must be fifty-five years of age or older and be willing to abide by the program requirements. They must be capable of serving children with exceptional or special needs without detriment to either themselves or the children. Eligibility to be a foster grandparent is not restricted on the basis of formal education, experience, race, religion, color, national origin, limited English proficiency, sex, handicap, or political affiliation. There is an income eligibility requirement to receive a stipend. This depends on the income eligibility guidelines for the state in which the foster grandparent resides. The Corporation for National and Community Service website, listed in the Resource section, has a link to each state's programs.

Additional Nationwide Youth Mentor Programs

There are many mentor programs looking for caring adults to help nurture resiliency and build strong potential in the lives of our youth. There are a variety of volunteer roles available, such as tutoring one-on-one, helping English learners, coaching sports programs, assisting with group activities and hobbies, supporting new mothers, teaching financial literacy, or helping with child care.

America's Promise

America's Promise has formed alliances with more than 360 nonprofits, educational institutions, corporations, associations, and faith-based groups working to decrease school dropout rates throughout the country. Under the leadership of founding chairman Gen. Colin Powell, America's Promise has become the nation's largest partnership focused on the well-being of young people and the commitment to reach the Grad Nation goals.

Boys and Girls Clubs of America

For more than a century, Boys and Girls Clubs of America (BGCA) have helped put young people on the path to great futures. Boys and Girls Clubs annually serve nearly 4 million young people, through membership and community outreach, in some 4,000 club facilities throughout the country and BGCA-affiliated Youth Centers on US military installations worldwide.

National Mentoring Partnership

The National Mentoring Partnership is a resource for the design, planning, operation, and evaluation of mentoring programs. The National Mentoring Partnership operates the only national online volunteer referral system for adults who want to volunteer as mentors and for those looking for mentoring programs for young people.

YMCA of the USA

For nearly 160 years, the YMCA of the USA has been an advocate for strong community-centered programs. With locations in 10,000 communities throughout the country, volunteers provide intergenerational programs, stressing youth development, healthy living, and social responsibility.

FASCINATING FACTS

- In fiscal year 2012, foster grandparents numbered 28,250 and served 215,700 young people.
- The combined effort of the CNC's three Senior Corps programs in 2012 equaled more than 360,000 volunteers contributing more than 80 million hours of service, serving 1.5 million Americans.
- Senior volunteering is at a 10-year high—1 in 3 volunteers in the United States is a senior volunteer—age 55 and older.
- Students who meet regularly with their mentors are 52% less likely than their peers to skip a day of school and 37% less likely to skip a class.
- Data from 2009 shows only 1/3 of all students entering high school are proficient in reading—only about 15% of African American students, and 17% of Hispanic students.
- In 2010–11, an estimated 4.7 million (or 10%) of public school students in the United States were English language learners.

Resources

Websites

America's Promise: americaspromise.org.

Boys & Girls Clubs of America: bgca.org.

Corporation for National and Community Service Programs: Foster Grandparents; Senior Companion Program; and the Retired & Senior Volunteer Program (RSVP): nationalservice.gov.

Federal and state-specific information on volunteering in America: uwgnh.org.

Information complied by 18 federal agencies that support programs and services focusing on youth: findyouthinfo.gov.

Find volunteer opportunities: volunteer.gov.

The National Mentoring Partnership: mentoring.org.

YMCA: ymca.net.

Videos

Foster Grandparent Program: http://bit.ly/WJ2AgZ.

Gang Member-Turned-PhD Mentors Youth on the Fringes: http://bit.ly/UvSQEW.

Mentoring Youth: 10 Successful Characteristics of Successful Mentors: http://bit.ly/1rJFP9g.

Reading

Gregory Boyle, *Tattoos on the Heart: The Power of Boundless Compassion* (New York, NY: Free Press, 2010).

Marc Freedman, *Prime Time: How Baby Boomers Will Revolutionize Retirement* (New York, NY: PublicAffairs, 2008).

Jean E. Rhodes, *Stand by Me: The Risks and Rewards of Mentoring Today's Youth* (Cambridge, MA: Harvard University Press, 2004).

PART FOUR

MECHANICS AND TECHNOLOGY

CHAPTER 19

Blogger/Vlogger

By giving people the power to share,
we're making the world more transparent.
— Mark Zuckerberg

Blogging and vlogging are all about sharing. They are about creating and being recognized for it. Both are a huge part of the social-media explosion in the twenty-first century. If you love to write, share stories and information, and identify resources and links that readers will enjoy and use, then try blogging. A *blog* (noun) is an online personal journal, a web page dedicated to your writing that links to other sites. You *blog* (verb) when you regularly update your narrative with new material.

Taking the idea of a blog to the next level is the *vlog*. *Vlogging* is the shortened word for "video blogging." Vlog entries can be a link to a video embedded in a blog or a short stand-alone movie created and uploaded to a platform such as YouTube. Many times vlogs are embedded in blogs for a total viewing experience.

Why Blog or Vlog?

People blog and vlog to share what they know and to recount their experiences. They may give opinions, talk about family history, or instruct on a topic of interest. Blogging and vlogging connects with others, establishes expertise and a reputation, and creates a following of readers and viewers. Blogs and vlogs can be instructional and entertaining and on any topic you can imagine. The main idea of these social-media tools is to communicate with your audience on a personal level.

Family Ties

Both blogs and vlogs can be a great way to share family memories and stay in touch. They allow readers to leave comments, and family members can add their own memories. These blogs can lead to vibrant family exchanges that each family member can read, process, and comment on at their own convenience.

Mannie, blogger and vlogger

Mannie, age sixty-two, is a park ranger at Antietam National Battlefield, in Sharpsburg, Maryland. He is currently writing his thesis for a master's degree in military history. Mannie is an experienced blogger and vlogger. He has several blog posts, but has pared those down to a few that he keeps current. He also has a YouTube channel, which currently contains 110 videos. See the Resource section for his blog and vlog links.

Mannie: I started my first blog when I became a park ranger at Antietam National Battlefield. I called it "My Year of Living Ranger-ously." I wrote and posted pictures of some of the area's famous Civil War battle sites and museums. My online journaling was equivalent to a personal diary. A diary is usually secret, but a blog is a diary that you want everyone to see. I think blogging and ego go together because a person has to think that what they have to say is interesting.

Mannie's Blogs

Mannie: Over time, I've written several blogs, but now I actively maintain only two, "Toy Soldiers Forever" and "Combat Helmets of the 20th Century." The toy soldier blog is just for fun. I write about 54mm Marxmen toy soldiers of the American Civil War. Many baby boomers grew up collecting a cadre of miniature figures produced by the US-based Marx Toy Company and others. Through that blog, I appeal to a lot of guys who have fond memories of playing with toy soldiers as kids. If my knees didn't hurt so much, I'd be on the floor playing with my toy soldiers. I built a table to compensate for that. The mind is the same as when I was ten years old, but it's the body that's changed.

I also blog about the combat helmets used in wars throughout the twentieth century. At one time, I had 111 combat helmets in my collection, but I'm paring back. I don't get rid of anything until I've photographed it and put it on my blog. There are a couple of helmet-collecting clubs online. It's an obscure and arcane niche. We mostly trade information. If you post something online, you'll get a dozen people come back with information. I get e-mails from people who have old combat helmets from war and ask for direction on selling them. I counsel them to keep away from gun shows and sell them on eBay, where the seller is more in charge.

Blogging is an affirming experience. I've become something of an expert on twentieth-century combat helmets. My blog is the book I always wanted to write. It's my online book. I don't have to worry about a publisher or an editor. I just go back and edit, as I want. You can immediately update the blog.

Earning Money from Your Blog

A May 2013 blog post on Mint.com written by Kelly Anderson discusses seven ways to earn money by blogging. One way is to add AdSense by Google, which places advertising on your blog. You can align with Amazon's Associates Program, which allows you to earn a portion of sales when people click through from your blog to Amazon.com and make a purchase. Ms. Anderson defines other Affiliate programs and private sponsorship as well. A final suggestion is to write an e-book and sell it on your blog.

Blogging Equipment

Mannie: Equipment for blogging is simple. Any interface to the Internet will do it. Many bloggers use computers, but there are some who use their smartphones exclusively. Blogging software has become so easy to use in recent years that no special knowledge beyond typing and basic computer skills is needed. I use Blogger.com, one of the oldest and most popular blogging platforms. It's simple and uncomplicated, and a good choice for beginners. It's from Google, so you can use Google's tools, such as Google Analytics that generates detailed statistics about your blog's activity.

Other blogging sites cater to different types of learning styles. I find myself gravitating to the platform that's easiest to use. I don't consider myself a tech-savvy person. I'm typical, so if I can use it, anyone can.

How did you get interested in vlogging?

Mannie: I picked up my video skills when I became friends with Chuck, a station manager of the local public-access television station. I volunteered my time there, and Chuck became my mentor. I owe all my expertise to him. I started making small, standalone videos, and it was a lot of fun. In August 2006, I discovered YouTube and put my first video up. Now I have my own YouTube channel with 110 videos so far.

When I first started, my videos were a half hour long. The television station manager taught me film production and editing. He taught me to shoot well and edit. That's the most important thing. Now most of my videos are two to three minutes long.

Vlogging Equipment

Mannie: I spend a lot of time outdoors, and I always have my camera with me to keep an eye out for fun events. It's a pocket camera and easy to operate. I used a much larger camera in the past, a big Pro Sony Camcorder, but the technology today makes a smaller camera just as good. Now I use a little Canon PowerShot. You can shoot video on a smartphone now, but I haven't learned that yet.

I take the digital footage and use the iMovie program to produce my videos. To get started, I would suggest spending $200 on a nice digital camera that shoots video, and $500 for a reconditioned Mac and software. A PC and Windows-compatible software can be used also.

How do you choose subjects for your videos?

Mannie: Anytime you have the urge to say to someone, "Hey, look at that!" that makes a good video. I always have my camera with me and it has always paid off. For example, I was at the park and watched a tractor go by and I saw the hay wagon it was pulling was on fire. I knew it was only a matter of moments before the fire department came, and I shot the episode. Little things like that. As they happen, you can turn it into an interesting forty-second video. It's taking someone along on a little trip even when they're not around. It's sharing an experience. It also makes you so much more aware of what's going on around you.

How do you get readers and viewers?

Mannie: I don't do anything special. People just find my blogs. Currently, I have over 100 followers on my "Toy Soldiers Forever" blog. As for my videos, I just put them up on the YouTube platform, and they take on a life of their own. I have 110 videos now, with over 600,000 views.

When I make a video that I feel special about, I'll post a link to Facebook and tell my friends about it. It evolves from there. One film that I think is very sweet, that I call CatBird Spring, chronicles the lives of a catbird family in my backyard. One bird became so comfortable with me filming that it perched on my finger. So far, I've had more than 2,900 views.

Search Engine Optimization (SEO)

Make your blog content SEO-friendly. In 2011, Google received over 3 billion daily searches from around the world, and that number is growing. Be sure to use names and key terms throughout your blog that will be picked up by heavy traffic and hit critical mass.

Mannie: I have no idea how many people I get who were at first looking for something else and discovered my blogs or vlogs. YouTube is easy to use. While you're uploading your video, a screen will pop up asking you to put in a title a description and keywords. This helps people navigate to your video.

Many bloggers and vloggers install Google Analytics, which is free, so you can see where visits originate, which key words are driving traffic, and what others might be saying about you and your content. Statistics will tell you if most of your followers are coming from a link off Facebook, a Google search, another blog, et cetera.

The YouTube Phenomenon

YouTube is free for all and has come a long way in a short time. In 2007, eight hours of video was uploaded to YouTube every minute. By 2011, it had increased to forty-eight hours per minute. In 2013, it's sixty hours per minute. In 2010, YouTube was watched 700 billion times. The objective is to become popular and "go viral," because 99 percent of the views were of only 30 percent of the videos.

Mannie: Frequently I will use copyrighted music in my videos as background. YouTube handles this well, helping the little guy, while protecting the copyright. It's a cool process. If the artist agrees, and they almost always will, YouTube will make a deal with the artist who owns the rights, place a small ad in the front of my video, and then share the profits from that ad with the artist. It's a win-win-win situation. I don't know about the copyright process for pictures, because all of the pictures I use either belong to me or are public domain.

How much time do you spend on your pursuit?

Mannie: My park-ranger blog, which has 750 posts and that I now post to only sporadically, has always been very photo intensive. About 40 percent of the posts have quite a bit of narrative and several include videos that I've done. My helmet-collecting blog comes next. I try to post monthly, but not as frequently during the winter. It has the most writing time, as I have to research the design and history of the particular helmet, pair that up with the photos, and then post it. I post to the toy-soldier blog the most frequently, sometimes twice a month. The amount of time spent writing is less than the amount of time photographing. All three of my blogs occasionally include content-specific videos that I've produced.

What is the most rewarding aspect of this activity?

Mannie: Getting other people to notice or comment on what I do. Anonymity is something that's never appealed to me. Recognition is the best compliment. I feel good when I know that I've helped someone through one of my blogs. For example, a woman who wanted to sell a combat helmet contacted me. A buyer was taking advantage of her. I helped her get the very best price through eBay.

Any final advice for future bloggers and vloggers?

Mannie: Yes, I would tell people there are no barriers. It's all become so easy to start a blog or create a video with the new technology. All you have to do is start.

FASCINATING FACTS

- The term *blog*, explained in Wikipedia, was coined in 1997, when Jorn Barger called his site a *weblog*. Barger coined the term weblog to describe the process of *logging the web* as he surfed.
- The top highest earning blog in 2013 is *The Huffington Post.* Owner Arianna Huffington has monthly earnings of $2,330,000.
- 6.7 million people blog on websites and 12 million people blog via social networks. Some 3 million new blogs come online every month.
- YouTube is streaming 4 billion online videos every day, up from 3 billion in May 2011.
- As of October 2013, the most watched video was Psy's "Gangnam Style," with 1,781,611,139 views.
- Winston Churchill and H. G. Wells can be seen in old photographs playing with little armies of Britain's toy soldiers on their rugs and lawns.
- Malcolm Forbes, former publisher of *Forbes* magazine, had a collection of over 90,000 toy soldiers.

Resources for Blogging

Additional blogging platforms

Free software designed to make blogging easy for beginners, and can be easily integrated with Google Analytics: Blogger.com; Typepad.com; and WordPress.org.

Squarespace is a blogging platform that charges a monthly fee, with apps for iPad, iPhone, and android. Pages and blogs can be linked to Tumblr, Facebook, Twitter, and Google+: squarespace.com.

Websites

A Newbie's Guide to Blogging: http://bit.ly/1rLFiDL.

Combat Helmets of the 20th Century blog: combathelmets.blogspot.com.

Elderblog Time Goes By website: http://bit.ly/1ChBRIo.

How to Syndicate Your Blog: http://bit.ly/1o7F02v; or How to Blog on Patch: http://bit.ly/1pxZaUU.

Toy Soldiers Forever blog: toysoldiersforever.blogspot.com.

The top 100 senior and boomer blogs and websites: http://bit.ly/1rUfljL.

Apps

Bloglovin: http://bit.ly/UHb3zl.

Evernote: http://bit.ly/1rZ1VCo.

Videos

How to Make a Blog—Step by Step for Beginners! by Tyler Moore: http://bit.ly/X6cZTD.

Reading

Rebecca Blood, *The Weblog Handbook: Practical Advice on Creating and Maintaining Your Blog* (Cambridge, MA: Perseus Pub, 2002).

James Hill, *Blogging: From Passion to Profits!* (Hill Tech Ventures Inc., 2014).

Resources for Vlogging

Websites

Mannie1952's channel on YouTube: https://www.youtube.com/user/mannie1952.

Some current alternatives to YouTube: Blip.tv, Vimeo, Flickr, Veoh, Viddler, DailyMotion, yfrog, ZippCast, Megavideo, Hulu, and Video Style.

Apps

Dropbox: http://bit.ly/1mSRPxB.

Adobe Photoshop Express: http://bit.ly/1rJGgk1.

Videos

How to Vlog: From the Vlogbrothers: http://bit.ly/1tepU36.

The 5 Deadly Sins of Amateur Video: http://bit.ly/1q0RBup.

Filmmaking Techniques: http://bit.ly/1o4JbMI.

How to Make Your Video Look Like Film: http://bit.ly/1l5ELFj.

Reading

Stephanie Cottrell Bryant, *Videoblogging for Dummies* (Hoboken, NJ: Wiley, 2006).

Michael Sean Kaminsky, *Naked Lens: Video Blogging & Video Journaling to Reclaim the YOU in YouTube* (Winnipeg, MB: Organik Media Press, 2010).

Alan Lastufka and Michael W. Dean, *YouTube: An Insider's Guide to Climbing the Charts*, ebook (Sebastopol, CA: O'Reilly Media, 2008).

CHAPTER 20

Craft Beer Homebrewer

You can't be a real country unless you have a beer and an airline. It helps if you have some kind of a football team or some nuclear weapons, but at the very least you need a beer.
— Frank Zappa

Homebrewing beer is a combination of art and science, and home beer makers are the foundation and grassroots of all craft beer. A 2012 American Homebrewers Association (AHA) survey found there are more than a million beer makers nationwide.

Growth of Craft Brewing

Americans have been brewing beer in their homes since colonial times. Both George Washington and Thomas Jefferson were homebrewers. Craft brewing expanded greatly in the United States in 1979, when the Carter administration deregulated the brewing of beer.

More than 90 percent of the professional brewers in this country started as homebrewers, and most of the new small breweries opening are being launched by homebrewers. Jim Koch, who founded Samuel Adams, started as a homebrewer and created the first batch of Samuel Adams Boston Lager in his kitchen. In 2012, total revenues for Jim Koch's company were approximately $629 million. The volume share for craft brewers in 2013 was 7.8 percent, up from 6.5 percent in 2012.

The recent explosion of interest in the hobby has created tricky questions for state alcohol regulators. As of July 1, 2013, homebrewing is legal in all fifty states, but it is not legal to sell homebrew. Many states still prohibit homebrewers from transporting their beer to club meetings or competitions. Some states also limit the amount a homebrewer can produce in a year. Homebrewers should check with their states for regulations.

Barry visiting the Mastra Brewery in Montevideo, Uruguay

Barry is a sixty-two-year-old retired schoolteacher and calls himself "The Ambassador of Beer." He arranges "pub crawls" in which ardent fans travel to local pubs and tour microbreweries tasting their unique brews.

Barry: *We share four-ounce tastes because the objective is not to get drunk but to enjoy the flavor of a variety of beer.*

How did you become interested in this pursuit?

Barry: When my father was young, he made beer with his dad during Prohibition days, so my younger brother and I thought it would be fun to give him a beer-making kit for his birthday. It was terrible stuff! So my brother and I decided to try making it ourselves. Together we brewed probably 250 batches of beer over the next fifteen years. And that's how I started making beer—in the kitchen of my one-bedroom apartment.

Barry has some funny stories about his homebrewing.

Barry: I once had a cork problem at the fermentation stage, and when I returned home from work, I found a six-foot circle of exploded hops on the ceiling. I had also burned up three of the four electric burners on the stove. I think my landlord was glad to see me move out. It's a good idea to use dedicated equipment and brew beer in the garage, on a porch, or out on the patio, if weather permits.

Coming up with names is a fun part for most homebrewers. One of our first beers was so cloudy, we called it "Dazed and Confused" from a Led Zeppelin song. My beer-making group called ourselves BRP Brewing, named for Barry, Rick, and Paul.

What expenses are involved?

Barry: Basic, beginning equipment kits cost $60 to $80; sometimes you can buy used equipment from friends at a beer club. Ingredients cost $25 to $45 per five-gallon batch, depending on the style being brewed. To purchase ingredients, look for local suppliers or use mail-order websites.

People store their freshly made beer in either a keg or bottles. Rather than storing it in a five-gallon tank, I save beer bottles with a regular lip, sterilize, and reuse them. Then I use a capper to put on new bottle caps. A capper costs between $10 and $20. Some people just label the caps of their beers, so they can easily clean and reuse the bottles. Now most people keg their beer because there is less work and cleanup. Then they label each keg. A total budget of $300 to start brewing beer would be generous.

How much time do you spend on your passionate pursuit?

Barry: For a two-year period, I was making beer once or twice a week and inviting my friends over to help consume my five-gallon production. I was winning competitions and getting obsessed with it. Then I reduced it to once or twice a month. You have to think about how much beer you actually need. Five gallons of beer is a lot of beer to go through every month. Right now, I'm taking a hiatus from homebrewing for a while to appease my wife.

A Word of Caution

Barry: The dark side of brewing beer is alcoholism. I know that I don't have to consume a lot of beer to taste it for flavor, and I'm very careful of how much I consume. I like to invite my friends over and share what I make.

We're looking at the flavor profile of the beer, and we drink only those that are interesting. Another problem to be aware of is DUIs. We take care when attending tastings at club meetings and pub-crawling. At the beer club, you must always be conscious of how many ounces of beer you drink and how much alcohol is in the drink. Designated drivers or using public transportation is advised.

What is the most rewarding aspect of this activity?

Barry: Having friends try my beer and hearing them say, "That's really good." It's the same feeling you have after cooking an elaborate meal for your family and friends, and they say it's just as good as the restaurant down the street. I puff up with pride. My goal would be to hear that my homebrew is as good as one of my favorite beers like Racer 5 or Parabola. For some people, that's enough. Others seek recognition through winning competitions or trying unusual styles of beer. One of the highlights of my beer making so far was winning Best of Show for my raspberry bock.

Beer Classification and Style

There are two basic beer classifications: ales and lagers. Ales use yeasts that are active at warmer temperatures and rise to the top during the fermentation process, which is only a matter of days. Lagers, on the other hand, use yeasts that are active at colder temperatures and ferments at the bottom of the tank. Lagers take a longer time to ferment, sometimes a month or more. This process is meant to create a crisp-tasting beer. Lagers are more popular and account for more than 90 percent of the beer consumed in the United States.

"Beer style" is a term used to differentiate beer by factors such as color, flavor, strength, ingredients, production method, or origin. The Brewers Association has defined 142 beer styles. Ales, for example can be porters, stouts, or dark ales. Lager styles include pale lager, pilsner, bock, marzen, dortmunders, and many more.

Barry: Experimenting with different styles of beer can be a lot of fun. I went to a liquor store and saw that a fellow in England is making a banana-bread beer. Supposedly when you take the cap off, it smells like banana bread. And that's the fascinating part about homebrewing. Beer has evolved so much from Washington and Jefferson's time. Every time I go to a brewery, I find someone else has put something else together. I had a porter (a dark-style beer) the other day with blood orange in it.

Production

The brewing preparation is similar to the canning process. Everything must be set up and sterilized; arrange to spend the whole day when you begin production. Plan on about four weeks before you can drink the beer you make, but the actual time from boil to beer depends on the style of beer you're making. Include two hours for brewing; two-plus weeks for the fermentation process; one hour to bottle your beer; and two to four weeks for bottle conditioning, which allows the beer to carbonate.

Barry: There are some new, incredibly great tools out there now, and it's more high-tech than when I first started. A task that took two hours now takes ten minutes. There are also mobile phone apps available that help you build your own recipes, tell you how much grain to add, step-by-step checklists, and a calendar to manage your batches. The materials weren't as good then as they are now. I was using non-food-grade tubing and my fifteen gallons of beer smelled like plastic. A friend who worked as a nurse in a burn unit of a local hospital started helping me, and she was a stickler for creating a sterile environment. My brew definitely improved with her help. After that, I started winning beer competitions.

Do you belong to an organization?

Barry: It's a good idea to join a local club. My local club, the Draft Board, is a very friendly crowd, and we all help each other. Beginning brewers can come to a meeting, ask questions, and have members taste their brew. That peer-review process is invaluable because these folks are good at what they do.

Brew Clubs

Brew clubs are the lifeblood of the homebrewing community. A local brew club provides an opportunity to meet other brewers, socialize, and learn from the club's collective experience. According to the American Homebrewers Association, there are over 1,500 registered brew clubs throughout the United States and around the world. The AHA website, listing clubs throughout the country, can be found in the Resources section.

Do you use the Internet in your hobby?

Barry: Yes, in several ways: to find new recipes, order ingredients, research, connect with my beer club, find competitions, read beer reviews, and announce scheduled pub crawls to my friends on Facebook. I like to go to the Beer Advocate on the web, which is a grassroots network where people review every beer that you can drink.

Competitions

Barry judges brewing competitions, and some of his former students are brewing beer and entering competitions now. There are many levels of competition at county fairs and club-only competitions. Clubs pick their best two or three beers in a category and enter them in statewide contests. Then they can see how they measure up to the best brewers in the state. Beer clubs will also have a seasonal brew focus, for example Oktoberfest beers. Club members will brew a specialty beer and members will critique one another's brew, discussing what they can do to make it better.

There are also national contests. The AHA website gives a list of all upcoming national events. All of the competitions provide valuable feedback from trained beer judges on their brews. While some homebrewers enter competitions for the recognition and awards, others enter simply to get an unbiased, objective analysis of their beer. Judges' feedback can give ~~you~~ information about sanitation procedures, ingredients, brewing process, and/or recipe formulation. Awards are usually ribbons or medals.

What do you see evolving in the future for your pursuit?

Barry: I've been offered jobs in microbrewers and have heard suggestions that I start my own brewery, but I enjoy being retired and I don't want to turn my hobby into a job. Instead, I prefer to incorporate my passion with travel. This year, my wife and I traveled to Alaska on the Celebrity Beer Theme Cruise, complete with an onboard beer festival, beer tastings, and beer-appreciation classes, including Beer 101, and visits to local Alaskan breweries. In two years, we are going on a beer cruise to Belgium, where they make more styles of beer than anywhere in the world.

FASCINATING FACTS

- *Zymurgy* is the branch of chemistry that deals with fermentation processes, as in brewing.
- The ancient Babylonians were the first to brew. In fact, they took their beer so seriously that if you brewed a bad batch, your punishment was to be drowned in it.
- The first professional brewers were all women.
- Store beer upright. It minimizes oxidation and contamination from the cap.
- Hops used in beer are in the same family of flowering plants as marijuana.
- The type of water used for brewing makes a difference. The best ales are produced with hard water (with more natural salts like calcium), while soft water is better for lagers.
- In the late 1800s and early 1900s, fresh beer was carried from the local pub to one's home by means of a small-galvanized pail. Rumor has it that when the beer sloshed around the pail, it created a rumbling sound as the CO_2 escaped through the lid, thus the term *growler* was coined.

Pairing Beer and Food

Barry: There is a big push of pairing food with beer, just like in the wine industry. There are specialists now whose whole job is pairing food with the right beer. For example, if you're dining on Indian food, you might want to have something crisp and light like a pilsner that will quench your thirst from the spicy food. You can download an app for your mobile phone that will give you suggestions for pairing beers with food. One of my favorite things to eat with beer is peanut brittle. And dark chocolate, too—that's good with dark beer.

Resources

Websites

American Homebrewers Association: homebrewersassociation.org.

Beer Advocate: beeradvocate.com.

Beer Style Finder: craftbeer.com/style-finder.

The Brewers Association: brewersassociation.org.

List of Brew Clubs: http://bit.ly/1qGuYgK.

Rate Beer: ratebeer.com.

Untapped: untappd.com.

Classes

The American Brewers Guild offers a Craft Brewers Apprenticeship Program (CBA), a 28-week program at the Vermont facility, or a distance-education version using DVDs, text, and their website. Also offered is Intensive Brewing Science and Engineering, a 23-week technical program: abgbrew.com/index.htm.

Craft Beer offers a free online Beer 101 course: http://bit.ly/1ptkhrg.

Apps

Apps for pairing food and beer: http://bit.ly/1mSTALb or http://bit.ly/1rs9Jey.

Eight Brilliant Beer Apps: http://bit.ly/1q63QTi.

Videos

The Craft Beer Channel on YouTube: http://bit.ly/1rJHmMw.

Beer America TV: beeramerica.tv.

Sam Adams Brewery Library of Videos: www.samueladams.com/video-library

Reading

Tom Acitelli, *The Audacity of Hops: The History of America's Craft Beer Revolution* (Chicago, IL: Chicago Review Press, 2013).

Jacquelyn Dodd, *The Craft Beer Cookbook: From IPAs and Bocks to Pilsners and Porters, 100 Artisanal Recipes for Cooking with Beer* (Cincinnati, OH: F+W Media, 2013).

Janet Fletcher, *Cheese & Beer* (Kansas City, MO: Andrews McMeel, 2013) (Pairing artisan cheese and craft beer).

Celebrator Beer Magazine: celebrator.com.

Zymurgy Magazine is the journal of the American Homebrewers Association: http://bit.ly/1rsbEzU.

CHAPTER 21

Ham Radio Operator

When everything else fails.
Amateur Radio often times is our last line of defense . . .
When you need amateur radio, you really need them.
—The Hon. W. Craig Fugate

According to the National Association for Amateur Radio, there are more than 704,000 amateur radio license holders in the United States. Often called *ham radio*; the amateur radio service has been around since the nineteenth century. *Ham* was a negative term used by professional radiotelegraph operators to suggest that amateur enthusiasts were unskilled. But amateurs embraced the name and adopted the word *ham* to describe their hobby and themselves.

Global Reach

Ham operators not only connect across town and across the country but also transmit globally, from Antarctica to remote islands in the Pacific Ocean. English is the standard language for ham radio traffic even overseas. The International Space Station uses amateur radio hardware. Astronauts and cosmonauts speak directly with teachers, students, parents, and communities, and answer questions while living and working aboard the Space Station.

Emergency Responders

In the event of a natural disaster or other emergency, amateur radio provides a means of communication when centralized systems such as cell towers, telephone lines, and power lines are down. During the 9/11 attacks, over five hundred ham operators provided emergency communications, such as coordinating contact between the search-and-rescue units. Within five minutes of American Flight 11 crashing into the North Tower, ham radios were operating. Private, nongovernment radio operators worked in shifts for two weeks. During Hurricane Katrina, amateur radio operators were functioning three days *before* the storm made landfall. At the request of the American Red Cross, seven hundred radio operators supplemented communications at two hundred shelters.

Ham Radio Is Not a CB

Ham radio is different from Citizens Band (CB), a favorite among truckers. CB radio allows only local communication, using strictly limited modes and frequencies. By comparison, ham radio operators have privileges all across the radio spectrum, from shortwave to microwave.

Ham radio enthusiasts are a worldwide community of licensed operators using the airwaves with every conceivable means of communications technology. Ranging in age from youngsters to grandparents, hams can transmit voice, data, and pictures through the air to faraway places without depending on commercial systems. When repeater towers are used, ham radio operators can communicate from city to city and throughout the world. When other communications systems fail in natural disasters, or during technological failures such as blackouts and other interruptions, amateur radio operators keep running.

Dave, ham radio operator

Dave, seventy-two years old, is a retired process-control technician and current president of the Green Bay, Wisconsin, Mike and Key Club. The club was founded in 1939 and Dave explains the meaning of the club name: *Mike* stands for microphone and *Key* stands for the Morse code key, both important elements in the history and tradition of amateur radio.

Dave: When I was a young Boy Scout, my older brother and I would use a buzzer to transmit Morse code messages back and forth to each other across the hall to our bedrooms. We also had an old RCA radio that could pick up shortwave and ship-to-shore radio information for boaters. That's how I got interested in radio transmission.

When I went into the Air Force, the aptitude tests showed electronics, so I had a choice of learning to be an electrician in Chicago or studying electronics in Biloxi, Mississippi. I went to Mississippi and was trained as a radio repairman during the Vietnam era. One of the things we would do was to provide radio communications for front-line commanders and call aircraft into designated areas. I got into electronics *just as technology was moving from tubes to transistors. Now we have moved to chips.*

How did you get started in ham radio?

Dave: After the Air Force, I worked in control systems and instrumentation. In 1988, I moved to the Kalamazoo area and my neighbor across the street, Alex, was a ham radio operator and worked for the Federal Communications Commission. I had dabbled with Citizens Band radio, and Alex became my ham radio mentor. In radio speak we call that an "Elmer" or someone who guides, encourages, and helps you out. He assisted me in all regards—how to operate a radio, how to make and put up an antenna, and how to pass the licensing test.

Morse code was required then for ham radio licensing [it is no longer required], and he was really good at it. The trick to learning Morse code is "Don't think about it." Let your mind do the work: "from your ear to your hand." Many people proficient in Morse code can listen to all of the transmission, then write it down by paragraph. Rather than letter-by-letter, they hear clumps of words.

Regulations and Licenses

Ham radio is a licensed radio service. Operators take an exam to get their operating license and call sign, which identifies the radio operator and location of the transmission. Since amateur radio equipment has the potential to interfere with other radio transmissions, operators must learn some information about radio, how it works, and the regulations governing amateur radio. The Federal Communication Commission (FCC) governs licensing.

Dave: I failed the test the first time. I was really nervous. One week later, I took the test again and passed it. That was a while ago; nowadays it's more advanced. There are three license levels in the US: Technician, General, and Extra/Advanced. Each subsequent level requires more knowledge and grants further privileges in permitted transmission bands. The tests cover the same topics—regulations, operating practices, electronics, propagation, antennae, and safety—but to increasing levels of complexity.

License Levels

If you're only interested in talking around town, you only need the Technician class license. This level allows all privileges in the very-high frequency (VHF) or ultra-high frequency (UHF) radio waves useful for local communications.

Dave: The lower level encourages beginners to earn a higher level to gain privileges on higher frequencies. At the Technician level, you can only go thirty miles out alone. You have "line of sight"; that means you can connect with whatever you can see. This might be a limitation if you live in a valley, but with today's innovations, if you live on flat ground you can use a repeater station, take a ten-watt radio, and broadcast it farther.

An amateur radio repeater is an electronic device that receives a weak or low-level amateur radio signal and retransmits it at a higher level or higher power, so that the signal can cover longer distances without degradation.

Dave: If you're interested in emergency communications, you need a General class license. High-frequency communication can be challenging, and it takes time to develop the required skills. If, like most hams, you are interested in talking all around the world on "shortwave" radio, you need the General class license.

With a General class, you can do everything the Technician does, plus use higher frequencies. You can use a bigger radio with more frequency power without depending on the Internet and repeater stations. One of the challenges in amateur radio is to see how far you can go to connect.

There is a third license. Extra/Advanced continues to expand frequencies, but's not a huge difference.

Ham Cram

Dave: The radio club offers a workshop called "Ham Cram," where members help each other study for their license preparation. "VEs," or volunteer examiners, administer all exams. The VE has to have a higher class than the exam that is given. All of the tests must be turned in to the FCC as the final authority.

Call Sign

Dave: After you pass the test, you receive your license and are assigned a call sign. Call signs consist of three parts. My call letters are N8KQS. The structure of the call sign is prescribed by an international committee and allows for localized assignment of unique IDs. The prefix of the call sign, usually composed of two or three letters and numbers, define the operator's country of origin, and often a specific region within the country.

Going back to my call sign, N8KQS, you can tell that the license was issued in the US, which uses the letters A, K, N, or W. The "8" indicates the Michigan area where I originally received my license [rather than his current home of Wisconsin, which is "9"]. Finally, the "KQS" is a unique suffix identifying the license holder. When you get to the Extra/Advanced level, you can request a vanity call sign such as a "two-by-two" [only two letters at the end instead of three], or even a one-letter designation.

What equipment and expenses are involved for start-up costs?

Dave: I have a dual-band Kenwood radio that operates UHF and VHF [$300]. It allows me to not only send voice messages but digital messages as well. Everything operates off a 12-volt power supply, which gives me the ability to use a battery when necessary. That way I don't need to use 110 volts, which is a typical residential power supply.

I have a smaller high-frequency radio [$800] as well, and a tuner. The tuner balances the standing wave ratio between my HF radio and antennae. It electrically changes the antenna length to make it resonate to the chosen frequency. My tuner was around $150. I can amplify the power from my radio with an amplifier [$800], from the normal 100 watts up to 600 watts. I never go that high, usually just to 150 watts, but it helps me get through the static in the area. I don't need to have the amplifier, but some days and in certain weather conditions and particular times of the day, some frequencies work better than others do, so it helps. The best time to talk depends on atmospheric conditions, but usually sunrise and sunset or really late at night you'll get clearer signals. Each frequency is a little different.

I use the microphone that came with the VHF/UHF radio and I have a headset with a microphone for my HF radio. I have a foot switch that I can press with my foot to talk. I like to keep my hands free to turn knobs and take notes. The headset is approximately $40, and the foot switch is $35. I also have a marine battery that I keep charged all the time in case of loss of electrical power.

The antenna is just a long piece of wire. I have two pieces of wire approximately 100 feet long saddled around my house. I have a five-band [frequency] vertical antenna that is 23 feet long in the backyard that looks like a vertical pipe. You can get more elaborate than that if you want. A fellow down the street has a 75-foot tower with a tri-bander antenna, but you don't need that. It's wants versus needs.

Figure start-up costs of $2,200 for all brand-new equipment, but you can get used equipment to start. It may not have all the bells and whistles, but it's enough in the beginning.

Some folks may want to get started with just a hand-held radio. There are new radios made in China that sell for $39 and look like a cigarette pack. It is 5 watts of power, but with local repeater stations, you can amplify that. Through some local repeater nodes, it is possible to connect from your radio to another radio in a foreign country through the node's computer connection.

How much time do you spend each day, week, or month on this pursuit?

Dave: With my involvement with emergency communications, as well as playing around, I'll spend a couple hours a day. My club duties as current president add another twenty to thirty minutes per day. We have monthly meetings and, together with a separate administration meeting, that totals one and a half hours per month. We also hold a half-hour class before the meeting for those interested in what new things are available.

Emergency Communication

Dave: The American Radio Relay League helped form the Radio Amateur Citizen Service, which is part of the FEMA plan during emergencies. Emergency coordinators work directly with each county's Emergency Management Department, and during an emergency begins a "log" or roll call of those radio operators who are on the air. For example, during a tornado, a "net" of available radio operators feeds information to Net Control, who is the liaison with the National Weather Service.

Amateur radio operators are known to be a reliable source. We are not reporters; we are communicators. In fact, when we are handed a message to send, we send it as it is . . . no spelling corrections or grammar. We do not have the right to interpret what the sender is trying to communicate. We are not allowed to give names of affected persons over the air unless through a digital transmission, to keep the information confidential.

What is the most rewarding aspect of this activity?

Dave: When something happens, I know I'm prepared and that I can provide help to my community. Also I enjoy just communicating with people. I keep in contact with old friends I haven't seen in a long time.

I've contacted people in many other countries as well. You can dial various frequencies. If you hear someone saying "CQ CQ," or "CQ Europe" or "CQ USA" it means, "I'm looking for someone to talk to." You just jump in and talk to them.

QSL Cards

Some hams collect QSL cards. *QSL* means "I confirm that I received your transmission." Amateur radio operators send them to one another to confirm that a two-way radio contact was received between stations. Each card contains details about one or more contacts, the station, and its operator. Some QSL cards have special value because they're not available anymore, for example, cards from Yugoslavia or the former USSR.

Dave: I have a three-ring binder full of QSL cards verifying contact. Some are pretty fancy. Some radio operators wallpaper their walls with them. Many clubs will issue the cards to celebrate a special event as well.

Any interesting stories about your activity?

Dave: One ham radio operator was also a sailor and he wanted to make sure he could get his messages home. He knew that often his voice communications on ship didn't reach far enough, but digital communications could go farther. So he developed a program that takes a message over the airwaves and stores it in a "dropbox" on the Internet. Anyone, family or friends can pick up the messages.

I was curious about how the program worked, so one day I signed on to make contact with a ship. I saw a map with little bubbles containing each sailor's call sign. You could track the location of each ship sending messages and see where the bubbles moved each day, tracking their progress all around the world. I found a ship sailing all by itself way out in the North Atlantic Ocean. I pulled up the message and the captain said he and his crew of two were trying to outrun a storm: "We're looking for contact and requesting storm information." I made contact and told the captain where the storm was projected to go. I sent the latitude and longitude so they could get out of the storm's path.

The next day he told me his present location and that they were headed to the Mediterranean. They requested that I please let the Coast Guard know their new location and that they were OK. Two days later, I received a message that they didn't escape the storm completely. Their main sails were torn and their generator used to charge the battery broke off, but they were limping along. Finally, I got a message saying, "Thanks for keeping track of us. We made it into port. Thank you for being out there."

FASCINATING FACTS

- The 26 code words in the NATO phonetic alphabet are assigned to the 26 letters of the English alphabet and used by hams: Alpha, Bravo, Charlie, Delta, Echo, Foxtrot, Golf, Hotel, India, Juliet, Kilo, Lima, Mike, November, Oscar, Papa, Quebec, Romeo, Sierra, Tango, Uniform, Victor, Whiskey, X-ray, Yankee, and Zulu.
- Thomas Edison proposed to his second wife in Morse code.
- Conversations lasting more than 30 minutes are called *rag-chewing.*
- In the United States, approximately 15% of amateur radio operators are women.
- The Amateur Radio Relay League (ARRL) Field Day held on the fourth weekend of June of each year, highlights the many roles of amateur radio.
- Japan has 1.3 million ham operators.
- Current and past celebrity hams include Joe Walsh (from the Eagles), Marlon Brando, Barry Goldwater, Walter Cronkite, Chet Atkins, Ronnie Milsap, and most astronauts.

Resources

Websites

The Amateur Radio Relay League: arrl.org.

Find exam location by zip code: http://bit.ly/1rJIYpF.

Four profiles of ham radio operator equipment: http://bit.ly/X0GQgb.

eHam.net is a community site designed and operated by and run for active Amateur Radio operators (hams): eham.net.

Identify clubs in your area: hamdepot.com.

A variety of groups on Yahoo!, Facebook, and LinkedIn. Search "ham radio."

Videos

A collection of ham radio videos from around the world: http://bit.ly/1mSX541.

The DIY Magic of Amateur Radio: http://bit.ly/1zk1Cp2.

How Stuff Works Videos, *How Ham Radio Works*: http://bit.ly/UDZw3B.

Reading

AARL, *Ham Radio License Manual with CD* (ARRL Ham Radio License Manual), (Newington, CT: ARRL, 2010).

Joseph Lumpkin, *A Complete Study Guide for Technician, General, Extra Class Ham Radio Exams, and the Volunteer Examiner Test: Including the Correct Answers to All . . . on Basic Theory, Rules, and Regulations* (Blounstville, AL: Fifth Estate, Incorporated, 2012).

H. Ward Silver, *Ham Radio for Dummies* (Hoboken, NJ: Wiley Pub, 2004).

CHAPTER 22

Motorcyclist

Four wheels move the body;
two wheels move the soul.
—Sasha Mullins and Trevor Finlay

Retirees are riding motorcycles in their fifties and sixties and beyond. *Wall Street Journal* writer Robert Johnson reported in December 2011 that the fifty-plus crowd is having a belated romance with motorcycles. The number of "graying riders" is increasing. He reports that the owner of a motorcycle safety school is seeing older, beginner riders in their seventies and eighties.

According to the Motorcycle Industry Council, motorcycling is growing and rapidly becoming more mainstream in the United States. The number of American households that own motorcycles jumped 26 percent from 2003 to 2008. During that same time, female ownership of motorcycles increased to 12.3 percent in 2008. Harley-Davidson reports that women purchase 9 percent of all new "Hogs."

Voni and Paul with their motorcycles

Voni and Paul call Big Bend, Texas, their home for eight months out of the year, then hit the road from mid-May until mid-September touring on their motorcycles. Voni is sixty-seven years old and a retired special-education teacher and Paul, age sixty-nine, retired from a career as a city planner. They have been riding motorcycles for many years. Voni belongs to the elite group of motorcyclists in the BMW Million Miler Club, and Paul has covered 825,000 miles and is still counting.

How did you become interested in this pursuit?

Voni: Back in the 1970s, we didn't have a lot of money and had two young children. Paul had been riding a motorcycle since he was fourteen. I decided to learn to ride so we could take the kids on vacations.

Paul: This way the children didn't fight in the backseat of the car. One rode with me, the other rode with Voni. It became a way we could go for a two-hour drive with nobody fighting. When our children turned seven and nine years old, we went on two-week vacations.

Voni: We like to travel and we like to camp. At first, I thought driving a motorcycle was a terrible idea, but it began to make sense to me. All I ever heard was how dangerous it was. One year, Paul gave me a motorcycle for Mother's Day. I intended to be as safe as I could be.

How did you get started?

Voni: I started on a 250 Yamaha, and never left the backyard for the first hundred miles. We lived in Iowa on a few acres in the country, and I rode the motorcycle around in an apple orchard. I was too scared to go on the back roads. When I finally got onto the pavement, it was a big step. I was fearful, but Paul was a natural teacher.

Paul: First, you have to learn the "muscle mechanics" of riding. You have to learn the operations first, such as "this is how you operate the clutch," "this is how you steer," "this is how you stop." Voni concentrated on that for the first hundred miles.

Voni: When we started, I would be on one motorcycle and Paul would be on another. That didn't help teach me to ride, so Paul went to Radio Shack and got a pillow speaker that's used on a CB radio. I would have the speakers and Paul had the microphone. He would talk to me and give me directions while he was driving behind me. I would go at a comfortable pace, and Paul would be the little voice in my head providing instruction and pointing out dangers. I could learn in that environment instead of reading instructions in a book.

Paul: The bigger part of driving a motorcycle is the mental part. It's visual, and you ask yourself questions such as "What is a threat?" and "Is that car going to turn in front of me?" When we got on the road to practice, it was natural for Voni to drive in front so I could point out things as they were happening in real time. I would say, "See that truck? He's not going to stop," or "Lean in and anticipate."

Voni: The timeframe was one year from beginning to ride until I drove on the road. If I were starting today, I would begin by taking a motorcycle safety class. Most classes provide the bike and the instruction. My advice is, when you start, spend a lot of time on roads where you don't have to deal with city traffic.

Paul: Learning to drive a motorcycle is no more difficult than learning to drive a car, with one huge exception—the effect of the weather. You always have to be cognizant of the weather. Forget riding in snow. If it's raining hard, you get pelted and water is running up your sleeve. If it is a hundred and five degrees going across the desert, you have to stay *cool; if it's windy, you're blown around. You have to be prepared for all of the elements.*

Where do you ride?

Voni: Cycling is so freeing for us both. When I am stressed, Paul suggests a ride out to Big Bend National Park. We look out over the vistas and the amazing sights bring life all back into balance.

Paul: My favorite kind of ride is during the summer. We typically travel north and west from Texas up to British Columbia. We love to ride in the mountains of Colorado and the Bighorn Mountains of Wyoming. We spend a lot of time in western Montana, Idaho, and British Columbia.

In Texas, we ride at 2,200-feet elevation up to 6,000 feet, or get on the road that follows the twists and turns of the Rio Grande. Sometimes we don't stop until we need fuel. A typical ride will be 300 to 350 miles. We drive a ways, then stop and get breakfast, bike some more, then eat snacks. Instead of going to a busy lunch counter, we pack a picnic and eat at a roadside rest stop looking at nature.

Voni: When we first retired, we thought we might like to be motorcycle tour guides, but it wasn't for us. We traveled to South Africa and four other countries in Africa. We traveled in New Zealand, Brazil,

Germany, and Spain. We rented our motorcycles when we traveled abroad.

Paul: For years, I only had two weeks of vacation and Voni had the whole summer off from teaching. So for twenty years she would take off and travel by herself. People would ask her all the time, "Aren't you afraid?" She finally started answering, "I teach in a public high school. Why would I be afraid?"

What do you bring on your trips and how do you pack?

Paul: Have you ever seen the TV show The Beverly Hillbillies, when the Clampetts arrive in their overloaded jalopy? We pack a tent and sleeping bags, and sleeping pads. We have saddlebags on each side of both motorcycles. We also have tank bags for frequent-access items. We carry snacks, food, and cooking-preparation bags. If the weather is too cold, wet, or windy we go to a hotel.

Voni: We pack clothes. Jeans take up too much room so we wear LD comfort tights that are designed especially for riding, under our riding clothes. They're easy to rinse out and dry overnight.

Paul: I bring hiking pants with zip-off legs, a couple of pairs of shorts, and sandals. Running shoes take up too much room.

Endurance Trips

Paul: We both like semi-competitive endurance rides and we like to participate in the Iron Butt Rally. It's a long-distance race, like a scavenger hunt, and held in the United States every two years. In the Iron Butt Rally, riders have to ride 11,000 miles in eleven days while trying to find proof that they arrived at designated checkpoints within a two-hour window of a designated time. They might have to take a picture of something, or get a receipt for a piece of pie at a specific restaurant. They might keep going for twenty-four hours at a time.

The Iron Butt Rally

No consideration is given for bad weather during the running of the Iron Butt. Riders can expect to ride through rain, sleet, snow, severe thunderstorms, hurricanes, and the occasional tornado. During the rally, temperatures routinely run 125 degrees or more in the desert Southwest. It's called the "World's Toughest Motorcycle Competition," and event organizers intentionally route the rally through such places as Death Valley or the Mojave Desert during the hottest part of the day. The race continues to extreme cold at the top of mountains like Pikes Peak in Colorado, where competitors may have to struggle up a muddy road to reach the peak's 14,110-foot summit.

Voni: Being on the bikes sixteen to eighteen hours a day is tough. Making sure we have good sleep every day and good nutrition is important. In one rally, we started in Missoula, Montana, and then drove to Nevada, on to Florida, and up to Maine in eleven days.

We drove in another event in which we tried to ride to forty-nine states in ten days—just for fun. That takes a lot of planning. Paul spent one winter planning how to touch every state in ten days. We ended in Juneau, Alaska.

What equipment and expenses are involved?

Paul: Motorcycles are our hobby run amok. We currently have nine motorcycles. They have so much mileage, we really can't sell them, and so we use them. One Christmas, we got together with our friends and frivolously started a group called Motorcycles Anonymous. We said we would meet once a year to talk each other out of buying more motorcycles. If at any time during the year anyone gets an irresistible urge to buy another motorcycle, he or she would call the support group. No one ever did.

Voni: Which motorcycle you use depends on your personality and whether you enjoy riding with someone or riding separately. My sister, for example, just wants to ride on the back; she doesn't want to drive. There are many clubs devoted to these "group riders." And for some people just beginning, it might be easier to start with another cycler and see if they like the traveling part.

Paul: You can spend $3,000 and get a very good used, reliable motorcycle. You don't have to spend $29,000 for a Honda Gold Wing, a Harley, or a BMW K1600.

Voni: Women don't have as much upper-body strength but because motorcycles are balanced so well, it isn't difficult to control them. You'd think it might be, but it isn't. If you don't want a two-wheel, you can also go for a three-wheel motorcycle.

Paul: There are also different styles of motorcycles. Touring bikes have a low center of gravity and are comfortable. There are also cruisers, where your feet are out in front of you. We use touring or sport touring bikes.

Voni: I use a sport touring, which has more of a forward lean and is easier on my back.

Paul: Mine is more a touring bike because it's easier on my neck.

Types of Motorcycles

The type of motorcycle you drive depends on what you want to do with it. The American Motorcycle Association suggests that the first step should be understanding the categories of motorcycles and the pros and cons for new riders. They describe the following motorcycle types:

A Standard is built for doing a little of everything. For new riders, the neutral ergonomics give the rider more comfort and a better sense of control. The lack of fairing (a shell placed over the frame to reduce air drag) makes tip-over less costly. Some larger Standards are well over 100 horsepower and can be intimidating to an inexperienced rider.

A Cruiser is built for relaxed rides. The low seat lets the rider get his or her feet down and has a low center of gravity, which offsets the heft. The engine is tuned for low-rpm power, which makes the clutch/throttle coordination easier. On the negative side, the long, low style means handling is a bit awkward.

A Sport bike is built for speed and handling, and is relatively lightweight. High power and strong brakes demand respect and a deft touch. The engine is tuned for high-rpm power and makes clutch/throttle coordination trickier. Drop it and the replacement plastic is costly and insurance costs are high.

Dual Sport motorcycles are built for riding on- and off-road. They are relatively lightweight and versatile—able to drive on trails and road. The relatively high seat heights take some getting used to.

The Touring is built for long rides on the open road. It is comfortable and has good weather protection and the convenience of integrated luggage. It is generally heavier and more expensive than the average motorcycle and has the most powerful engines that demand respect.

The Scooter is built for urban transportation and practicality. There is no clutch or gears to shift, just twist and go. You get 50 to 90 miles per gallon, depending on size. Scooters are typically more affordable than motorcycles; however, scooters with smaller wheels can be less stable at higher speeds. If a motorcycle is your ultimate goal, the skills you learn on a scooter may not translate as precisely as those you would learn on a small starter motorcycle.

A Trike is a three-wheeled motorcycle that has grown in popularity in recent years, expanding from a do-it-yourself niche to a lucrative market for major manufacturers. In 2013, Harley-Davidson sold the Tri Glide at prices starting at $30,000. Because of the stability of three-wheelers, riders aren't required to lean into curves or hold them steady at stoplights, activities which can challenge weak knees and muscles.

Paul: Tires are more important on a motorcycle than a car. Each tire is putting down on a spot that is smaller than your fist. That's where you stop and start. Depending on your bike, there will be two or three good brands. It's important to learn how to change a tire.

What special clothing do you wear?

Voni: Specific clothing is important because it mitigates the weather, and I shop online for deals. You need clothing that is rain-proof, and is vented for heat. Leather is still used, but another option is "textile" pants and jackets that are more versatile for cool and warm weather.

Textile Clothing

The textile motorcycle jacket has vents that allow it to breathe in warm weather and liners that can be added when the weather is cold. It also disperses rainwater better than leather, has more pockets, and is easier to clean. A textile motorcycle jacket contains some protective armor within it to help protect jacket wearers in the event of an accident, but does not provide as much protection as a leather jacket.

Voni: You can buy an outfit for $200. You need boots and a helmet. Buy motorcycle-specific boots that go over the ankle and give ankle support. Helmets can cost $70 to $1,000. As long as the helmet is Department of Transportation rated, there isn't much of a difference except for comfort.

Paul: I like a helmet that cost $200. A face shield is important.

Most of the clear shields are treated to block ultraviolet light. They are made of a hard polycarbonate and are replaceable. The newer models don't get scratched too often now.

Voni: I have several pairs of gloves: vented, waterproof, and leather gloves. Having several pairs is important to me. Gloves protect my hands from getting calluses from turning the throttle. We bring four pairs with us when we travel for cold and warm weather. Gloves with mesh protect the knuckles and palms but allow airflow. I use midweight deerskin gloves too.

Paul: You need tools. Most people carry the tool kits that come with their motorcycles. I carry enough tools to take the motorcycle apart and put it back together again. I'm a maintenance junkie.

Voni: Paul has been writing for BMW Motorcycle Magazine for eighteen years. He wasn't a mechanic, he just learned because we couldn't afford to spend lots of money having the dealership service the bikes all the time. In the winter, Paul would take the motorcycle apart, label all the parts, and then put it back together. You should also include a training class in the budget.

Paul: So figure $5,000 for a total budget for start-up costs. A used motorcycle for $3,000; $1,000 for tires, tools, and additional gear; $600 for good riding clothing, boots, and a helmet; $120 for a training class; and $280 for miscellaneous items.

What are some problems of this activity?

Paul: Weather and traffic.

Voni: We've done a lot to be safe drivers and stay current on the traffic rules. We took a rider's advanced training school class at Laguna Seca and learned from a trained motorcycle racer. I've never been involved in an accident and Paul was involved in only one.

What is the most rewarding aspect of this activity?

Voni: I taught high school kids and I would tell them, "There are no drugs that come anywhere close to what you feel when you do something you love, whether it's running or hiking or motorcycling."

Paul: I like the people we meet. When we're traveling and stop at a gas station, someone will walk up to you and talk to you. When you drive a car or travel in a group, you won't meet people. They don't come over and interact.

Voni: We've been invited out to dinner or to stay at homes of people we've met at a gas station. The motorcycling has grown into other things as well, such as writing for magazines. Paul and I also enjoy spending our time and energy teaching young riders.

Do you belong to an organization connected to your hobby?

Paul: Yes, we belong to the BMW Motorcycle Owners of America. There are 40,000 members. The median age is probably fifty years old. For the last ten years, the chronic discussion topic at the board meetings is how we will attract young riders, because we're all getting older.

Our local motorcycle group is the San Antonio BMW Riders. We're also part of the 53,000-plus members of the Iron Butt Association who have completed an endurance run. The Iron Butt rally is held every other year.

Voni: For eight years, we headed the GEARS program. GEARS stands for Gaining Early Advanced Riding Skills and is for young people from the ages of sixteen to twenty-six. For the last four years, we have taught classes at Camp GEARS. Now some of our graduates run the program.

Is there anything I haven't asked you that you'd like to add or think is important for readers to know?

Voni: Find your passion and go. It keeps us young just thinking about it. We are so blessed that we have a shared passion. It's wonderful to share those memories.

Paul: There are a dozen different ways of having fun on motorcycles. Not everyone will be as hard-core as we are. There are lots of people who ride on a weekend. They may take a weeklong trip and that's a big deal. Or they may take small rides. Some people get smaller, dirt-oriented bikes and never go on pavement. They just ride on trails, in the desert or in the woods. You will find what you like. It will evolve.

FASCINATING FACTS

- Erin Doherty-Ratay of Boulder achieved a Guinness World Record when she and her husband rode their motorcycles through 50 countries on 6 continents on a 4-year world tour.
- More than 500,000 people participated in the 2012 Sturgis Motorcycle (FF) Rally in South Dakota.
- *Vespa* means "wasp" in Italian. *Cucciolo* (the name of the first Ducati) means "puppy."
- Steve McQueen didn't do the famous 65-foot motorcycle jump in the movie *The Great Escape*. American Triumph dealer Bud Ekins did it in one take.
- The Fonz (aka Henry Winkler) couldn't actually ride a motorcycle.
- The first Harley used a tomato can for a carburetor.
- The front tire provides 75% of a bike's grip when cornering.

Resources

Motorcycle Rallies

The Travel Channel's best motorcycle rallies: http://bit.ly/1nMdSMi.

The Cannonball Endurance Run in September: cannonballism.com.

Daytona Bike Week in March and Bikertoberfest in October: officialbikeweek.com and http://bit.ly/1tf3Aq0.

The Harley Love Ride in October in Glendale, California: https://www.facebook.com/theloveride.

The Iron Butt Rally in June in South Dakota: ironbuttrally.com.

The Red Bull Indianapolis GP Motocross in August: http://bit.ly/1pl0EV3.

Rolling Thunder, held each year on Memorial Day weekend at the Lincoln Memorial in Washington, DC, to honor American veterans: rollingthunderrun.com.

Sturgis Motorcycle Rally, held in the Black Hills of South Dakota every August: sturgismotorcyclerally.com.

Websites

100 Best motorcycle roads: http://bit.ly/1ki8ZtU.

Trike Owner Club, Brothers of the Third Wheel: btw-trikers.org.

Apps

Best Motorcycle Apps for Your Smartphone: http://bit.ly/1pl0SLO.

Videos

Hard Miles and Hard Miles 2. Two full length DVDs about the Iron Butt Rally: http://bit.ly/1o4YLrB.

The History Channel's video on the *Sturgis Motorcycle Rally, Only in America with Larry the Cable Guy:* http://bit.ly/1tf4J0Y.

Official Rolling Thunder Rally video: http://bit.ly/1o4YQeX.

Reading

Ron Ayres, *Against the Wind* (North Conway, NH: Whitehorse Press, 1997).

Philip Buonpastore, *Shifting Gears at 50: A Motorcycle Guide for New and Returning Riders* (Irvine, CA: BowTie Press, 2012).

David Hough, *Mastering the Ride More Proficient Motorcycling* (New York, NY: BowTie Inc, 2012).

CHAPTER 23

RV Traveler

Kilometers are shorter than miles.
Save gas; take your next trip in kilometers.
— George Carlin

In 2010, the Recreational Vehicle (RV) celebrated its 100th birthday. According to a 2011 University of Michigan study, 8.9 million households own RVs. Owners travel for twenty-six days and average 4,500 miles annually. The institute estimates 450,000 travelers consider their RV as their full-time residence.

The Silver Bullet Airstream Trailer

Park an Airstream trailer or a "Silver Bullet" anywhere and this icon of Americana is likely to attract a crowd. The Airstream Company tells its history: In 1929, Wally Byam purchased a Model T Ford chassis, built a platform on it, towed it with his car to a campsite, and painstakingly erected a tent on it. The effort was tiresome and unpleasant, especially when it rained. Wally then built a teardrop-shaped permanent shelter on the platform that enclosed a small ice chest and kerosene stove. He published an article that ran under the headline "How to Build a Trailer for One Hundred Dollars." Readers wrote Wally for more detailed instruction plans, which he sold at a cost of $1 each. The response was extraordinary, earning him more than $15,000.

After building several trailers for friends in his backyard, he rented a building. Airstream Trailer Company went into full production in 1932, when fewer than forty-eight trailer manufacturers were registered for business. Five years later, nearly four hundred companies competed against each other. Today, of those four hundred, only Airstream remains.

Airstream announced a 59 percent sales increase in calendar year 2013. The polished aluminum exterior has made Airstream an American icon and "Airstreamers" share a community spirit. In the early 1950s, the Airstream company founder began leading groups of owners on travels all over the world. Currently, 5,800 owners belong to the Wally Byam Caravan Club International Inc. (WBCCI). Local, regional, and national groups organize weekend and weeklong rallies and longer trips, called caravans. International rallies are held annually.

Shirley and John with Cooper and their vintage Airstream

Shirley and John are both sixty-four years old and have been retired eight years. Shirley worked as a certified public accountant and retired three different times. She thinks it's finally for good now. John still owns an antique shop and works two days per month.

How did you become interested in this pursuit?

Shirley: I always wanted a vintage Airstream. They're iconic. I think Airstreams are cool. But I didn't really think about traveling around in it. We both love and collect antiques.

John: In fact, Shirley was my best customer at my antique store.

Shirley: I looked around for a couple of years and found that my nephew's partner had an Airstream that she wanted to sell. It was two thousand miles away in Minnesota. My next-door neighbor went and picked it up for us. It sat on our property for eight months before our neighbor decided to teach us how to hook it up to go camping. Our first trip was in 2008 for the weekend and we didn't go too far from home. We had never camped in an RV before.

John: It is a 1965 Safari Airstream twenty-two-foot trailer. It was left in a very nice "as-is" state. But it was old. After forty-six years, the floor and refrigerator had to be replaced. We bought new tires and propane tanks. We spent a lot of money fixing things and restoring the interior. When you own a vintage Airstream, it seems like you are the caretaker for the next person who will own it. This is an ongoing process.

Shirley: Our first trip was to an Airstream rally. We woke up the first morning and found a lake of water underneath our trailer. All the pipes under the belly of the trailer had leaks. It cost over $1,000 to redo all of the plumbing.

Who buys Airstream trailers?

Shirley: Quite a variety, I think. Many well-educated professionals, engineers, pilots, schoolteachers . . . We've met firefighters, a newspaper editor—very interesting people, very culturally inclined.

John: People who love to travel. Many people we've met have traveled all over the world.

Shirley: Airstreams have a lot of history and a large following. Some people may even call it a cult. People either really love them or they don't get it. As a towable, the Airstream is considered very expensive, like the Mercedes in the auto world. You can buy another RV for one-third the price, but it will fall apart in five to ten years. The Airstream is built like an airplane and something like 70 percent of all Airstreams ever built are still going.

If you own an Airstream, your name is included in the membership directory. Each member has a unique number and most put that number on their trailer. If you see another Airstream driving down the road, or parked close by, you can look up the number in the directory, find out who it is and where they're from, and perhaps go and introduce yourself. There is a real strong bond with Airstreamers. I don't think you'll find that with any other RV make.

Do you belong to an organization connected to your hobby?

Shirley: We belong to four different Airstream clubs. Two clubs represent specific areas, such as Northern and Southern California; one is the international club; and the fourth is a club for vintage Airstream owners. Each club has their own rally. We belong to the Wally Byam Caravan Club International club as well. As a WBCCI international member, you can go to any rally, but the number of participants is limited, so as a local member you get first sign-ups. Usually there are eighteen to thirty people in a rally. Some clubs have many members and so space is sometimes limited. The rally is usually four days long and held in a state park or wherever the current club president chooses.

What do you do at these rallies?

Shirley: Each rally is in a different location, depending on who organized it. We go to museums, theaters, and on tours of all the local attractions. We've toured several unique sights, such as a Nike missile site and a mushroom factory. In our home state of California, we've seen more things in the eight years of touring than in the thirty years we've lived here.

As a group, we always have coffee together in the morning and we eat several dinners together as well. Also, every day at 4:30 p.m. at an Airstream event, happy hour is held rain or shine. That tradition started with Wally Byam, the founder, because he always wanted his cocktail. In the '50s, it was cocktails, now it's usually wine and hors d'oeuvres. Of course, you don't have to drink.

In the 1950s, people would go camping and they would meet for dinner all dressed up—the men in suits and the women in heels and gloves. We looked at some of the old pictures of the caravan trip through Africa and they're all dressed up for dinner. It's hilarious to think about it.

We're taking up playing the ukulele because there are a lot of uke players in the Southern California Airstream group. They sing, play, and have a lot of fun. One friend wrote a song about Airstream traveling.

What start-up costs and ongoing expenses are involved?

Shirley: Of course the cost of the trailer, gas, and food. We honestly don't spend a lot more than if we were at home. There are parking fees, but then if we were home we would be spending that money on utilities. We live outside of town, so we spend a lot of money on gas when we're home. We have a friend who keeps her horse on our property and she looks in on the house to make sure everything is secure. We pay all of our bills online. Most locations have a wireless Internet connection.

John: I have a toolbox that I bring with me. All the traveling puts a lot of wear and tear on the trailer. We replaced the heater in our trailer with a little fireplace. One trip it snowed and we brought the fireplace out and we sat around it at the campground.

There are always other owners around to help you. One of the nice things about having an Airstream is that some of these people have had them for thirty to thirty-five years. With all of this expertise, somebody has run into about any problem that can exist. Collectively, we could build one from scratch.

Dreamers and Streamers Budget

An Airstream is considered vintage if it is at least twenty-five years old. More than two-thirds of all Airstreams manufactured since 1936 are still on the road, so many opportunities exist for modern owners to adopt and adapt a vintage Airstream trailer. Prices can range from $3,000 to $20,000 or more, depending on the size, the year, and the condition. The r's (reconditioning, repairing, remodeling, and replacing parts) are all extra.

In 2014, a new Airstream, depending on the size and options, begins around $40,000 and can surpass $140,000. Add a vehicle with a trailer hitch to tow the Airstream. Fuel is a big budget item. Consider 10 mpg to an optimistic 17 mpg to tow, and figure out the cost of your trip.

Where do you travel?

Shirley: We will travel six to seven months total this year. We usually go for a month, then head home. We spend a little time at home, then hit the road again. This year we will be traveling throughout California and down to Phoenix and Tucson, Arizona. Then we go to a vintage Airstream rally in Colorado, and then on to the international rally in Wyoming. So far, we've been as far east as Mississippi and Minnesota.

John: We bring our chocolate Lab, Cooper, with us on our trips. He's twelve years old and blind in one eye. He's perfect for me. He picked me out and adopted me.

Shirley: There is an Airstream event every month. We belong to WBCCI, which is the official Airstream organization. It has a long history. The founder, Wally Byam, would organize huge caravans and the international organization continues to hold them. Rallies are a weekend to four days long and caravans can be weeks or a month. Caravans are held all over the world. People ship their trailers around the world. One caravan I know of, the Airstreamers transported their trailers to Africa and traveled the continent.

We use technology when we travel. I have an app on my phone that I use to find good RV park locations. We have iPhones, iPads, and computers with us all the time. We take care of all of our business via the Internet while we travel.

How do you prepare for a long trip?

Shirley: When we get ready to travel, we go through a checklist and make sure that everything we will need is there. We do the same thing when we return. We do all of the laundry and make sure all everything is clean and the pantry is restocked and ready for the next trip.

John: In fact, we live in a dry area that is subject to forest fires, so in case of a fire all we would have to do is hitch up the trailer and go. Everything we need is already stored in the Airstream. We keep it stocked with dry goods and toiletries.

What problems or difficulties arise in this activity?

Shirley: Well, we've had our catastrophes. Once when we were in South Dakota, John forgot to unplug the electrical cord before we left. We drove forward and pulled out the whole electrical system.

John: We had no electrical at all—no lights, turn signals, et cetera. Luckily, I had a spare part, we were with some friends, and they helped us fix it. We would have had no clue on how to fix it on our own. So now we always ask, "Are you unplugged?"

Shirley: Also like in any organization, some people get too caught up with the politics of it. Some people have been involved for thirty or forty years. One woman has been involved since the 1950s, when her father was one of the early members. They may have given up the suits and heels, but some of the old-timers want to run things the way they were run in the past. For example, they want strict adherence to having meetings at each event. It's not necessary. We have one member who always wants to write and rewrite the bylaws.

John: That's why we join different clubs, because they're all run differently. One of the groups is more about having fun and exploring. We try to avoid all the politics and intricacies of bylaws.

What is the most rewarding aspect of this activity?

John: The fun part for me is meeting people and becoming good friends. We keep in touch with friends we've made. We traveled to Australia once to visit some friends we made at a rally and they came to our house as well.

Shirley: We've made good friends with people all over the country. In fact, our first stop this year will be to our friend's house in Sun City, Arizona, on our way to Phoenix. I love the travel. Always seeing new things and doing new things.

John: Our favorite trip so far was on a Cajun caravan. We traveled around all of the Cajun areas of Louisiana with people from all over the country for two weeks. Lots of sightseeing, tours, and great food.

We were in Louisiana on another trip having a wonderful seafood buffet, then we went to an old barn where people once bid at cow auctions. It was now a club with a band and music. They were playing

Cajun music and they invited me to play my harmonica with them. All of our other rally members were surprised because they didn't know I played. That was a lot of fun.

Do you have any advice for future RV owners?

Shirley: Remember, if you buy a vintage trailer, you're going to have to spend a lot of money fixing it up, but you can save quite a bit of money by buying used.

John: I think you should follow your own passion. There's a whole world that will come your way. Being retired is not the same thing as being old.

FASCINATING FACTS

- For decades, NASA has used a fleet of Airstream motorhomes to transport astronauts to the launch pad.
- As part of its Silver Bullet program, the Air Force Research Laboratories transformed a series of Airstream trailers into mobile communications modules.
- RVs are made by American companies, employing American workers, located in America. In fact, more than 80% of recreation vehicles are made in Elkhart County, Indiana. Another 12% are produced in Oregon, California, Iowa, and Michigan.
- The average camper travels 190 miles to go camping.
- The average RV owner is 48 years old and more than 9.3 percent of those 55 years old and older own an RV.
- Some celebrities who own a Silver Bullet are Mathew McConaughey, Tom Hanks, Johnny Depp, Brad Pitt, and Sean Penn.
- The 2013 5 most popular RV destinations, according to GoRVing.com are (1) North Rim of the Grand Canyon, Arizona; (2) Devils Tower, Wyoming; (3) Mt. Rushmore, South Dakota; (4) Disney World, Florida; (5) Outer Banks, North Carolina.

Resources

Websites

Airstream factory tours in Jackson Center, Ohio (1 hour north of Dayton): airstream.com.

Airstream owners' association: wbcci.org.

Go RVing: gorving.com.

A meet-up site for full-time or part-time RVers: nurvers.com.

Recreational Vehicle Industry Association: rvia.org.

RV Travel Newsletter and Blog: rvtravel.com.

RVing Women is a national network across the country that offers camping, educational, and social events: rvingwomen.org.

Apps

Gas Buddy: http://bit.ly/1rsLSLG.

Satellite Finder: http://bit.ly/1o4ZoBt.

Roadside America by This Exit: http://bit.ly/X17BBa.

Videos

YouTube RV Travel Channel: youtube.com/user/RVtravel.

Reading

Good Sam Enterprises, *Good Sam RV Travel Guide & Campground Directory: The Most Comprehensive RV Resource Ever!* (Ventura, CA: Good Sam Enterprises, 2013).

Steven Fletcher, *Best RV Tips from RVTipOfTheDay.com* (Yuba City, CA: Fletcher 2012).

Bob Livingston, *RV Repair and Maintenance Manual* (Englewood, CO: Trailer Life Books, 2002).

The RV Bookstore sells several titles on RVing: rvbookstore.com.

CHAPTER 24

Woodturner

Creativity is putting your imagination to work,
and it's produced the most extraordinary
results in human culture.
— Ken Robinson

Woodturning is a unique form of woodworking that uses a lathe, which is a machine used to spin a block of wood. In all other forms of woodworking, the wood is held still and it is the tool that moves to create cuts. In woodturning, the wood is turning and the cutter is relatively stationary.

History

The earliest lathes date back to ancient Egypt, when they used a bow to rotate the block of wood. Modern lathes use electricity, but use the very same principles as the ancient lathes. A block of wood is clamped into place and spun rapidly, allowing the craftsman to work on the entire diameter of the block at one time. By *turning* wood, artisans create many intricate shapes that are smooth, round, and even.

In the Middle Ages, a woodturner worked alongside a joiner and a carver in the castle to create the fancy chairs that were popular among nobility and the growing merchant classes. *Turned* architectural elements continued to proliferate during the Renaissance throughout Europe. By the time of the English colonization of the Massachusetts Bay, woodturners from England and Holland were creating finials, drop finials, balusters, newels, and other architectural building elements.

According to the American Association of Woodturning, the practice of woodturning quietly grew in popularity in the years following World War II as a means of therapy to help soldiers heal. By the early 1980s, woodturned art began to appear in galleries and craft shows, and woodworking magazines discussed techniques and featured new work of this old craft.

Photo by Don Varney

Kevin, displaying his woodturned bowls

Kevin, age sixty-four, lives near Worcester, Massachusetts, and belongs to the Central New England Woodturners Association. Before he retired, he owned a construction company specializing in pipeline excavation.

Kevin: *I've been interested in woodworking my whole life. I have a 1953 photograph hanging in my barn of me at four years old at my father's workbench. I would watch my father putter around with his tools, and it fascinated me.*

How did you get started?

Kevin: In 2004, in preparation for my retirement, I built a twenty-two-by-thirty-foot addition with a full cellar on an old barn on my property, just for woodworking. Then in 2007, while I was still working, I took a course in woodturning and that's all she wrote! I was hooked.

The class was on Tuesday nights from 7:00 p.m. to 10:00 p.m. at the Worcester Center for Crafts, an adult education program. In the ten-week class, I learned how to use all the tools and equipment needed to create woodturning pieces. The first thing I made was a spurdle, a spoon for stirring porridge. It was a simple project to learn how to use the lathe. The wood is positioned on a spinning axis and the tool is presented manually. I guide the tool over the wood. It's similar to using a potter's wheel. Touch and timing are important to creating a well-done piece.

I made someone a gift and I wouldn't take any money for it, so that person bought me a gift certificate for another woodturning class. The second class was with the same instructor, but you could go at your own speed and work independently. Learning woodturning is just like everything else. If you have the desire, you can learn it. I jumped in with both feet and bought an expensive lathe. In addition to the two classes, I watch a lot of videos online.

How do you decide what you're going to make?

Kevin: In woodturning, the piece of wood you get determines what you will make out of it. I use native wood. In my area that's birch, maple, and walnut. I like maple burl. Out where I live, we have many trees and I can use wood from a downed tree, or I look on Craigslist under "materials" or on some other websites to purchase nice pieces of wood.

Tell me about the wood that you use.

Kevin: Looking for wood can be an interesting experience. I'll drive a hundred miles to find beautiful wood. One day I'll find someone living in a trailer up in the woods who will have great pieces, and the next day I'll find a fellow living in a mansion trying to purge his supply of beautiful stuff. I only buy the best wood. Birdseye maple is my favorite wood. It produces a nice finish. It's beautiful to look at, beautiful to touch. Not too many people have access to Birdseye maple. When I finish a piece, I use walnut oil on the natural wood.

I have a process I use to prepare wood. Wood takes one year to dry for each inch of thickness, so a four-inch piece of wood will take four years to thoroughly dry. This prevents the wood from warping or cracking when I work with it. First, I separate the wood. All the maple goes in one area, oak in another, standing up vertically. Then I store the wood outside. The next year I put it in the cellar, then onto a shelf, then to a work area. It's all over the place, so I make a path.

You can turn wet wood or wood that is not completely dried if you want to create a warping. Some artists like to incorporate that look in their design. I don't work with wet wood.

Describe your workshop and the equipment you use.

Kevin: I live in Central Massachusetts and I work in a 150-year-old barn that was moved onto my property in 1900. That old barn and the addition I built comprise my workshop. I have a 20-inch Powermatic lathe and a 16-inch Oneway lathe that are both high quality. At today's prices, they would cost $5,000 each. However, I'm a "bottom fisherman." I bought them both used and got good deals. You can get started with a mini-lathe for about $300. A band saw is also necessary to get the wood close to round. You can get one for $300.

As far as a budget, I'm like all enthusiastic hobbyists: "The bucket has no bottom." But seriously, $800 will get someone started with *a lathe, a band saw, and all the tools and accessories needed to start some nice projects.*

The Basic Tools

In addition to the lathe, the basic tools needed in woodturning are gouges, skew chisels, scrapers, and parting tools. Gouges remove large portions of material from the wood and are available in various types and sizes. The roughing gouge may be used after the band saw to round the piece from a square to a circle. Spindle gouges have smaller, arc-shaped tips that resemble fingernails. Spindle gouges are more suitable for finishing the surface. Bowl gouges remove excess material from the right angle of the grain.

Skew chisels smooth the rough surface and remove long ribbons of wood as they taper and shape the material. They're also used to make decorative cuts. Skews can have round, oval, or square tips, which are used to smooth the end and right angle of the grain.

Scrapers are blunt and non-beveled and finish the face, edges, and raised bands of the material during the final turning stages. Shear scrapers smooth and shape the interior curves of a bowl. The long-hook tool smooths tight internal curved surfaces, such as vases, and the short-hook tool is for smoothing bowls and other items with gradual curves. Ring tools create hollow spaces in boxes and vases, and they are available in three standard sizes.

Parting tools cut the finished product away from the lathe, cut a deep groove into the material, and reach areas that are not accessible with the skew chisel.

Sharp Tools Are Safe Tools

Kevin: Sharp tools are the keys to woodturning. A woodturner needs a good grinder and must learn know how to sharpen the tools. Turning with sharp tools is much easier than with dull ones. Cuts will be cleaner and not grab or gouge the wood. I might sharpen a tool ten times while making one bowl.

Safety is important. The wood is turning at 2,000 rpm. I wear an apron with a snap-collar around the neck, and a full-face shield to protect against flying chips.

Is there an organization connected to your hobby?

Kevin: I'm a member of a woodworking guild. It's called the Central Massachusetts Woodturners Association. There are three associations in our state. We have sixty members and typically, 15 percent of the membership is women. We meet the first Thursday of every month. We have a little business meeting first, then a "show and tell." People bring in what they've made and share any experiences, such as announcing that they received a contract to make several items or something new they've tried. Recently, we had a visitor come to our meeting and request fifty pepper grinders made.

How much time do you spend on this pursuit?

Kevin: I'm in my workshop every day. I spend between two and ten hours a day working on projects. It probably averages out to four to five hours each day. I like to make usable items rather than solely artistic pieces. I especially like to make bowls.

Woodturning is a solitary hobby. You have to like to be by yourself. I have a 300 CD player and since I'm a "burnt-out '60s guy," I listen to all the old classics as I work. I'm also a big blues fan. Woodturning is dusty and a hobbyist shouldn't be afraid of getting a little dirty.

How do you make a bowl?

Kevin: I cut the wood round, and then mount it on the lathe. Using a variety of tools, I "turn" the outside, then "turn" the inside. After that, I rotate it over to do the bottom. I'll make ten bowls at a time. It's easier to mass-produce, because you're doing as many as six steps to create each bowl. This way you do step one ten times, then you do step two ten times. I finish each bowl with a walnut-oil rub.

I give them as gifts and I sell a lot. I sell at two farmers' markets a week during the summer and I participate in many arts-and-crafts shows during the holidays. November and December are very busy. I don't have a website because I feel you have to see the bowl and touch the smooth finish. I encourage touching at the shows.

My bowls sell for $10 for a small "ring dish," all the way up to $300 for a family-size salad bowl. The bowls that are more expensive are usually "segmented" pieces. I like to combine maple and walnut together in stacked rings or variegated bands very precisely cut and fit together. I make enough money on my hobby to pay for materials, enough to fill up the gas tank. I don't do it for the money, just for the enjoyment.

Every bowl comes with instructions for care. I tell people to "treat the bowl the way you treat your hands." You never put your hands in the microwave; you never put your hands in the dishwasher, and never in boiling water. Wash the bowl with a mild soap and water. It will be fine as long as you dry it immediately.

Do you make any other items?

Kevin: Yes, I make bottle stoppers, corkscrews, bottle-opener handles, pastry scoops, rolling pins, and cutting boards. One of my specialties is a gift set, which includes a plate, a cutting board, a knife for cutting cheese, and a corkscrew to open a nice bottle of wine. I prefer to make items I choose rather than commissioned items. I find people aren't aware of what they really want. I never have a problem selling all the items that I make.

What is the most rewarding aspect of this activity?

Kevin: One woman bought a $185 bowl from me, and I asked her if it was a gift. She told me it was her birthday. She was returning from a spa, where she just had her hair and nails done, and my bowl was a gift to herself.

Another time, a neighbor stopped me when I was out walking the dog and asked me if I had a bowl she could buy for a gift she needed. I was in the process of making several for a show I had coming up, so I told her to stop by and she could take her pick before the show. She chose a mahogany bowl. I just saw her and she told me she received the nicest thank-you from the recipient and it was hands-down the best present at the shower. Those compliments are better than money!

FASCINATING FACTS

- Ed Moulthrop, (1916–2003) a self-taught woodturner, is known as the "father of modern woodturning." He was most famous for his large-scale turned bowls, made from domestic woods, usually spherical or elliptical with polished clear finishes. He designed and built his own equipment to accommodate the size of his pieces.
- In the United States, most hardwoods grow east of the Mississippi River.
- The oldest living tree east of the Mississippi is believed to be an angel oak on John's Island, South Carolina, which is about 1,400 years old.
- The screwdriver was invented a hundred years before the screw. It was originally used to extract nails.
- *Zinzulation* is the sound made by a power saw.
- Many drugs are produced from trees. The aspirin was originally developed from willow bark. Some chemotherapy drugs are made from the yew tree.

Resources

Websites

American Association of Woodturners: woodturner.org.

Find a chapter: The 350+ worldwide chapters of the AAW: http://bit.ly/1nMgFVN.

Center for Art in Wood: centerforartinwood.org.

Central New England Woodturners: www.cnew.org.

Woodturning Online: worldwide forums, list of courses and schools, clubs and associations, projects, and DVDs: woodturningonline.com.

Classes

Arrowmont School of Arts and Crafts: arrowmont.org.

John C. Campbell Folk School: https://www.folkschool.org.

Gary Rogowski, Northwest Woodworking Studios: A school for woodworkers: northwestwoodworking.com.

Videos

Woodturning Demystified—Basic Education Demonstration to Get You Turning: http://bit.ly/1zkmdJH.

Over 440 free videos on all aspects of woodturning: http://bit.ly/1rON4LC.

Reading

Mark Baker, *Woodturning Projects: A Workshop Guide to Shapes* (Lewes, UK: Guild of Master Craftsman, 2003).

Suzanne Ramljak, Michael W. Monroe, and Mark Richard Leach. *Turning Wood into Art: The Jane and Arthur Mason Collection*. New York, NY: H.N. Abrams, in association with the Mint Museum of Craft + Design, 2000.

American Woodturner Magazine: woodturner.org.

Wood Magazine: woodmagazine.com.

PART FIVE

PHYSICAL ACTIVITY AND SPORTS

CHAPTER 25

Backpacker

In Wildness is the preservation of the world.
—Henry David Thoreau

Hiking refers to a single-day walk in the woods with minimum gear. Most people refer to *backpacking* as a longer trek, at least overnight, carrying needed supplies in a pack on the back. Hiking and backpacking are wonderful ways to exercise. Thousands of miles of trails crisscross America, where the tradition of long-distance hiking started. The terrain can range from steep climbs over rocks to flat lakeshore paths. It's an easy, low-cost way to discover the great outdoors, and there are hiking opportunities for almost anyone at any age and ability level.

Our National Trails System

The National Trails System Act of 1968 made it federal policy to recognize and promote hiking trails by providing financial assistance, support of volunteers, and coordination among states and other authorities. Congress designates National Scenic Trails, National Historic Trails, and National Recreation Trails throughout the United States.

National Scenic Trails are 100 miles or longer, continuous, primarily non-motorized routes of outstanding recreation opportunity. One example is the Appalachian Trail. Laid out as early as 1937, the Appalachian Trail runs for over 2,000 miles through fourteen eastern states. It was a major inspiration for the first British long-distance trail, the Pennine Way.

National Historic Trails commemorate historic (and prehistoric) routes of travel that are of significance to the entire nation. The Pony Express National Historic Trail traces the route that young men once used to carry mail on horseback from Missouri to California. The trail navigates through eight states.

National Recreation Trails are regional and local trails that requested recognition by the federal government. These trails bring communities together and offer nature and wildlife settings close to home. The Tahoe Rim Trail, running through California and Nevada, is one example. The National Parks System website contains information on all of the designated trails and a US map of all of the trails.

Much of the splendors of our national parks can only be seen by traveling off the beaten path, where majestic panoramas, waterfalls, glaciers, wildflowers, and wildlife are in full display. By traveling into the backcountry, it is possible to see grandeur that few people see. In Yosemite National Park, 95 percent of the visitors never leave the valley and see only 1 percent of the park. It's time to get in shape, strap on the backpack, and adventure into the wilderness.

Before You Begin

Talk to your doctor about your plans and know your limits. Backpacking can be exhausting after a certain length of time if you're not acclimated. Learn about the terrain of your trail in terms of hills and increase in elevation. You might want to start on a path that is level so that you can enjoy your hike while getting an appropriate workout relative to your progress.

Deb, backpacking in the Grand Canyon

Deb lives in Boise, Idaho, and is sixty years old and semi-retired. As a former teacher, she runs her own business tutoring students in grades kindergarten through eighth grade.

Deb: Having my own business gives me some income and the time to take off for backpacking adventures. I work twenty to twenty-five hours per week. I've always been a hiker, backpacker, swimmer, and bicyclist.

Where do you backpack?

Deb: I live in Idaho, which offers a lot of beautiful outdoor sites. Three-fourths of Idaho is mountains. Here in southern Idaho, in the Snake River Plain, we have a variety of terrain. We're not far from the desert, and we have the foothills close by. A little farther out, there are canyons, rivers, and mountains. The outdoors and the wilderness are always accessible; it doesn't take much time to get there. I'm three hours away from the Sawtooth and the White Cloud

Mountains, which are both part of the Rocky Mountain range. Before moving to Boise, I lived in northern Idaho for sixteen years, so I've covered many areas of this state.

I've had many wonderful outdoor experiences. My hiking excursions involve bringing a backpack and are usually a couple of days. A typical trip involves leaving on a Friday afternoon, hiking in eight to ten miles, setting up camp for the night, and spending the next day hiking in a loop to return on Sunday.

Some people may not want to spend long periods of time or aren't sure about this activity. I don't think they should let that stop them. There are also "in-and-backs," which are short trips, if time allotment is limited. There are no rules. A hiker may choose a three-mile hike and camp. There's a huge movement going on right now called the "twenty-*four-hour trip" or "overnighter." For some hikers it might be a good place to start.*

What special clothes do you use?

Deb: First, hiking and backpacking require good shoes. They are the most important thing. If a hiker has sore feet or develops blisters, then the whole show stops, so it's important to invest in quality shoes. My personal preference is a sturdy boot. I look for the lightest boot I can find with arch and ankle support. I use an Italian leather boot by Zamberlan. There are other good brands as well. They come in a variety of styles. Boots can cost $150 to $300. Look for end-of-season sales. I use SmartWool socks, wool or wool-blend.

When I backpack, I don't carry too many clothes. I try to keep my pack as light as possible. My favorite clothes are anything that "wicks" moisture away. I don't wear any cotton clothing. I wear the long pants that have a zip-off leg that converts to shorts. Some people wear a capri pant with bike leggings instead. The idea is to be able to pull off clothing if it's too warm. I always wear a hat, sunscreen, and sunglasses, and always bring water for hydration.

What special equipment do you use?

Deb: There is a big difference between car camping and backpacking. The equipment is completely different. How much something weighs is not a problem in the trunk of a car; it's a big factor when it's on the hiker's back.

Backpack

Deb: A backpack is a very personal purchase. Salespersons at specialty sports stores will measure customers for a proper fit. They fill the pack with heavy items so the hiker can feel how it will perform during use. I recommend an internal-frame backpack. I have five or six different packs. I use an ultra-lite that has hardly any frame at all. I have a Deuter-brand backpack that I like very much for multiday backpacking. Others use the Osprey brand.

Again, it's a personal thing. It's a good idea to spend some time and try on different packs. A woman under five-eleven should buy a backpack specially designed for a woman instead of trying to wear a man's pack. It just won't fit correctly. I am five-four and weigh 110 pounds. For a two night, three-day backpack, I'll carry approximately twenty-five pounds. When I went to the Grand Canyon on a six-day trip, I carried forty-three pounds. I'm strong and in good shape, and my pack fit me so well, I didn't feel the weight. We did a forty-three-to fifty-mile trek down and then back up again. A good backpack is around $200.

Trekking Poles

Deb: I can always pick out everyone over fifty years old on the trails because we all use trekking poles to save our knees. I try to get the lightest poles I can find. I get locking rather than the screw type. The screw type is called "collapsible"—and they do, always at the wrong time! For a two-mile hike, it doesn't matter, but for a weeklong hike, it matters a great deal. Locking, adjustable poles provide a comfortable fit; they can be adjusted shorter for going up hills and longer for going down. I like the cork grips, not the black carbon handgrips that make my hands sweat and turn black. The price is between $90 and $100.

Sleeping Bag and Tent

Deb: A sleeping bag is another important item to consider. I use both down and synthetic sleeping bags. My bags weigh two and three pounds. If a hiker lives in a dry climate and can only get one sleeping bag, he or she should get a down bag. A down bag is light and provides more warmth than a synthetic bag. The problem with a down bag is if it gets wet for whatever reason, such as a leaky tent or a pack that falls in the river, it will not loft or provide warmth until it's thoroughly dry. It will cost $300 to $400 for a good bag.

I use a solo quarter-dome tent. I think it's the best value for a light tent. That costs around $110. A half-dome tent is available to fit two people. It's best to buy a tent at a store that specializes in camping gear. My tent is three pounds. Some of my friends use eight-ounce tents.

Global Positioning System (GPS)

A Global Positioning System (GPS) is a navigation system that communicates with satellites to provide location and time information in all weather conditions anywhere on Earth. Thirty-one satellites orbit the Earth on six orbital planes at an altitude of 12,600 miles in a fashion that puts nearly all points on the planet in line of sight with at least six satellites at any given time.

Deb: I have a Garmin GPS with a touch screen. You can find them on sale for $125 to $150. Extra batteries and a paper map are good contingencies. A budget for good equipment: shoes, backpack, poles, sleeping bag, tent, and GPS is $975 to $1,250.

Do you belong to an organization connected to your hobby?

Deb: I belong to several hiking clubs, and I would strongly recommend that anyone who is new to this activity join a club and find fellow enthusiasts. Meet-up groups that have specific kinds of hiking and backpacking activities are in every state. I belong to the Boise Trailheads and the Idaho Hiking Club. From those clubs, I've met other people and we have planned our own trips.

Hiking clubs attract all ages, from twenty to sixty years old and older. Since it's all volunteers, everyone gets together and organizes trips. If the group is adventurous, the trips will reflect that. If the group is at a beginner level, perhaps they'll plan a trip through a greenbelt or local recreational area. Usually a Meet-up group is based on whoever steps up to lead the trip and their skill level. Remember, these are not paid guides—just volunteers, maybe with a little more experience. Hikers should look for a group that is in sync with their expectations and a group that they can contribute to as well. I think the best-size group for backpacking is between two and six people, and the best size for a hiking group is up to ten people. Many groups have as many as twenty hikers, which can become more of a party than a hike.

How much time do you spend on this pursuit?

Deb: I'm lucky because I'm semi-retired and have lots of time. I spend four out of seven days either backpacking or preparing for a trip. I start backpacking in May when the weather is warm. In Idaho, you can go south to the warmer areas if there is still snow in the northern areas.

My favorite trip so far was to the Grand Canyon. I was the lead with organizing the trip and told the group "All brains are on": everyone needs to pitch in and help plan. I went with four other people and we all had never been there before, so a friend who had hiked the Grand Canyon many times helped us plan. We planned a ten-day trip to Arizona that included a six-day excursion for an intermediate-to-advanced backpacker. We went in the beginning of November. It was perfect weather.

We started at the 8,000-foot elevation level and hiked down to Phantom Ranch at the bottom. We stayed there one night, then hiked to several places, gradually working our way up. Our longest day was an eleven-mile hike; our shortest day was seven miles. We ran into a boulder slide and had to climb over rocks for ten minutes to get through. The very last day was all up—and very challenging.

What is the most rewarding aspect of this activity?

Deb: Just being outside and seeing the beautiful views is rewarding to me. Once I buy my equipment, everything else is free. I've done most of my backpacking in Idaho because it's so accessible. I enjoy trekking around my beautiful state. I'm proud of the fact that I've climbed all of Idaho's "Twelvers," which are the twelve mountains that are higher than 12,000 feet elevation, from Hyndman Peak at elevation 12,009 feet to Borah Peak at 12,662 feet. Not too many women have done that.

Any advice for future backpackers?

Deb: Idaho has some rough terrain, and my fear of heights was holding me back when backpacking trips required climbs or when I was near cliffs with sheer drop-offs. Just looking over the edge of a cliff would scare me and I would freeze. So at the age of fifty-eight, I decided to do something about it. I started by learning rock climbing in a gym. I learned that if I took little baby steps I could overcome the challenge that heights gives me. Anyone new to backpacking should take baby steps.

I've also had times in my life when I just wasn't as active as I'd like to be. I think anyone can identify with that. Instead of being physically active and staying fit, I got caught up in daily activities and found I was not in shape. I would wonder, Could I ever do this again? Yes, I can! The body is resilient and, if not beaten up too badly, it's amazingly responsive. Lack of time or experience should not stop anyone. If individuals start small, soon, in a year or two, they can be on their way.

FASCINATING FACTS

- More than 6,000 volunteers help to maintain the Appalachian Trail and its 165,000 painted markers that show hikers the way.
- The Pacific Crest Trail spans 2,650 miles from Mexico to Canada through three western states: California, Oregon, and Washington. It crosses 26 National Forests, 7 National Parks, 5 State Parks, and 3 National Monuments.
- The longest hike in the United States is the North Country National Scenic Trail, 4,600 miles from Lake Sakakawea, North Dakota, to Crown Point, New York.
- A man weighing 190 pounds will burn 517 calories in one hour of hiking; a woman who weighs 163 pounds will burn 440 calories in the same time.
- According to a 2008 study of search-and-rescue missions in Utah national parks, fatigue, darkness, and insufficient equipment accounted for about 42% of rescue calls.
- The top 5 famous trails in the United States are (1) Appalachian National Scenic Trail, (2) Pacific Crest Trail, (3) Continental Divide National Scenic Trail, (4) American Discovery Trail, and (5) North Country National Scenic Trail.

Resources

Websites

The American Hiking Society: americanhiking.org.

Hiking Meet-up groups: hiking.meetup.com.

Hiking over-50 Meet-up groups: hiking-over-50.meetup.com.

Hiking trips for women: http://bit.ly/1uwYGpX.

National Park Service list and map of National Scenic and Historic Trails: http://1.usa.gov/1l5UVhX.

The National Recreational Trails database: http://bit.ly/1lL1p5Q.

Sierra Club: sierraclub.org.

The Wilderness Society: wilderness.org.

Apps

US Army Survival Guide http://bit.ly/1o50tJu and http://bit.ly/1oypv8N.

My Tracks shows where you have been, how fast you went, and how big those hills were: http://bit.ly/Uw6VSV.

Videos

Go to YouTube and search "hiking with seniors." Not only will you be inspired, but you'll see a great many trails throughout the United States: youtube.com.

Reading

Jan D. Carline, PhD; Martha J. Lentz; and Steven C. Macdonald, *Mountaineering First Aid: A Guide to Accident Response and First Aid Care* (Seattle, WA: Mountaineers Books, 2004).

Adrienne Hall, *Backpacking: A Woman's Guide* (Camden, Me: Ragged Mountain Press, 1998).

Harvey Manning, *Backpacking One Step at a Time* (New York, NY: Vintage Books, 1986).

Jason Stevenson, *The Complete Idiot's Guide to Backpacking and Hiking* (Indianapolis, IN: Alpha Books, 2010).

Chris Townsend, *The Backpacker's Handbook, 4th Edition* (Camden, Me: Ragged Mountain Press, 2011).

Premier hiking/backpacking spots in the United States

Appalachian Trail: appalachiantrail.org

Arches National Park: nps.gov/arch/index.htm.

Denali National Park: nps.gov/dena/index.htm.

Glacier National Park: nps.gov/glac/index.htm.

Grand Canyon National Park: nps.gov/grca/index.htm.

John Muir Trail: johnmuirtrail.org.

Mount Whitney: mount-whitney.com.

Pacific Coast Trail: pcta.org.

Sawtooth Forest: fs.usda.gov/sawtooth.

Yosemite National Park: nps.gov/yose/index.htm.

Zion National Park: nps.gov/zion/index.htm.

CHAPTER 26

Dancer

Dance is the hidden language of the soul.
—Martha Graham

Do your moves mirror the grace of Fred Astaire and Ginger Rogers? How about the saucy style of John Travolta or Rita Moreno? On the other hand, are you one of the thousands who describe themselves as a dancer with "two left feet" but secretly wish you could dance? Even just a little? Maybe it's time to try!

Types of Dance

Dance is like ice cream; there are lots of different flavors. Some types of dancing require a partner to twirl you around the dance floor; in other types you normally tap, stomp, and shimmy all by yourself. Here are some popular dances and styles:

- Ballroom: Foxtrot, quickstep, and waltz
- Classical: Ballet and tap
- Cultural: Belly dancing, hula, and clogging
- Latin: Cha-cha, salsa, mambo, rumba, samba and zumba
- Rock-and-roll: four-step, six-step, and freestyle
- Sequence: Line dancing and square dancing
- Swing: East Coast and West Coast swing; boogie-woogie; lindy hop; Charleston, and jive

Choose Your Style

The best way to find the style of dancing you most enjoy is to experiment. Take a group class and stick with it for at least a month. Give it some time before deciding you don't like it. You can find dance classes at a dance school or studio, a health club, or a community recreation center. Some YMCAs, churches, or synagogues offer group classes followed by a social hour.

Michelle and Jody dancing the West Coast swing

Michelle and Jody are in their early sixties and live in Las Vegas. Michelle retired after thirty-five years as a special-education teacher in an elementary school. Jody taught high school special education and finished his thirty-seven-year career in school administration.

Michelle: When we were first married, thirty-eight years ago, we took ballroom dancing at the university and had a blast. We progressed to semi-private lessons and continued that for another year until we had children. Then we became involved in raising our family. We always loved to dance and move to music. But raising a family while maintaining our careers meant we didn't have a lot of extra time or money to invest in dancing.

When we were ready to retire, we thought we would like to travel and discussed a cruise to Alaska. So we saved and saved. We received a gift certificate for private dance lessons from a friend as a retirement gift. Dance lessons rekindled that passion. We took a hard look at how we wanted to spend the money we saved for the cruise, and then decided to forgo the cruise and spend the money on dancing.

How did you get started?

Michelle: Our goal for dancing was just to have fun. All we remembered from past lessons was steps to the East Coast swing, because it's versatile. We learned some very basic rumba and cha-cha. We wanted a fun dance teacher. We found one that encouraged us to explore West Coast swing. It seemed difficult to me at first because there was so much freedom in it, and I don't consider myself a creative person.

In the past, we learned ballroom dancing, which involves many different dances, including many Latin dances. Dancing is an amazing journey for us because there's so much more we want to learn. We have a little bit of all of them under our belt, but we are most comfortable with the West Coast swing.

West Coast Swing

Michelle: West Coast Swing actually developed out of the lindy and jitterbug. What makes it so unusual is that the dance is always evolving. What it was five years ago is not what it is now. West

Coast swing is known as a "slot" dance. The woman goes back and forth in an imaginary narrow area, as opposed to East Coast swing, where the woman goes around in a circle. It's a versatile dance. You can dance West Coast swing to jazz, blues, and some country, pop, rock, and contemporary music. That's what sucked us in. You can dance to any music.

After group lessons, we decided to try some private lessons. In the back of my mind I kept thinking, "Maybe I'm too old to do this." During that time, Jody was diagnosed with diabetes. This shocked us because we both eat healthy meals and we're not overweight. When we researched ways to exercise and meet people, dancing kept coming up. It doesn't matter if you do ballroom dancing or West Coast swing, dancing is one activity that has benefits both physically and mentally. We can do it together and we have fun and laugh all the time.

In the past, we also learned some country two-step. Then we came across the Rhythmic Souls dance studio that offered cowboy cha-cha lessons, which is a country-western partner dance. We said, Wow, this is great! We can learn country dance and use our cha-cha.

We love our dance instructors; they are such fun people. We are getting out, exercising, relieving stress, and meeting many people. Many of the other dancers are younger but we enjoy that too.

Describe the typical dance scene.

Michelle: The majority of the people that we dance with are in their mid-twenties and thirties, but one of the things that impresses us with this community is that it does cross so many age spans. There is no barrier. It's all about the dance, having fun, and expressing yourself. I'm not sure I could say the same thing about many other sports. There's no judging; everyone is there to have fun. That's what we really like. We've met some nice people. When you meet couples who are as young as your children are, they bring a different outlook to the table.

Jody: There are many different venues and activities. Dance studios arrange dance parties. Some instructors rent a large room and invite groups of people. The groups change week to week. There are maybe forty to eighty people coming to dance.

Michelle: There are dances at community centers and private studios. Some people open their homes, move back the furniture, and host dancing.

How much time do you spend on this pursuit?

Jody: My wife is obsessed with dancing. If she could take lessons every night, she would do it.

Michelle: We dance at least two nights a week; we dance three to five hours each time. We've been doing this for almost nine months now. I've lost twenty pounds, and I wasn't even trying. The doctor told me I needed to "bulk up" a little.

Jody: I've lost about ten pounds. I have to be careful about what I eat, and I feel a lot healthier. I should be practicing a lot more than I do. When we're learning a new pattern, I should practice every night just to get the moves down.

Michelle: I go to YouTube often to watch the champions dance. There are also free videos of all of the competitions. I study the different moves.

What expenses are involved?

Michelle: To get started, check your local dance studios and dance halls. Many offer free half-hour to forty-five-minute introductory lessons. Maybe you'll pay an entrance fee of $5, so it doesn't cost you much. After you've tried different dances and you find one that you like, then I would suggest you take a group lesson.

Community recreation centers and private dance studios offer lessons. We paid a monthly charge of $40 each for a group lesson. Private lessons in our area range from $40 to $125. The price varies depending on the location of the studio and if the dance instructor attained a championship level. Typically, our dancing includes one private lesson a week. We pay $75 a lesson right now. If you buy a package, you get a discount.

We started at a recreation center and had a great time. It depends on what you're dancing for and what your goals are. I'm seriously considering entering the competition circle for West Coast swing, even though I'm sixty years old. You should have a dance instructor that meets your goals. For competitions, I will need someone who knows that arena and understands how West Coast swing competition works.

Jody: I like to dance just to have fun. I'm not into the competition circuit. I want to learn new things, but I'm not as obsessed.

Michelle: Last year we went to Palm Springs for a four-day beginners West Coast swing boot camp. It turned out to be one of the best vacations we ever took. You can take whatever classes you want and they have competitions going on. Champion instructors attend, and it's a good value for the money spent. We plan to make this an annual trip.

What clothes do you wear dancing?

Michelle: For West Coast swing most people wear jeans. Ballroom or competition—that's a whole other thing. When I taught school, I wore skirts or slacks, so I had to go buy jeans.

Jody: Shoes are the biggest expense. You need a comfortable, leather-soled shoe. I have some foot problems, so I buy a special dance shoe. It's a dance tennis shoe with a high back and a soft heel. You can buy them at a dance store or online for $100 to $125.

Michelle: It depends on what dance you're doing. For West Coast swing women use a flat shoe. When you finish doing a dance pattern, you do an anchor step, settle back, and put weight down on the heel. If you can't get your heel down, it throws you off a little. It's not like a ballroom cha-cha or rumba, where you would wear a higher two- to two-and-a-half-inch heel.

What is the most rewarding aspect of this activity?

Michelle: I've spent the most romantic times dancing with my husband. Even though I'm obsessed, the best part is that we spend time together. Even though West Coast swing isn't close like the foxtrot or waltz, there is a lot of fun music to dance to. It's opened up another line of communication for Jody and me. In dance, there's a lead and a follow, and that's added another way of communicating with each other.

Jody: The most rewarding aspect is when I try something totally new and I succeed. I may get frustrated at first when I don't know the pattern, and then all of a sudden it clicks and I say, Oh, I get it now! That's what I like about it.

As the man, I have to know how to lead. I have to have a plan and know what the cues are. I have to be thinking all the time. A wonderful thing about dancing is if you make a mistake, you just start again. Many times our instructor will tell us, "All the girl has to do is follow; you guys have the hard part of leading." If I turn my hand one way and my partner turns her hand the other way, I can wind up hurting her. Dancing partners can't be going in different directions. I'm very conscious about that. I hold the hand lightly. In West Coast swing, I don't grip my partner's hand. I make sure my hold is loose in case we're not in sync.

No Partner? No Problem.

Michelle: There's a huge single community of dancers where we live. Some women might say, "Oh, I don't want to venture out because I don't have a partner." At our West Coast swing group class, you don't need a partner. When you're having a lesson, a dance pattern will be introduced, you practice it, and then the instructor will say, "Everybody rotate." Of course, you don't have to; you can stay with the same partner, but even more advanced dancers like to rotate to the next dancer because it helps improve your dance.

Jody: Sometimes there are more women than there are men; sometimes it's the other way around.

Dave Weston's blog on Salsacrazy.com is worth reading. An article called "A Salsa Dance Guide for Women: 19 Easy Ways to Attract More Men to Dance with You" has some great tips for any style of dance.

Health Benefits

In a September 2013 examiner.com article, "Dancing Your Way to Health," Eli Madrone cited several studies that discussed how dancing yields better health. One study in the Journal of Aging and Physical Activity showed tango dancing improves balance in aging adults. Dancing requires a lot of fast movement and good posture, so frequent dancing will help you stabilize and gain better control of your body.

Dance is a great activity for those at risk for cardiovascular disease. An Italian study noted that people with heart failure who took up waltzing improved their heart health, breathing, and quality of life significantly, compared to those who biked or walked on a treadmill for exercise. Additionally, a 2003 study in the New England Journal of Medicine declared people were less likely to develop dementia if they participated in ballroom dancing at least twice a week.

Michelle: To me, the most interesting thing about dance is that it's a whole mind-body experience. Not only are there physical benefits, but cognitive benefits as well. Dancing is responsible for the highest risk-reduction of dementia of all the sports.

How You Dance Changes the Way You Think

Dr. Peter Lovatt, head of the Dance Psychology Lab at the University of Hertfordshire in England, reported that dancing has an effect on the cognitive process, and in particular, how we dance changes the way we think. His research on Parkinson's disease found that physical structured movement (learning choreographed dance steps) improves *convergent thinking*, which is used to come up with a single answer to a problem. But improvised dancing improves *divergent thinking*, which encourages alternative or creative problem-solving. The research found this was a useful way of developing new neural pathways to limit the damaging effects of Parkinson's disease. See the Resource section for dance classes offered specifically for those affected by Parkinson's disease.

Any advice for beginner dancers?

Michelle: Dance has given us so many opportunities for meeting new people. West Coast swing is popular all over the world, not just in the US. There are competitions in Australia, Korea, and Canada. We've made good friends with people from different parts of the world that we probably would never have met otherwise.

Dancing has allowed us to accomplish quite a few things that we wanted to experience. I encourage people to give it a try. You can't go just one or two times. You have to invest some time in it. If you're not happy with the lesson, try a different place.

Jody: Everyone who retires needs to put dance on his or her bucket list. Even if it's just for a little bit.

Do you have any plans that may evolve within this hobby?

Michelle: I might put a dance competition on my bucket list. I don't understand how it works yet, but I've heard once you get into it, you never want to give it up. You would think someone who started at this so late wouldn't consider this, but there are competitions for people fifty-five and older.

FASCINATING FACTS

- The waltz was a shocking dance in its day. It only became acceptable in English society when the young Queen Victoria took to it with a passion.
- You don't have to able to walk to dance: wheelchair dancing is popular, particularly in Europe. There, ballroom and Latin American dancing competitions have divisions for wheelchair-bound dancers in separate competitions or in combinations with partners who do not have a disability that requires a wheelchair.
- Dance marathons reached their height during the 1930s Great Depression, when dancers went to great lengths to compete for monetary prizes. The longest recorded marathon lasted 22 weeks and 3 days.
- According to the *Guinness Book of World Records*, Michael Flatley held records in the late 1990s for 35 taps per second, and was the highest-paid dancer in the world, earning $1,600,000 per week.
- "I Could Have Danced All Night" (from the musical *My Fair Lady)* was the 24th most-performed song of the 20th century.

Resources

Websites

Access Dance: Where to go dancing in your area: accessdance.com.

Dancing for the Dream: a nonprofit that works with those over 45 years old and promotes health physically and emotionally using line dance as its chosen form of exercise: https://www.dancingforthedream.com.

Dance for Parkinson's (Dance for PD), an innovative dance therapy program in more than 100 communities in 9 countries: http://bit.ly/1rsRMwv.

Find a dance partner: dancepartner.com.

Dance Studio Connect: dancestudioconnect.com.

Find a dance studio: findadancestudio.com.

Dance Meet-Ups: Many dancers get together for classes or dance events through meetup.com.

"A Salsa Dance Guide for Women: 19 Easy Ways to Attract More Men to Dance with You": http://bit.ly/1q46Yz0.

Square dance clubs and organizations: http://bit.ly/1kib7ll.

USA Dance promotes ballroom dancing in the local community. Find a local chapter: http://bit.ly/1oyrJoA.

Apps

DanceApp uses a combination of animations, videos, visual/sound effects, music, and text instruction to build a solid foundation for learning ballroom dancing, beginning with the six core dances of waltz, foxtrot, tango, rumba, cha-cha and East Coast swing: http://bit.ly/1o51t0j.

SeeDance is a free app for Apple and Android devices. Using a dancer's current location, the app scouts out dance studios, dancewear stores, dance performances and events, and many other needs the dancer may have: seedance.com.

Videos

Beginner Dancing: http://bit.ly/1kibaO2.

Salsa videos: http://bit.ly/UEg3EN.

West Coast Swing videos: wcsvideos.com.

Reading

Robin D. Chmelar and Sally S. Fitt, *Diet for Dancers: A Complete Guide to Nutrition and Weight Control* (Pennington, NJ: Princeton Book Co, 1995).

Rusty Frank, *TAP! The Greatest Tap Dance Stars and Their Stories 1900–1955* (Cambridge, MA: Da Capo Press; REV edition, 1995).

Lindsay Guarino and Wendy Oliver, *Jazz Dance: A History of the Roots and Branches* (Gainesville, FL: University Press of Florida, 2014).

Elizabeth A. Seagull, *Ballroom Dancing Is Not for Sissies: An R-Rated Guide for Partnership* (Charleston, SC: BookSurge Publishing, 2008).

CHAPTER 27

Softball Player

Baseball is ninety percent mental
and the other half is physical.
—Yogi Berra

The game of softball is a variation on baseball, using a larger ball and a smaller infield. A tournament held in 1933 at the Chicago World's Fair spurred interest in the game. Of the two types of softball, slow-pitch is more popular than fast-pitch in recreational leagues.

The standard ball used in softball is twelve inches in diameter, compared to a nine-inch baseball, and less dense. The ball is pitched underhand with an arch approximately ten to twelve feet on its path to the batter. Seven innings rather than nine constitute a regulation game. The infield is smaller than a baseball diamond; the distance between the bases is sixty feet rather than ninety feet in regulation baseball.

Most town and city recreation departments around the country organize men's, women's, and coed slow-pitch softball teams. Some teams play year-round, others begin in spring and continue through fall. Softball teams follow the rules of the Amateur Softball Association, the national governing body of US softball. To accommodate the needs of the older crowd, there are modifications made for the leagues for players fifty and older that emphasize safety.

Nationwide, about 2 million Americans over fifty years old play recreational softball, according to Terry Hennessy, CEO of Senior Softball USA, and he predicts a 10 percent annual growth rate. On February 18, 2014, Senior Softball USA announced that it launched a division for players eighty-five and up.

Ray, defending second base

Ray is sixty-seven years old and lives in Baltimore, Maryland. He is a retired transit-district information agent, a job he loved for thirty-five years.

Ray: I worked in the information and service department. In addition to administration, I would go out into the community once a week and visit companies to promote the bus service, hand out schedules, answer questions, and occasionally field complaints.

Love of the Game

Ray: I've always been involved in playing ball. I played junior varsity and varsity ball in high school. Then I played fast-pitch for years. I've slowed down a little and now I play senior slow-pitch ball. Brooks Robinson, who played third base for the Baltimore Orioles from 1955 to 1977, was my idol and always will be. When I was young, I wanted to walk like Brooks, talk like Brooks, and play like Brooks! And my uniform today—I don't wear any other number but the number 5.

I wanted to be a Major League ball player. I'm a small guy, but I'm still gifted with my hands. When I was growing up, I'd take a ten-cent rubber ball and practice throwing it. I'd beat that ball on the side of the brick school wall for hours, no matter what the weather, and drill myself on ground balls. Just today, playing second base, I made a diving catch straight out in the air and caught the ball!

What position do you play?

Ray: Mostly, I play second base, sometimes the infield as short-stop, and I can play the outfield because I'm still fast. I've been blessed and I love doing what I'm doing.

How often do you play ball?

Ray: I play on two teams for players sixty years old and older organized through the Parks and Recreation Departments of two areas. One team plays doubleheaders on Monday and Wednesday mornings. I play for a second team and play a doubleheader on Tuesday evenings. That's six games a week.

The season starts in April and goes through August. Some leagues then start another season called "fall ball." My group starts practicing in November or December to get ready for our April start. We go to an indoor facility and warm up for two hours, choose sides, and play.

How old are most of the players?

Ray: You have to be sixty years old or older to play in the league. A lot of these men that are playing ball never became "couch potatoes." Maybe they played ball in high school, but they're all ball fanatics like me. On the Tuesday team, I'm the oldest player. We don't win a lot of games, but we have each other's respect; we have camaraderie and a fellowship that's hard to find. The Monday/Wednesday team is very competitive. Some of the guys are seventy years old. One of our players is seventy-nine. Another team in the league has an eighty-seven-year-old player and you cannot get him out at the plate.

How are the leagues organized?

Ray: My Tuesday league for sixty years and older has eight teams. The Monday/Wednesday league has fourteen teams; and that's just the "A" division. There is also a "B," "C," and "D" division. All the divisions probably add up to over four hundred players. On each team, there are twenty players on the roster. The team plays with eleven men on the field. Everybody gets to bat until there are three outs.

Senior League Modifications

Ray: One reason for the popularity of softball for seniors is the modifications to the rules for senior teams. The modifications make the game safer and provide more protection against injury. For example, each team is allowed one courtesy runner per inning. If the batter has trouble running, one of the other players gets behind the plate and runs for the hitter. Or if the batter wants to run to first base, another player can pick it up and run from there. In some leagues, the number of home runs that can be hit by a team are limited.

Also the majority of leagues use a double first base—one white and one orange. The white base is in the field and for the defensive player. The orange base is on the other side of the line and that's for the runner to run through. A play at first requires the defense to touch the white base, while the runner must go to the orange base; otherwise, an out is recorded. There is also an additional base by home plate. When a runner leaves third base and runs home, he runs to the base four feet to the left of home plate for safety reasons.

A player on base must have one foot completely on any base at all times until the ball is hit; there's no leading. If the player moves off the bag before the hit, he will be called out, and stealing of bases is prohibited. Some leagues prohibit sliding, but I know one fellow, seventy years old, who slides into the base all the time. He's used to sliding and says it's instinct.

All batters start at bat with a count of one ball and one strike. They're allowed one foul ball and there's no bunting. This speeds up the game. In some of the other leagues, a pitcher has a screen in front of him to protect him against the hit ball. With some of these new alloy bats, it's hard to move fast enough to get out of the way. Some leagues use a single-walled aluminum bat. Others use a double-walled aluminum bat, and in tournaments some batters will use a titanium bat. If you hit the ball right with one of those bats, it can go three hundred feet.

What expenses are involved?

Ray: The cost varies by recreation departments. Players on the team I'm on are asked to pay $110 to play on a team for the regular season. That covers entry fees for league play, balls, uniforms, and umpires. Each player is responsible for his own equipment.

Tournaments

Ray: There are tournaments going on all through the season, and some even before the start of regular play. Many are held on holidays. On Memorial Day weekend, the "World's Largest Softball Tournament" is held in Richmond, Virginia, where five hundred teams compete.

Years ago, a team would go to a tournament based on their merit. Now that's all changed. The website for senior softball lists all of the tournaments by month for men's and women's ball. It costs between a $300 and $500 entry fee for a team to play in a tournament. That doesn't include travel and hotel expenses. Additionally, each player is asked to pay $200 to cover the cost for balls and uniforms and umpires. There are softball fund-raisers going on all the time. My Monday/Wednesday league has an annual fund-raising dinner. We raise a couple thousand dollars to pay for the team's tournament costs. It's a great deal of work but worth it.

This year my team will do six tournaments. Around the first of the year, we have a softball meeting and advertise for team players; then we decide on the tournaments. Distance and price of entry determines the list. Sometimes the prize is a trophy, sometimes they give out "goodies" like rings, jackets, and ball bags. When a tournament gives out goodies, you know it's going to cost $500. One year we traveled to Las Vegas for a tournament. You can go to tournaments in Hawaii, Japan, or New Zealand if you can get the money together. But that's not typical.

My Worst Game

Ray: One year, we were playing in a tournament and leading the game 29 runs to 7. It was the last inning, with two outs. I wasn't playing that day, just sitting on the bench. The opposing team was up at bat, we needed one more out, and we would win the tournament. The batter hit a ball to third base that had backspin on it—uncatchable. The next batter got a base hit. Then it became a chain reaction.

Our team managers didn't know what to do. They kept the same pitcher on the mound. As a former manager, I knew you had to do something to stop the momentum. Years ago, when I was manager, I was faced with the same problem of trying to stop the momentum, went up to the pitcher, and with a serious face asked him, "How do you like your cheesesteaks?" I just tried to relax him a bit, change his state of mind. But the current managers didn't know what to do and we lost that game 30 to 29. That game was a nightmare.

Looking Good

Ray: A while back when I was managing a team, we were going to play in the Richmond, Virginia, tournament. We didn't have any uniforms and we didn't have any money, so I went to the Big Lots store and looked for something we could wear. I found some shirts, but they were football jerseys, not baseball attire.

The shirts had a V-neck, and were red at the top on the shoulders, and gray down to the waist. I bought twenty shirts for $1 each. Then I bought iron-on transfer letters and numbers and there I was, ironing on "SF," letters that stood for the team name, and big numbers on the backs of twenty shirts.

As the game progressed and the guys ran around the bases, all of the numbers started peeling off. We looked a little ragged, but we won that tournament by one run. That allowed us to advance to the nationals in Atlanta. I still have a couple of those shirts.

The Negro Baseball League

Ray: The Negro Baseball League is another passion of mine. I knew nothing about the Negro League until 1996. Mrs. Geraldine Day lives in our area, and her husband was the great Leon Day, the only Negro League player from Baltimore inducted into the Hall of Fame. He was inducted in Cooperstown in 1995. I met Mrs. Day and some of the other Negro League ballplayers at a park dedication and I became involved with the Negro Baseball League organization.

I'm known as the Negro Baseball League's Goodwill Ambassador. I created an exhibit of memorabilia and I give presentations about the history of the League. With the help of Baltimore County, the League moved the exhibit to a permanent home in the Owens Mills branch of the Baltimore County Public Library.

March 27, 2014, was the grand opening of the Hubert V. Simmons Museum of Negro League Baseball, named after Hubert "Bert" Simmons, who played for a Negro League team called the Baltimore Elite Giants. The grand-opening celebration drew several former players, including Luther Atkins, who played second base for the Satchel Paige All-Stars from 1955 to 1960 and Mamie "Peanut" Johnson, one of only three women to pitch in the Negro Baseball League and who played with the Indianapolis Clowns from 1953 to 1955.

As an acknowledgment of all of the wonderful players from the League throughout the years, I was proud to be among the fifteen people invited to the White House to meet President Obama in August 2013. That was thrilling.

What is the most rewarding aspect of this activity?

Ray: I've kept a ball from every tournament win over the years. The ball has on it the name of the pitcher who pitched the game, the year, the date, and the score. I save scorebooks from the past as well. I keep T-shirts. I'm a pack rat. My wife won't let me bring anything else in the house!

Softball is a big part of my life. Through softball, I've participated in many fund-raisers for hospital programs, the March of Dimes, and Christmas Giving programs. I derive a great deal of satisfaction from helping people.

I wouldn't have traveled to Fort Myers, Florida, and Las Vegas if I wasn't playing softball. One year I was fortunate to play ball in the Senior Olympics. In 2008, I was inducted into the Anne Arundel County Softball Slow-Pitch Hall of Fame, and in March 2013, I was inducted into the Maryland Slow-Pitch Hall of Fame.

Any advice for those interested in playing softball?

Ray: Playing softball can open up a new adventure, especially when you get up in age and you don't want to become idle. It keeps you alive. You stay connected and you gain many friendships along the way. If a player on the opposing team gets hurt, everyone signs a get-well card. Being involved in softball teaches you what life is all about. It's not about winning all the time. It's about being grateful that you're able to get up every day and play this game.

FASCINATING FACTS

- George Hancock, a journalist for the Chicago Board of Trade, invented softball in 1887. He designed the game to be a form of indoor baseball to be played during the winter.
- The original softball was actually just a rolled-up boxing glove.
- A backwards *K* in scorekeeping means the player struck out by not swinging at the last pitch.
- In 1991, softball was officially named an Olympic sport for women. It debuted as a medal event in 1996 in Atlanta.
- The USA Women's National Softball Team won 3 consecutive Olympic gold medals (1996, 2000, 2004) and a silver medal at the 2008 Olympic Games.
- In 2014, the Softball Players Association reported over 17,000 players over the age of 50 registered with the organization. More than 100 are over 80 years of age.

Resources

Websites

Amateur Softball Association (ASA): asasoftball.com.

International Senior Softball Association: seniorsoftball.org.

The Hubert V. Simmons Museum of Negro League Baseball: http://on.fb.me/UEh5Rg.

Meet Up groups for softball (slow-pitch, coed, and pick-up games): softball.meetup.com.

Senior games: seniorgames.net/sports/softball.

Senior Softball USA (find a league): seniorsoftball.com.

Slow-Pitch Nation, nationwide softball tournaments posted online: slowpitchnation.com.

Softball Players Association Men's and Women's Program: softball-spa.com.

Women's softball message board: http://bit.ly/1nO2des.

Tournament listings: http://bit.ly/1nO2kqm.

Apps

Amateur Softball Association Official Rules of Softball Mobile App: http://bit.ly/WJaYgk.

Videos

Slow-Pitch Hitting Tips: http://bit.ly/1AnRE7u.

Slow-Pitch Softball Mechanics: http://bit.ly/X1gHOq.

Reading

Amateur Softball Association, *Official Rules of Softball* (Oklahoma City, OK: Amateur Softball Association of America, 1996).

Rainer Martens and Julie S. Martens. *Complete Guide to Slow-Pitch Softball* (Champaign, IL: Human Kinetics, 2011).

Kadir Nelson, *We Are the Ship: The Story of Negro League Baseball* (New York, NY: Jump At The Sun/ Hyperion Books; 1 edition, 2008).

CHAPTER 28

Target Shooter

Fast is fine, but accuracy is final.
—Wyatt Earp

Target shooting is a game of movement, action, and split-second timing. It requires the accuracy and skill to repeatedly aim, fire, and break a clay disc hurled through the air at a speed simulating the flight path of a bird. In 2012, some 30.25 million Americans participated in target shooting.

Shooting in America

According to USA Shooting, an organization headquartered at the US Olympic Training Center in Colorado Springs, Colorado, the first forms of shooting competitions in the United States were called *rifle frolics* or *turkey shoots*. Held sometime between 1790 and 1800, the prizes were typically beef, turkey, or other food items. A single shot was fired from a distance of 250 to 300 feet from either the standing or resting position. The firearms used in these matches featured 38- to 40-inch barrels, double-set triggers, and target sights similar to those that were used for European target arms.

Rifle makers used new percussion caps in 1825 and target accuracy greatly improved. Formal match shooting began shortly thereafter and competitions in all parts of the United States drew large attendance from shooters and spectators. One particular match in Glendale Park, New York, in the 1880s attracted more than 600 competitors and 30,000 spectators for the one-day event. In 1898, a shooting festival at the same location offered $25,000 in cash prizes.

Olympic Competition

French nobleman Baron Pierre de Coubertin orchestrated the first modern Olympic Games in 1896 in Athens, Greece. It began with nine competitive sports, including shooting. The number of Olympic shooting events has ranged from a low of two at the 1932 Los Angeles Games to a high of twenty-one events in Antwerp in 1920. Beginning in 2008 at the Beijing Olympic Games, the Olympic program now includes fifteen shooting events: six for women and nine for men. The athletes compete in shotgun, rifle, and pistol disciplines.

Nancy, target shooter and instructor

Nancy, who lives outside of Chicago, retired at age fifty-five. She had been a vice president of a Fortune 100 company and a self-proclaimed workaholic.

Nancy: I was terrified and wasn't sure what I was going to do with my time. My husband and I both took up target shooting and became very involved in it. Now, three years later, I'm also a certified pistol and rifle instructor.

I thought a lot about what I was going to do with my time after I retired. I didn't want to be a couch potato and I like to stay busy all the time. I've always been interested in being outdoors; I always had a dream to be a forest ranger. I wanted an outdoor sport that I could do physically. I'm only five-one, so I wanted something that wasn't gear-intensive and not be limited by my height. Turns out I do have a lot of gear because I keep buying more. Together my husband and I have more than thirty firearms and we target shoot with all except two.

How did you get started?

Nancy: I learned to shoot a rifle when I was in the military, so I had some exposure. However, I didn't use a firearm during my six years active duty and three years civil service. I was in military intelligence, stationed in Germany for three years serving on a former Luftwaffe post. After that, I was stationed at Fort Hood, Texas.

I already knew that I might be comfortable around guns and I knew I wasn't going to be afraid of them. My husband and I decided to do this together, and started looking locally for what classes were available. We went to a nearby gun club and began by taking lessons with an instructor. We had six one-hour lessons, one-on-one with the instructor, then attended a series of two-day classes. It took me about six months to a year before I felt I really understood the fundamentals and developed the muscle memory to stand consistently holding the gun correctly.

Golf with a Shotgun

Nancy: I decided a shotgun was more interesting to me than pistols because you shoot clay targets, and the moving targets seemed like it would be more fun. Once I started breaking those things, I really liked it! It was instant gratification. You know immediately whether you're doing something right or wrong. I've heard the same attributes apply in golf. Once you feel you've got your swing just right, you can actually feel that your body did it the correct way. It's the same kind of movement. It's all about eye-hand coordination, keeping your eye on the target. And it's about follow-through. It's similar to golf, but for me it's more fun.

Target-Shooting Games

Nancy: The three main shotgun target shoots are skeet, trap, and sporting clays. My husband likes shooting skeet best; I prefer sporting clays. Each game has different target presentations depending on your position standing on the field.

The word *skeet* is derived from the Scandinavian word for *shoot*, but the sport is an American invention. In 1920, a group of American bird hunters started shooting clay targets to practice wing-shooting. Originally performed using a 360-degree area, the field was changed to a half-circle to avoid disturbing a nearby chicken farm. Skeet shooting uses two different *houses*, one high, one low, to release the targets along a left-right plane, and shooters fire from eight stations.

Trap shooting is older than skeet, dating back to the late nineteenth century. Targets, called *birds*, are launched at forty to forty-five miles per hour from a mechanical house, flying at an angle away from the shooter. One of the greatest trap shooters of the nineteenth century was Annie Oakley. In a one-day exhibition, Oakley shot 4,722 of the 5,000 glass balls released.

Sporting clays is the closest thing to actual field shooting because the machines are constantly moving. It's more unpredictable and challenging. Rather than having clay birds thrown from standardized distances and angles as with skeet or trap, each sporting-clays station replicates a different animal. Targets may be thrown from literally any angle. One target may come out flying like a pheasant, another rolling on the ground like a rabbit.

Other forms of target shooting include the newer 5-stand, which uses a wide variety of launch positions, and international skeet, the Olympic-style format that uses a different gun position, a delayed bird release, and faster targets.

What special clothes and equipment do you use?

Nancy: You don't need to wear special clothes or shoes. I wear a hat to shade my eyes, and a shooting vest with big pockets to hold shells. Eye and ear protection is very important. Before you go buy your first gun, you need to decide how important it is to you to absorb the recoil, also referred to as the "kick." Borrow other peoples' guns to see how they feel. Many classes will supply the shotgun for each student.

Some new shooters may favor a single-barrel, 20-gauge or 28-gauge, semiautomatic because of reduced kickback, which is the sharp recoil that occurs as the gun fires and thrusts backward into the shooter's shoulder. When the shot is fired, a semiautomatic takes the gases that are created and uses them to cycle the next shot, thereby reducing the kick.

I use a Beretta shotgun, which ensures a good fit, especially for individuals with smaller hands. I don't mind the kick, so I use a 12-gauge shotgun with an over-under barrel, which is two barrels aligned vertically, one over the other, rather than horizontally. My shotgun uses one shell at a time, which differs from the semiautomatic, which kicks the shell out and puts the next one in the barrel automatically. While it's doing that, you don't feel the kick as much. In an over-under or double-barrel shotgun, the energy has nowhere to go and so you get the kick.

Traditional shotgun shooting requires movement, speed, and allowing your arms and gun to swing along the trajectory of a moving target. You don't aim a shotgun; you plan your shot placement, and point and shoot with your eyes on the target. It can be instinctive, and is very much about hand-eye coordination. Trigger control is not important, nor is minimizing body movement by managing normal breathing.

What expenses are involved?

Nancy: Shooting instructors certify at different levels, so the higher the level, the more expensive their lessons are. Our instructor charged $40 per hour. I borrowed the shotgun that I used for the lessons. Often you can find a club where you can rent a gun, or it comes with the instruction. Many shooting clubs give free clinics each month just to get people interested in the sport. Also many states' Natural Resources Departments offer wing-shooting clinics in preparation for a safe hunting season. The retailer Orvis, and the National Rifle Association, also offers classes for all age groups.

Until you figure out what you want to shoot, you shouldn't spend a lot of money. A newcomer to this sport can typically learn how to shoot and can get into the hobby for under $600. You can pay $350 for a decent used semiautomatic shotgun; new ones cost $500 to $600. Ammunition is currently $8 per box for twenty-five shells. One game of trap or skeet uses one box. Sporting clays uses a hundred shells, but you don't have to finish the whole course. You can complete half or a quarter of the course.

Buy safety glasses that wrap around your eyes and are made of polycarbonate [$10]. You want to prevent the shards of clay in the wind from getting in your eyes. Earplugs are very inexpensive. A shooting vest with big pockets to hold the shells costs $20. The clay targets are consumable and our club charges non-members $7 per round; members pay $5. Club membership is not necessary when you are just beginning. My club membership is currently $280 per year. Once a firearm is purchased, the ongoing expenses are the cost of the clay pigeons and ammunition. Like any hobby, a beginner or amateur will spend much less than an enthusiast.

Do you belong to an organization connected to your hobby?

Nancy: I belong to several organizations: the National Rifle Association, National Shooting Sports Foundation, the National Sporting Clays Association, trap leagues, and skeet leagues.

Target shooting has many dimensions. Many participants enjoy skeet and trap shooting purely as a recreation, but you can join leagues and participate in serious competition. USA Shooting, the sport's national governing body, has authority over all levels of shooting from local events up to the Olympics. You can be anywhere on the continuum. It's an individual choice as to how involved you want to be.

I also belong to three shooting clubs. Each offers me something different. Many clubs have groups of shooters that have individual perspectives. Some of the "legacy clubs" expect you to be proficient in the sport and know what you are doing. They are very formal. They expect you to know all the protocols. Other clubs are much more relaxed. Call and ask if the club is more or less formal. You can quickly get the sense of it by just going once.

You meet a lot of people while shooting and it opens the door to continuous mentoring. Someone will always give you a pointer if you're open to it. Skeet and trap shooting evolved from "gentlemen's sports." It's common in clubs to shoot a round, then go into the clubhouse for coffee, then go out again and shoot another round.

Describe the demographics of one of your shooting clubs.

Nancy: One club I belong to has 1,500 members, but less than 50 percent are active. More than 80 percent are men; however, we do have a woman chairperson who is over seventy years old. But that's unusual. It's a varied age group. Most use the pistol range and 25 percent use shotguns.

One growing group I've noticed is what we call "Blackgunners." These are mostly guys in their thirties or younger. They come decked out in camouflage, bulletproof vests, and magazines strapped to their sides, using sporting rifles [assault rifles] and tactical shotguns. Why? I've asked myself the same question. I think many are former vets, having served in Afghanistan and Iraq. Then there are those "wannabe" soldiers, and then there are the videogamers. We have this generation that grew up playing videogames. Now they're old enough to buy guns, so they are coming to the clubs to shoot.

Hollywood Shooters

Nancy: It's hard to watch Hollywood actors and extras handle guns sometimes, because it's obvious they have no training. When the movie Superman: Man of Steel was filming six miles away from the club, the director sent over sixty of the extras and stunt actors for a three-day workshop on proper gun handling. I coordinated the agreement and organized six instructors and we went through the basics with them: "Here's how you hold it, how you stand, et cetera." We had them fire some live bullets so they could get the real experience, because when you're firing blanks, it's not the same.

What is the most rewarding aspect of this activity?

Nancy: I'm a certified instructor and I find teaching very rewarding. I especially enjoy working with young people. I volunteer to coach scouts working on their merit badges. Our club, as well as national organizations, places special emphasis on involving non-traditional shooters, such as minorities, women, and the disabled in the sport.

A couple of times per year, I instruct at Annie Oakley Days. This clinic is designed for those who don't know anything about shooting, or people who are afraid of guns. We explain safety and different kinds of shooting. We introduce shotgun, pistol, and rifle shooting, and after the clinic, most people find they enjoyed it and are not afraid anymore. The clinic usually has had more women, but the last class had an equal number of men and women.

During one Annie Oakley Day clinic, one of the students was a woman in her early fifties who had never shot before. After introducing the basics, the students started with a stationary target. We try to make them feel comfortable and gain confidence. There happened to be some hornets flying around that day and this woman hated hornets. She was really nervous. She saw one of the hornets land on the target. She said, "I hate those things," picked up the gun, and fired. Our jaws dropped and in collective silence; we realized she took out the hornet and plastered it on the target. It was her first shot!

Is there anything else that you think is important for readers to know?

Nancy: Yes. I want people to know that target shooting is not about politics. It shouldn't affect it, but too often, it does. Target shooting is a fun sport and an individual choice. It has nothing to do with crime or killing. When I encounter people in our classes who are afraid of firearms, it's usually not from personal experience. They've seen it on TV. Shooting has been tainted and bears an unfair stigma. My sport is all about my eyes being able to judge distance and speed and my hands being able to react. It's a skill.

FASCINATING FACTS

- First recorded use of a firearm was in 1364.
- In 1835, Samuel Colt developed the first mass-produced, multi-shot, revolving firearm.
- In the past, the clay pigeon was made of clay. Targets used now are composed of a mixture of lime and pitch. The petroleum in the pitch is what produces the very satisfying black puff when a solid hit is made. New biodegradable targets are now appearing that use no pitch and produce a grayish puff when hit.
- The fastest time shooting 25 clay pigeons is 37.2 seconds and was achieved by Tyler Jackson Leinbach (USA) in North Carolina, January 2013.
- Americans Kimberly Rhode and Vincent Hancock won gold medals in the Women's and Men's Skeet competition at the 2012 London Olympics.
- In Olympic skeet competitions, there is a random delay of between 0 to 3 seconds after the shooter has called for the target. Also, the shooter must hold the gun so that the gun butt is at mid-torso level until the target appears.

Resources

Websites

Amateur Trap Shooting Association: shootata.com.

Find a place to shoot: wheretoshoot.org.

Clay Targets Online: claytargetsonline.com.

First Shots. Many ranges across the country offer free introductory classes to firearm safety and the shooting sports called "First Shots": http://bit.ly/1mTip9Q.

National Rifle Association (NRA) classes: http://bit.ly/1tRee3L.

National Skeet Shooting Association & National Sporting Clays Association: nssa-nsca.org.

National Shooting Sports Foundation (NSSF): nssf.org.

Orvis retailer wing-shooting schools: http://bit.ly/X1im6u.

Trapshooters: http://bit.ly/1rW8PZ2.

USA Shooting: usashooting.org.

Apps

NSSF Where to Shoot mobile app for iPhone and iPad: wheretoshoot.org/iOS; and for Android: wheretoshoot.org/Android.

Videos

Firearm Safety for Everyone: http://bit.ly/1kicOzf.

Free videos from the National Shooting Sports Foundation on a variety of topics: http://bit.ly/1nxgA7j.

Safety videos: nssf.org/safety/video.

Reading

Chris Batha, *Breaking Clays: Target Tactics, Tips & Techniques* (New York, NY: Quiller, 2005).

Mark Brannon, Tom Hanrahan, and Matthew Brannon. *Shooting Sporting Clays*. Mechanicsburg, PA: Stackpole Books, 2011.

Rick Sapp, *The Gun Digest Book of Trap & Skeet Shooting* (Iola, WI: Krause Publications, 2009).

CHAPTER 29

Triathlete

If you set a goal for yourself and are able to achieve it, you have won your race. Your goal can be to come in first, to improve your performance, or just to finish the race—it's up to you. —Dave Scott

Triathlon has exploded in popularity over the past ten years. A 2012 Sports & Fitness Industry Association study reported an estimated 1,992,000 individuals completed at least one triathlon in 2011. USA Triathlon is the national governing body for the multisport disciplines in the United States. The organization's former president, Bob Wendling, reported that the numbers of older athletes competing in "Sprint" triathlons seen a significant increase in 2012, and that more than 50,000 people older than fifty now compete in at least one sprint triathlon a year, a tenfold increase since 2005.

It's All About Endurance

Triathlon is a timed sporting event that combines swimming, biking, and running in consecutive order. This also includes the transition times between each event. The multisport race format is designed to test the endurance of its participants, much more so than swimming, biking, or running alone.

To accommodate different skill levels, there are four triathlon races. The shortest form is the *Sprint*, in which you swim

1/4 mile, bike 10 miles and run 3.1 miles. The *Olympic* contains a swim of 1.5 kilometers (just under 1 mile), bike 25 miles, and run 6.2 miles. Next is the *Half-Ironman*, with a 1.2-mile swim, 56-mile bike, and 13.1-mile run. In the *Full Ironman*, athletes swim 2.4 miles, bike 112 miles, and then run a marathon of 26.2 miles.

I'm Too Old for This . . .

According to USA Triathlon, the number of triathlon participants aged sixty to sixty-nine is fully twice that of athletes in their late teens. More people seem to take up triathlon later in life and stay with it longer. The American Association of Retired Persons (AARP) began the TriUmph Classic series in 2003 for people over fifty. Although most participants are in their fifties, a substantial number, up to 30 percent in some areas, are between ages sixty and seventy-four.

Margaret Hawkins, TriUmph Classic manager, thinks the combination of the three sports appeals to more participants. People who can't imagine themselves running an entire marathon, may find it less daunting to cross-train for shorter distances in three sports. A triathlon calls on mental strength just as much as physical strength.

Team In Training

The Leukemia & Lymphoma Society's (LLS) Team In Training (TNT) program is the largest endurance sports charity-training program in the country. During the past twenty-five years, 600,000 participants have helped LLS raise more than $1.4 billion to find cures and ensure access to treatments for blood cancer patients.

TNT's training programs, available throughout the country,

prepare athletes to participate in a marathon, half-marathon, century ride, hike adventure, or triathlon. Dedicated websites help with fund-raising, and TNT offers clinics on topics such as gear, apparel, nutrition, and injury prevention. The Team In Training program provides coaching and manages all the arrangements for the event so participants can focus on their race.

Patrick, the triathlete

Patrick is a retired financial executive who lives in Tampa, Florida. He competed in his first triathlon at age fifty-five and now, at age sixty-three, has completed fifteen triathlons so far.

Patrick: I was very busy smoking and drinking at the beginning of my career in my thirties and I knew this had to change. A friend introduced me to running. My buddy and I would get up at five in the morning and run through the streets of New York, where I lived. I started running a mile and built up from there.

Then one New Year's Eve a whole group of us made a drunken commitment to sign up to run the Long Island Marathon in 1984. I had no idea of what I was getting myself into. I started running in 1983 and one year later, I was running in a marathon.

Back in 1984, we didn't know anything about training and the need for water. We'd bring the equivalent of two cups of water with us for an entire run. We had no idea about hydration and electrolytes. We weren't taking enough fluids; we weren't eating correctly. I finished the race anyway.

How did you get started?

Patrick: When I moved to Florida, I wanted to take advantage of the great weather and get passionate about running. Team In Training provides a training program and coaches for their events, so I signed up to be a running coach. That's how I learned about the TNT triathlons. I became the coach for the running part of the race.

I knew how to swim, but for me, as well as 90 percent of triathletes, the swim is the most technical part. The swim coach became my mentor and our team started the training program. He would coach us: Here's how much time you have to devote to running, how much time to swimming, and to biking . . . It was a challenge going from the single discipline of running, where I felt comfortable. Now I had to do three sports.

Your training level depends on which level triathlon you do. Our group trained six months to prepare for an Olympic distance triathlon. Even if you don't live close to a TNT program they have the "Flex" option so you can train the same way as traditional TNT does, with coaches, workouts, nutrition, and hydration advice—all on your own schedule.

When you sign up for a TNT triathlon, you are required to raise a target amount to participate in the event. However, the Leukemia & Lymphoma Society's fund-raising program is a well-oiled machine. They have a template request letter that you can use and the organization helps you mail out the first 100 letters. There are lots of other ways people raise the funds, but I get the minimum required amount needed just from the letters. My dentist alone contributed $100. It's amazing that there is always a connection and people want to give to a good cause. When you tell them what you're doing, that it's for cancer, people are always looking for an opportunity to help. TNT is the biggest of the groups, but charity runs are very popular and there's a lot of competition now.

You've done fifteen triathlons so far. Which were your favorite and least favorite?

Patrick: My favorite is a Sprint triathlon called "Escape from Fort De Soto." It takes place on what I consider one of the top-ten beaches in the country. It's a lot of fun, a beautiful setting, and close to home. I've done that one four times.

The worst triathlon I ever raced was a Half-Ironman in Camp Wilderness, Florida. Every racer hates the three h's—hills, heat, and humidity. It was a difficult course on a dirt path. It didn't have hills, but with no shade and with the humidity, the temperature felt like 101 degrees. I guess it's the nature of us crazy people to do things we shouldn't be doing, so I finished the race. I've only had one DNF [did not finish] so far.

USA Triathlon

USA Triathlon is the national governing body for triathlons and other multisport disciplines. Headquartered in Colorado Springs, Colorado, it is a member federation of the US Olympic Committee and the International Triathlon Union. It is responsible for the selection and training of teams to represent the United States in international competition. It conducts national camps and clinics and provides coaching education programs.

Patrick: USA Triathlon is the umbrella organization for all sanctioned events, and they publish standings and offer insurance. Anyone who participates in a sanctioned race has to buy a one-day membership and obtain the insurance coverage. Anything can happen. It's a crazy sport. I've never been seriously hurt, but the more aggressive you are, the more risk.

The Mind of the Triathlete

The Tribe Group conducted the "Mind of the Triathlete" study in late 2008 for USA Triathlon, and their findings present a picture of the triathlete. Although the average age is thirty-eight years old, 6 percent of triathlon participants are fifty-five years or older. Many participants are male (59.6 percent). Ninety-five percent of the athletes say they participate for the personal challenge, 87 percent also say they do it to stay in shape. The Sprint triathlon remains the most popular, with 75 percent of the respondents.

Patrick: Triathletes tend to be very successful people because they're organized, they plan, and they do what they set out to do. There's a deep desire to finish what they've worked for and committed to do. Sometimes the people who win races are not the best athletes but the ones that can withstand the most discomfort. When you get into the later stages of the race, it's a mental challenge. The work really comes in at the end, and you have to be prepared. At the late stages, 70 percent of the effort is mental.

I was running in the St. Anthony's Triathlon in April, the first race of the season. A lot of the pros show up for the race testing their fitness, so you get to see some good athletes. I saw a guy on a bike fly over his handlebars; he did a "face-plant" and was very bloody. He was my age. The guy got back up, took three Advil, and finished the race. That gives you a good idea of what these people do.

"Good Shape"

The Mayo Clinic gives good advice about precautions to take before beginning to exercise. Although moderate physical activity, such as brisk walking, is safe for most people, health experts suggest that you talk to your doctor before you start an exercise program.

You should also check with your doctor if you have symptoms suggestive of heart, lung or other serious disease. These symptoms include pain or discomfort in your chest, neck, jaw or arms during physical activity; dizziness; shortness of breath; ankle swelling; a heart murmur or a rapid or pronounced heartbeat; or muscle pain when walking upstairs or up a hill that goes away when you rest.

Patrick: What shape you want to achieve depends on your objectives. It may take some people a much longer time to complete the race than others, but their objectives may be making good changes in their lifestyle rather than making good time. I know people who are in much worse shape than I am, but they're out there doing it.

One of the unique things about a triathlon is that the participant's age is written in black marker on their calves. So as you're racing, you can see how old the person is that you're gaining on or who's passing you. If you're my age or older, you may feel tremendous if you pass a forty-year-old; on the other hand, you also may have someone older passing you!

Equipment and Expenses

A triathlon combines three sports: the swim, bike, and run. Some expenses and equipment are necessary, even as a beginner. As you progress in the sport, you can add to it, and it can become an expensive pursuit.

Swim

Patrick: You need to have access to open water, or at least a pool with a minimum length of twenty-five yards. Since all swims in a triathlon are in open water, the ability to access an open-water source is important; otherwise, you'll get too focused on looking at the lines in a pool. I call swimming in a triathlon "combat swimming." You need to learn to swim defensively, always keeping an arm out so you aren't kicked. You need to learn to become accustomed to water currents, temperatures, and winds.

Swimmers wear a competitive swimsuit, usually made of Lycra, goggles, and a bathing cap. You will be racing in a cap, so wearing one during practice helps you get used to it. Buy a rubber cap, not Lycra. For those people living in areas where the waters remain chilly throughout the spring and summer you may want to consider wearing a wetsuit. But before you buy, see if you can borrow. If you do buy, do not purchase a dive suit or surfing wetsuit. The material is much thicker and the suits tend to be looser-fitting. A triathlon wetsuit is light and skin-tight and allows for terrific mobility. The cost is approximately $200.

Bike

When you first begin, any bike with gears will work. In fact, many of today's Sprint races have a *fat-tire* division for those with mountain bikes or hybrids. It is important, however, to have a bike that fits your body.

Patrick: If you want to buy a bike, you can get a basic road bike good for most Sprints for under $1,000. I bought a Trek for $600. You can spend a lot of money on a bike. Some enthusiasts spend $20,000 for a bike. You also need a helmet and a computer that hooks up to your wheels to count your cadence. When training, you want to count how many strokes you're making per minute. You're trying to maximize your cadence. If you're going too slowly, you want to lighten the gear up; too fast, you need to switch to a heavier gear. Don't worry about speed.

I do recommend purchasing a couple pairs of cycling shorts for your training. Your derriere will be glad you did. You can also buy special "tri" pants that don't have as much padding, but together with a "tri" shirt, they breathe and dry fast.

If you decide to stick with this sport, you will need a pair of clip-on bike shoes. For your first race, however, you can cycle in your running shoes. Make sure the bike pedals on your bicycle do not require specific cycling shoes. If they do, you will have to make a decision: either purchase different pedals or invest in some bike shoes. If your bike does have cycling-specific pedals, I recommend having them switched out for a pair of basic pedals with a toe clip. A new pair of bike shoes can run you between $100 and $300, whereas a set of standard pedals would probably only set you back about $30. The bike shop will be able to change them out in a matter of minutes.

Water bottles and bicycle-repair equipment are needed too. Water is vital! You will need water bottles and bottle cages that attach onto your bike. At a minimum, you need to learn how to perform some repairs. Having spare equipment will do you little good if you do not know how to change a tire. Your best friend is the guy at the bike shop.

Run

Patrick: You need a good pair of running shoes. This is very important. If possible, try to purchase your first pair from a knowledgeable source. That is, someone who can look at your feet and determine what you may need. If there is a running-specific store in your area, use it even if the shoes are expensive. Once you find a pair you love, then you can order online for future pairs and save money. I go through three to four pairs of shoes per year. I track my mileage. When I get to four hundred miles, I start looking for new shoes.

It's important to wear comfortable, weather-appropriate clothing. Also, if it is sunny and hot, a good cap is a plus to shade your face. Find one made with mesh. This will allow heat from your head to pass through.

A total budget of $1,500 to $2,000 for swim, bike, and run will get you started.

How much time do you spend each week on this pursuit?

Patrick: I spend approximately fifteen hours a week on all three sports when I'm seriously training. Depending on what kind of triathlon I'm doing, I'll train to go the distance that I'm racing. The distance for a Sprint will be less than an Olympic triathlon. I run very early in the morning to avoid the Florida humidity.

For example: On Monday morning I'll run at an easy pace for fifty to sixty minutes with a fifteen minute pre/post stretch with the goal to build endurance. In the afternoon, I'll do a strength class for an hour. Tuesday is a thirty-minute easy bike ride. Wednesday morning I'll swim 2,500 yards for one and a quarter hours with the goal to improve form, then take a yoga class for one hour to increase flexibility and core strength. That afternoon is an optional easy run of thirty minutes. Thursday morning is a ninety-minute bike ride, to work on cadence. Friday morning I'll swim 2,500 yards for one and a quarter hours to work on pacing, then I'll take a yoga class for one hour. On Saturday morning, I'll do a long run for ninety minutes to build endurance and work on pacing. Saturday afternoon is an optional swim of 1,500 yards for forty-five minutes. Sunday morning is a two-hour-long bike ride, followed by a half-hour run, to work on bike-to-run transition. Total hours for the week equals approximately fourteen hours and fifteen minutes.

Do you have a special training diet?

Patrick: I try to keep a consistent diet year-round. I eat lots of carbs, fruits, and vegetables, but my calorie count goes up during peak training. Because I live in Florida, maintaining a good fluid balance is very important. So I drink a lot of water, Gatorade, and an electrolyte replacement. In addition, I have now added a daily protein shake to my diet in hopes of improving my strength. The one item I really have to watch during training is alcohol consumption—my wife and I both love wine! But as I get deeper into training I try to eliminate any alcohol during the week and just have a glass or two over the weekend.

What is the most rewarding aspect of this activity?

Patrick: Getting across the finish line in a difficult race! The first thing I sometimes say to myself is "I'll never do this again," but endurance athletes have short memories. What pulls me to sign up again and again is the team of people I coach and train with. Before I know it, we're going to do this together. We help each other and become a team during training. But when you go to a big event 90 percent of the time you're not with your training team. You're grouped according to age. I'm tentatively planning a Half-Ironman in Augusta, Georgia. If that goes well, I might try the full Monty [the Ironman].

Do you have any advice for a beginner?

Patrick: My advice is don't give up. You have to have a short memory. There are always bad days. Don't worry about it. When you have a good day, burn that in your memory bank. That's just the nature of what we do. Go on to the next day. There's always a breakthrough around the corner. Patience and persistence are great values to cultivate for a triathlete. You have to have resiliency.

FASCINATING FACTS

- An athlete who has *bonked* has reached the point where they can go no further; fatigue has taken over and exhaustion has set in.
- Sister Madonna Buder, a 71-year-old nun has completed more than 340 triathlon races.
- A recent study of 44,500 health professionals showed coronary heart disease (CHD) risk was reduced by 18% in men who walked 30 minutes per day, but men who ran for just 1 hour per week decreased their risk by 42%. The men who engaged in *any* form of vigorous exercise enjoyed a whopping 30% risk reduction. Unfit men who became fit had a 52% CHD reduction in risk.
- Half-Ironman races can also be referred to as Ironman 70.3s, with the number 70.3 representing the total mileage of the race.
- A *brick* is a workout where a bike ride is followed immediately by a run.
- If the water temperature for the swim is over 78 degrees, the USA Triathlon rules prohibit wearing a wetsuit.
- *T1* is the term used for the swim-bike transition. *T2* is the bike-run transition.

Resources

Websites

Beginner Triathlete: beginnertriathlete.com.

Find a Team In Training program near you: teamintraining.org.

IronApp is the home for triathletes on Facebook: https://www.facebook.com/IronApp.

Online Triathlon Communities: active.com; beginnertriathlete.com; or trinewbies.com.

Training programs: http://bit.ly/1tfki8Y.

USA Triathlon: usatriathlon.org.

YMCAs have triathlon training programs: ymca.net.

Apps

Beginner Triathlete: http://bit.ly/1lL8mnD.

GoSwim: http://bit.ly/1AnUSYO.

Jog Log—Couch to Marathon Training: http://bit.ly/1o54fmc.

Map My Ride (Cycling app): mapmyride.com/app.

Video

AARP Triathlon Championship: http://bit.ly/1tfkViJ.

Team In Training informational video: http://bit.ly/1l5ZvwP.

Top 10 inspiring cycling/Triathlon videos for training: http://bit.ly/WJbGu6.

Triathlon Training for Beginners: http://bit.ly/1rWbQIE.

Reading

Meredith Atwood, *Triathlon for the Every Woman: You Can Be a Triathlete. Yes. You.* (Swim Bike Mom 2012).

Dan Golding, *Triathlon for Beginners: Everything You Need to Know About Training, Nutrition, Kit, Motivation, Racing, and Much More* (GoldingTriathlon Success, 2012).

LAVA Magazine: lavamagazine.com.

Triathlete Magazine: triathletemag.com.

Notes and Sources

First-person narratives presented in *Energize Your Retirement: Stories of Passionate Pursuits* were conducted in person, on the phone, and over e-mail from September 2013 through June 2014, and edited for clarity.

In addition, I consulted a great many primary and secondary sources for this book. In order to give credit to those sources and guide a reader's further interest, I have listed my sources below in alphabetical order in in each chapter.

Introduction

A search of Amazon books was conducted on the subject of "retirement" on February 7, 2014, in which 37,424 results were found.

Bankers Life and Casualty Center for a Secure Retirement. Last modified August 2012. http://bit.ly/1o0XGkB.

Bernard, Dave. "The Baby Boomer Number Game." *US News & World Report* (blog). March 23, 2012. http://bit.ly/1rSgOX3.

Creative Commons, SA. "Baby Boomer Lead Generation, Facts and Fiction—Resources—50-Plus, Baby Boomer Marketing." Immersion Active. Last modified 2014. http://bit.ly/1kfHFMN.

Goyer, Amy. "The MetLife Report on the Oldest Boomers Healthy, Retiring Rapidly and Collecting Social Security." Met Life Mature Market Institute. http://bit.ly/1opdMcs.

Lloyd, Janice. "Key to a Healthy, Happy Retirement: Having Fun." *USA Today*, October 21, 2013. http://usat.ly/1t61p8o.

Pittman, Genevra. "Use It or Lose It? 'Cognitively Active' Lifestyle Tied to Better Memory Test Performance in Older People." *Med City News*, July 4, 2013. http://bit.ly/1pVfMHm.

Powell, Alvin. "Decoding Keys to a Healthy Life." *Harvard Gazette*, February 2, 2012.

US Department of Health and Human Services Centers for Disease Control and Prevention, *Promoting Active Lifestyles Among Older Adults* (report). Last modified 2001. http://1.usa.gov/1nqj33A.

Chapter 1: Amateur Astronomer

Arias, Tomas. "CCMR - Ask A Scientist!" Cornell Center for Materials Research. Last modified May, 2001. http://bit.ly/1AhDiWa.

Boquist, Geertsen, Hasenauer, Maisler, Randall, Torres, and Wagoner. "Urban Club - Tips." The Astronomical League. http://bit.ly/UsL9zs.

Collins English Dictionary. "Syzygy (astronomy)." In *Wikipedia, the free encyclopedia*, 2012. http://bit.ly/1rFS1Gu.

Cooper, Larry. P., C.A. Morrow, R. A. Pertzborn, J. Rosendhal, and P. Sakimoto. "Explanatory Guide to the NASA Office of Space Science Education & Public Outreach Evaluation Criteria." Space Science Institute. Last modified March, 2004. http://bit.ly/1zdHPHK.

Mann, Adam. "Amateur Astronomers Help Scientists Map Over 42 Million Stars | Science." WIRED. Last modified June 12, 2012. http://wrd.cm/UsLh1X.

Plait, Phil. "Astronomy facts: Complete archive of the daily astronomy factoid BAFacts." *Slate Magazine* (blog). http://slate.me/1kfHWPR.

Rifkin, Karen. "Astronomy for Everyone: Promoting scientific literacy at Ukiah Library." *The Ukiah Daily Journal* (Ukiah), July 30, 2013. http://bit.ly/1phqCbY.

Northwestern University. "Space Environment: What is escape velocity?" http://bit.ly/1nHCDt1.

Chapter 2: Beekeeper

"All About Bees Website: Explore the Types of Bees." http://bit.ly/1usEPIC.

Haley, Stephen. *Sugar and Sweeteners Outlook: March 2012* (report). USDA Economic Research Service, 2012. http://1.usa.gov/1l3QjZy.

Johnson, Kirk. "Scientists and Soldiers Solve a Bee Mystery." *New York Times*, October 6, 2010. http://nyti.ms/1rIkcpO.

Linnay, Jessica. "The Buzz About National Honey Bee Day." *Greener Ideal* (blog). Last modified August 19, 2013. http://bit.ly/1lI1p6P.

National Agricultural Statistics Service, Agricultural Statistics Board, US Department of Agriculture. "Honey Industry Facts, National Honey Board." Last modified March 21, 2014. http://bit.ly/1lI1p6P.

National Honey Board. "Honey Varietals." Last modified 2014. honey.com/about/about-nhb.

Seed in Context (blog). "The U.S. Department of Agriculture (USDA) and the U.S. Environmental Protection Agency (EPA) Released a Comprehensive Joint Scientific Report on Honey Bee Health on May 2, 2013." May 7, 2013. http://bit.ly/1zgTiGE.

Texas A & M AgriLife Extension. "What Is a Neonicotinoid? Insects in the City." http://bit.ly/1ntFiFy.

York County Beekeepers. "Honeybee Facts and Trivia." http://bit.ly/UuxPue.

Chapter 3: Bird Watcher and Conservationist

"Native American Indian Crane Legends, Meaning and Symbolism from the Myths of Many Tribes." Native Languages of the Americas, 2012. http://bit.ly/WWGvLv.

American Birding Association. "ABA Checklist Version 7.5." Last modified December 2013. http://bit.ly/1ro2Qec.

Answers.com. "What Does the Crane Symbolize in Korean Culture?" http://bit.ly/1AkwLtY.

Bird Watcher's Digest. "Cool Bird Facts." Last modified March 2014. http://bit.ly/1nJa6lb.

Bremner, Lynn. "Bird Watching Tips and Interesting Facts About Birds—DesertUSA." DesertUSA and Digital West Media, Inc. http://bit.ly/1nJIGNG.

National Audubon Society. "Birding Basics." Last modified 2009. http://bit.ly/1xhKQDW.

Science for Kids. "Fun Bird Facts for Kids—Interesting Information About Birds." Last modified January 24, 2014. http://bit.ly/1q1aPgn.

Sullivan, George. "White House Pets, Adapted from Facts and Fun About the Presidents." Scholastic, Inc. Last modified 1987. http://bit.ly/1k1yWh1.

Chapter 4: Habitat Restorer

American Rivers. "Fun Facts About Rivers." Last modified 2014. americanrivers.org/rivers/fun/.

BAMONA. "Butterflies and Moths of North America." Butterflies and Moths of North America. http://bit.ly/1kgVNWf.

Coulter, Lynn. "Find Out Fascinating Facts About Soil." HGTV Gardens, Scripps Network, LLC. Last modified 2014. http://bit.ly/1usFOZd.

Earthwatch. "Volunteer Opportunities, Volunteer Vacations." Earthwatch Scientific Research Expeditions. http://bit.ly/1kgVSt8.

ESchoolToday. "What Is an Ecosystem?" Last modified 2010. http://bit.ly/1tOfvJ8.

Hill, Ryan L. "Habitat Restoration." *Encyclopedia.com*. HighBeam Research Inc., 2002. http://bit.ly/1qFDk8c.

Leland, Toni. "Did You Know? Fun Facts in the Garden." Dave's Garden. Last modified October 30, 2008. http://bit.ly/1rIkI7d.

Mikula, Rick. "FAQ." The Butterfly Website. Mikula Web Solutions. Last modified May 7, 2014. http://bit.ly/WWHprB.

National Wildlife Federation. "Habitat Loss." Last modified 2014. http://bit.ly/1q1bGOa.

———. "Making Wildlife Habitat at Home." Last modified 2014. http://bit.ly/1qFDlJz.

Nature Conservancy. "About the Nature Conservancy." nature.org.

US National Park Service. "Replanting Poached Ginseng." http://1.usa.gov/1q1bNJB.

Chapter 5: Mushroom Hunter

Cairns Mushrooms, Queensland, Australia. "Healthy Fresh Mushrooms Nutritional and Mineral Information." http://bit.ly/1otIAc4.

Ivors, Kelly. "The History of Mycology in the United States." Mycological Society of San Francisco. October 2003. http://bit.ly/UuybkM.

Mateljan, George. "What's New and Beneficial About Crimini Mushrooms?" The George Mateljan Foundation. http://bit.ly/1kgW37x.

Oklahoma State University, Oklahoma 4-H Programs. "Ag Facts: Mushrooms." http://bit.ly/1xhLNfy.

O'Malley, Julia. "Secrets of the Fungi Forest." *Anchorage Daily News*, August 18, 2013. http://bit.ly/1tOg2KW.

Ratkowsky, David. "Classification of Fungi in the Age of DNA." *S.F.S.G. Newsletter* 16(5): 4–5. Last modified 2004. http://bit.ly/1AkyoYA.

School of Medicine at the University of Virginia. "The Blue Ridge Poison Center." http://bit.ly/1zgV3nf.

Stamets, Paul. *Mycelium Running: How Mushrooms Can Help Save the World*. Berkeley, CA: Ten Speed Press, 2005.

Stewart, Terra Brie. "Fungi—The Hidden Kingdom." http://bit.ly/1taguWw.

Summerfield, Robin. "Food Fans Resurrect Local Slow Food Movement." CBC News (Manitoba), November 10, 2010. http://bit.ly/UBTa4P.

Yahoo Groups. "Big D MycologyGroup." Last modified April 25, 2010. http://yhoo.it/1AkyLlL.

Chapter 6: Service Dog Trainer

Author interview with Ms. Heidi Voight, director of communications at Fidelco Guide Dog Foundation, October 1, 2013.

Adams, Kristina, and Stacy Rice. "Brief Information Resource on Assistance Animals for the Disabled." Animal Welfare Information Center, National Agricultural Library, United States Department of Agriculture. Last modified September 19, 2011. http://1.usa.gov/1xhMR3a.

Answers.com. "Guide Dogs Frequently Asked Questions." http://bit.ly/1k1zrHL.

Dalziel, D. J., et al. "Seizure-Alert Dogs: A Review And Preliminary Study." *Seizure European Journal of Epilepsy*. Last modified March 2003. http://bit.ly/1rU0WmJ.

Fidelco Guide Dog Foundation, Inc. "Fidelco FAQs." Last modified June 2013. http://bit.ly/1mQKRco.

Guide Dogs for the Blind. "Guide Dog Breeding and Whelping." Last modified 2014. http://bit.ly/1lI3iAl.

Pet Assure. "50 Fascinating Facts About Dogs." http://bit.ly/1rU12en.

Please Don't Pet Me. "What Is a Service Dog?" Last modified February 14, 2014. http://bit.ly/1lI3nEc.

The Dog Fact Information Center. "101 Amazing Dog Facts." Last modified 2013. http://bit.ly/WIpchw.

US Department of Justice, Civil Rights Division, Disability Rights

Section. "Commonly Asked Questions About Service Animals in Places of Business." ADA.gov homepage. Last modified January 14, 2008. http://1.usa.gov/1nJcUPl.

Chapter 7: Calligrapher

Adams, Henry. "A Tribute to a Great Artist." Smithsonian. Last modified October 6, 2001. http://bit.ly/1qFDFYG.

Calligraphy for Beginners. "Calligraphy for Beginners." Last modified March 23, 2012. http://bit.ly/1tOgFUW.

Canada Tibet Committee. "Longest Calligraphy Scroll: Jamyang Dorjee Chakrishar Sets World Record." Last modified August 4, 2010. http://bit.ly/1AkzvYn.

H. Child, "Calligraphy Today"; D. Miner, ed., "2,000 Years of Calligraphy"; A. Baker, "Calligraphy"; P. Standard, "Calligraphy's Flowering, Decay, and Restoration"; Z. Ouyang and W. C. Fong, "Chinese Calligraphy" In Calderhead, C., and H. Cohen, eds., "The World Encyclopedia of Calligraphy" and "Calligraphy." All available at TheFreeDictionary.com. Columbia University Press, 2013. http://bit.ly/1otK2vk.

International Association of Master Penmen, Engrossers and Teachers of Handwriting. "Engrossing and Illumination." http://bit.ly/1q1ewmh.

Kvernen, Elisabeth. "An Introduction to Arabic, Ottoman & Persian Calligraphy." 2009. http://bit.ly/1xhNMQZ.

Manohar Vitthal Desai. In *International Exhibition of Calligraphy*. Moscow: Contemporary Museum of Calligraphy. http://bit.ly/1ppKQgZ.

Saint John's Abbey. "The Saint John's Bible." Last modified 2014. http://bit.ly/1l3SigF.

Vitolo, Dr. Joseph M. "Script in the Copperplate Style." Zanerian College, Columbus, Ohio. http://bit.ly/1pjnZXb.

Chapter 8: Crossword Puzzle Constructor

Bellis, Mary. "Arthur Wynne—History of Crossword Puzzles." About.com Inventors. Last modified 2014. http://abt.cm/1tOh1L9.

Collins, Nick. "Why Some People Are Amazing at Crossword Puzzles." *Business Insider.* September 10, 2013. http://read.bi/1ntHXPN.

Courtland, Jindra. "Wordplay: Why Are Crossword Puzzles so Popular?" *Yahoo Contributor Network* (blog). June 25, 2006. http://yhoo.it/1o2Xod3.

Cruciverb. "Crossword Software." http://bit.ly/X6fV2J.

Frater, Jamie. "25 English Language Oddities." *Listverse* (blog). December 3, 2007. http://bit.ly/1rIlEsd.

Leggett, Tabatha. "15 Fascinating Facts About Crosswords." *BuzzFeed* (blog). September 4, 2013. http://bzfd.it/1ntI3XI.

Shortz, Will. "A Philosopher of Puzzles." Last modified 2012. http://bit.ly/1ro669x.

Snyder, Thomas. "Dr. Sudoku Prescribes: A Modest Proposal." *WIRED.* Last modified January 9, 2012. http://wrd.cm/1l3SBIj.

Stoddard, Samuel. "Fun with Words: Numbers." *RinkWorks* (blog). 2014. http://bit.ly/1ro6d54.

Wordplay. Directed by Patrick Creadon. Featuring Will Shortz, Jon Stewart, and Ken Burns. 2006. DVD.

Chapter 9: Magician

Jones, Chris. "The Honor System." *Esquire* (Digital Edition), August 7, 2012. http://bit.ly/1tOhjSe.

Mail Online. "Now That Really Is Quite Interesting: The Answers to Questions You Thought You'd Never Ask." Last modified November 3, 2012. http://dailym.ai/1otLnCh.

Sanders, Dal. "The Society of American Magicians—SAM." Last

modified 2014. http://bit.ly/1rU1Pvz.

Teller Speaks! YouTube. January 29, 2008 http://bit.ly/1nJenoO.

The Magic Academy of Australia. "Interesting Facts About Magic." http://bit.ly/WWL2NW.

White, Jack. "History: A Proud Heritage, Starting in 1922." The International Brotherhood of Magicians. http://bit.ly/UBUl4a.

Chapter 10: Performing Arts Usher

Americans for the Arts. "National Findings: Economic Impact of the Nonprofit Arts & Culture Industry" (report). http://bit.ly/1tanDWS.

Dirda, Michael. "'The Ninth: Beethoven and the World of 1824,' by Harvey Sachs" (book review). *The Washington Post,* June 17, 2010. http://wapo.st/1AkEqZ4.

Green, Aaron. "What Is the Longest Opera?" About.com Classical Music. http://abt.cm/1zh0VNk.

Lincoln Center. "Overview and History." 2014. http://bit.ly/UBXeCa.

San Francisco Ballet. "History: San Francisco Ballet." Last modified 2014. http://bit.ly/UuB7hj.

Chapter 12: Stone Sculptor

Antonova, Irina. "Gina and Her Sculptures." Gina Lollobrigida Sito Ufficiale. Last modified 2011. http://bit.ly/1mQPgvX.

Barton, Eleanor Dodge. "The History of Sculpture from *The New Book of Knowledge.*" http://bit.ly/1robrh1.

Custom Stonecarving. "Tallest Statue in the World." *Biggest Stuff* (blog). http://bit.ly/1qFEOzj.

de Young Museum. "About the de Young." http://bit.ly/1otSZEX.

Giacometti Sculpture 'L'Homme qui marche I' Fetches $104.3 Million, World Record: Sotheby's." *The Huffington Post*, April 5, 2010. http://huff.to/1pjpXqE.

King, Hobart. "Mohs Hardness Scale: Testing the Resistance to Being Scratched." Geology.com. Last modified 2014. http://bit.ly/1kgYl6L.

Legion of Honor. "History of the Legion of Honor." http://bit.ly/WIqLMg.

Murray, Monika. "10 Interesting Art Facts." *Monika Murray's Artistic Affairs* (blog). April 13, 2011. http://bit.ly/1k1BLys.

The J. Paul Getty Museum. "About Sculpture in Western Art." http://bit.ly/1AkEVTb.

Chapter 13: Disaster-Response Worker

American Red Cross. "Disaster Relief at a Glance." http://rdcrss.org/1ntMAt7.

———. "A Brief History of the American Red Cross." http://rdcrss.org/1lI8gNp.

Emergency Management Institute. "IS-288: The Role of Voluntary Agencies in Emergency Management." National Preparedness Directorate National Training and Education Portal. http://1.usa.gov/1rU50U3.

Mixner, David. "Ten Most Expensive Disasters in United States History." *DavidMixner.com—Live From Hell's Kitchen* (blog). August 10, 2013. http://bit.ly/WWQLU8.

Chapter 14: Medicare Counselor

Federal Bureau of Investigation. "FBI — Health Care Fraud, Rooting Out Health Care Fraud Is Central to the Well-Being of Both Our Citizens and the Overall Economy." http://1.usa.gov/1usOX41.

Medicare. "Ask Medicare." http://1.usa.gov/1otU4wd.

MMAP, Inc. "Assistance with Medicare." Last modified 2013. http://bit.ly/1ppRHHg.

———. *Medicare Advocate Volunteer Brochure*. (Michigan: Michigan Medicare Assistance Program IMMAP, 2014). http://bit.ly/1l3VTes.

Seniors Resource Guide. "Find Your State's State Health Insurance Assistance Program (SHIP)." Last modified 2014. http://bit.ly/1rIowp1.

Chapter 15: National Park Volunteer

US National Park Service. "Bighorn Sheep—Rocky Mountain National Park." Last modified April 2, 2014. http://1.usa.gov/1rIoxtf.

———. "Forest Health: Mountain Pine Beetle—Rocky Mountain National Park." Last modified May 2, 2014. http://1.usa.gov/1nJlA8h.

———. "Frequently Asked Questions." Last modified April 31, 2013. http://1.usa.gov/1lI8ILL.

———."National Park Service Press Releases." Last modified April 3, 2013. http://bit.ly/1pjqn01.

National Parks Conservation Association. "Parks in Jeopardy." Last modified September 2012. http://bit.ly/1nJO5EG.

Chapter 16: Nonprofit Board Director

BoardSource. "Nonprofit Board Statistics" (report). Bohse and Associates Inc. Last modified 2007. http://bit.ly/1tapvP7.

Bureau of Labor Statistics. "Volunteering in the United States, 2013." http://1.usa.gov/1ppSrw5.

Cisco Systems Inc. "Nonprofit Board Orientation." Cisco 2009. http://bit.ly/1otV2bP.

Giving USA Foundation. "Charitable Giving Statistics." National Philanthropic Trust. Last modified 2013. http://bit.ly/1nJm4eR.

NCCS Core 2012 Public Charities File. "Display Largest Public Charities." http://urbn.is/1rodamG.

Smith, Robert. "Buffett Gift Sends $31 Billion to Gates Foundation." NPR. Last modified June 26, 2006. http://n.pr/1k1C6RW.

The Chronicle of Philanthropy. "A Look at the 50 Most Generous Donors of 2013." Last modified February 9, 2014. http://bit.ly/1mQQFT7.

———. "Sharing the Wealth: How the States Stack Up in Giving." Last modified August 19, 2012. http://bit.ly/1nJOkPU.

US Office of Personnel Management. "Combined Federal Campaign (CFC)." Last modified 2014. http://1.usa.gov/1rIoMo1.

Vermeulen, Greg. "10 Questions to Ask Before Joining a Nonprofit Board." *The Huffington Post*, August 23, 2013. http://huff.to/1zh337G.

Chapter 17: Ombudsman

Administration on Aging. "Long-Term Care Ombudsman Program." http://1.usa.gov/1nJOreu.

Duggan, Maeve, and Aaron Smith. "Social Media Update 2013." Pew Research Center's Internet & American Life Project. Last modified December 30, 2013. http://bit.ly/1mQQRBL.

Hobbs, Frank B., and Bonnie L. Damon. *65+ in the United States*. US Bureau of the Census. Current Population Reports, Special Studies, 1996. http://1.usa.gov/1rIoPAg.

Miller, Mark C. "Volunteer Consultants: Extending the Reach of Ombudsman Programs." National Long-Term Care Ombudsman Resource Center. Last modified May 2003. http://bit.ly/1l3WxsF.

Ombudsman Services of Contra Costa. "Ombudsman Services." http://bit.ly/1nJn42w.

Social Security Administration. *Top names of the 1920s*. Last modified 2013. http://1.usa.gov/1q1qJau.

The Center for Brain Health. "Study Finds Aerobic Exercise Improves Memory, Brain Function and Physical Fitness." *Center for BrainHealth* (blog). November 12, 2013. http://bit.ly/1rKkTxg.

US Department of Health and Human Services, Administration on Aging. "Long-Term Care Ombudsman Program." Washington DC, 2011. http://1.usa.gov/1l3WOeZ.

Wegerer, Jennifer. "Oldest Oscar Nominees and Oldest Academy Award Winners." Senior Living News and Trends. Last modified February 27, 2014. http://bit.ly/1taqT4k.

Chapter 18: Youth Mentor

Center for Addiction and Mental Health. "Youth Mentoring Linked to Many Positive Effects, New Study Shows." *Science Daily*, January 15, 2013. http://bit.ly/1rKlM9d.

Corporation for National and Community Service. "Foster Grandparents." http://1.usa.gov/WWTJbd.

Freedman, Marc. *Prime Time: How Baby Boomers Will Revolutionize Retirement And Transform America.* (New York: Public Affairs, 2008).

National Mentoring Partnership. "The Value of Mentoring." Mentor. http://bit.ly/1zh4seq.

Scholastic. "Facts about Kids and Reading." http://bit.ly/1kgZgEi.

US Department of Education. "Fast Facts: English Language Learners." National Center for Education Statistics (NCES). Last modified 2011. http://1.usa.gov/1roeXIa.

Chapter 19: Blogger/Vlogger

Admin Solutions Mobile Web Design Company. "Interesting Facts About Blogs from Hubspot." Last modified May 31, 2012. http://bit.ly/1nJPfQq.

Anderson, Kelly. "7 Ways to Make Money from Blogging." *Mint-Life Blog Personal Finance News & Advice* (blog). May 23, 2013. http://bit.ly/1rU6DBl.

Conor, John. "Top Blogging Platforms on the Internet." *Blogging Tips* (blog). August 13, 2013. http://bit.ly/UuCxbw.

Dunlop, Michael. "Top-Earning Blogs." *Income Diary* (blog). http://bit.ly/1l3XpgE.

Fishkin, Rand. "21 Tactics to Increase Blog Traffic." *Moz* (blog). January 17, 2012. http://bit.ly/1pjrbCc.

Fun Trivia Quizzes. "Toy Soldiers—Fun Facts, Questions, Answers, Information." http://bit.ly/UBZSaS.

Jarboe, Greg. "60 Hours of Video Is Now Uploaded to YouTube Every Minute." Reel SEO. Last modified January 23, 2012. http://bit.ly/1lIaHzG.

Karr, Douglas. "Infographic: The Blogconomy Blogging Statistics." *Marketing Technology* (blog). Last modified August 25, 2013. http://bit.ly/1l3XxwO.

Nielsen. "Buzz in the Blogosphere: Millions More Bloggers and Blog Readers." Last modified March 8, 2012. http://bit.ly/1pjrflr.

SeniorsForLiving. "Top 100 Senior Blogs & Web Sites." http://bit.ly/UC03mG.

Sniderman, Zachary. "7 YouTube Alternatives & Why They Make Sense." Mashable. Last modified April 11, 2011. http://on.mash.to/1xhYMhv.

The Toy Soldier Company. "A Brief History of Toy Soldiers from the Toy Soldier Company." http://bit.ly/1zh5pDq.

YouTube. "Statistics." http://bit.ly/WIruNM.

Zern, James. "Official Blog: Mmm mmm Good Videos Now Served in WebM." YouTube Official Blog. April 2011. http://bit.ly/1rofREG.

Chapter 20: Craft Beer Homebrewer

Al. "Fun Facts About Beer!" Blue Pants Brewery. Last modified June 8, 2013. http://bit.ly/WIrFse.

American Homebrewers Association. "American Brewing History." Last modified 2014. http://bit.ly/1AkIAQG.

Beer Drinkers of Wisconsin. "Fun Beer Facts." Last modified 2012. http://bit.ly/1roh8LR.

Grayson. "24 Fun Facts About Beer." *Daily Infographic* (blog). April 1, 2013. http://bit.ly/1kgZRFX.

Hieronymus, Stan. "History of Beer | Timeline." CraftBeer.com. http://bit.ly/1tOo3zB.

Inman, Mathew. "20 Things Worth Knowing About Beer." The Oatmeal. Last modified 2014. http://bit.ly/1zh6GdG.

KegWorks. "13 Fascinating Beer Facts." http://bit.ly/1mQTkfI.

Nason, Adam. "American Homebrewers Association Estimates 1 Million Homebrewers in U.S." Beerpulse. Last modified February 15, 2012. http://bit.ly/1usUcRt.

OMG Facts. "8 Mind-Blowing Facts About Beer." Last modified March 29, 2012. http://bit.ly/1q1w95s.

Richard. "What Is the Difference Between an Ale and a Lager?" *Beer-FAQ* (blog). September 4, 2007. http://bit.ly/1kgZVWh.

The Kegman. "Beer Classification 101: There's a Beer for Everyone." *The Official Blog of the Kegman* (blog). February 15, 2012. http://bit.ly/1q1wipx.

Chapter 21: Ham Radio Operator

American Radio Relay League (ARRL). "2012 Continues to Show Growth in Amateur Radio Licensing." http://bit.ly/1AkJ49z.

Carver, Hanby. "Floods and Wireless." *Technical World,* August 1915, 806–07, http://bit.ly/1tOomul.

Edison Museum (Beaumont, TX). "Edison Files: Edison's Two Families." http://bit.ly/1o36juX.

Harker, Ken. "A Study of Amateur Radio Gender Demographics." American Radio Relay League. Last modified March 15, 2005. http://bit.ly/1ntRGpl.

Maxwell, W6CF, Jim. "Amateur Radio: 100 Years of Discovery." American Radio Relay League, Inc. Last modified 2010. http://bit.ly/1qFGf0I.

N2GJ, and W2SG. "Famous Hams and ex-Hams." Tellurian Networks. http://bit.ly/UC1mlD.

NASA. "Amateur Radio on the International Space Station." http://1.usa.gov/1ntRMwU.

Nelson, Patrick. "Why Ham Radio Is Still Handy." *Tech News World*, August 8, 2012. http://bit.ly/1mQTVOf.

Tate, John D. "Proper Phonetics!" eHam.net. Last modified May 14, 2009. http://bit.ly/1AkJn4f.

Chapter 22: Motorcyclist

American Motorcyclist Association. "What Type of Bike Is Right for You?" Last modified 2013. http://bit.ly/1nJtOgX.

Iron Butt Association. "The Iron Butt Rally." Last modified April 25, 2014. http://bit.ly/1o37t9L.

Johnson, Robert. "When Heaven Is a Harley: The 50-Plus Crowd Is Having a Belated Romance with Motorcycles." *Wall Street Journal*, December 19, 2011. http://on.wsj.com/WWYJwp.

Libaw, Oliver. "Baby Boomers Put the Vroom in Motorcycles." ABC News. Last modified June 17, 2014. http://abcn.ws/1rU9bzn.

Motorcycle Industry Council. "Motorcycling in America Goes Mainstream Says 2008 Motorcycle Industry Council Owner Survey." Last modified May 18, 2009. http://bit.ly/1tOq12O.

Newsquest (London) Ltd. "10 Motorcycle Facts to Mark Anniversary of First Ever Motorbike Race." News Shopper. Last modified November 2013. http://bit.ly/1rKrlo4.

O'Connor, Colleen. "New Documentary: Women Motorcycle Riders a Fast-Growing Trend." *Denver Post*, November 24, 2013. http://dpo.st/1rKrrvS.

PF Motorcycle Salvage. "Fun Bike Facts." Last modified 2014. http://bit.ly/1zh8WSi.

Template, Johnny. "10 Amazing Facts About Harley Davidson Motorcycles." What D Facts? Last modified 2012. http://bit.ly/1ou4hc4.

Chapter 23: RV Traveler

"Celebrities Love Their Airstreams." YouTube http://bit.ly/UC2DZW.

Airstream, Inc. "Airstream, Inc.: History." http://bit.ly/1rok7Ea.

Beckley's Camping Center. "15 Fun RV Facts and Figures." Last modified September 21, 2013. http://bit.ly/1ou4uMu.

Official Amish Country Visitors Guide. "RV Travel in Elkhart County, Northern Indiana." http://bit.ly/1l4075W.

Parade. "Top 5 RV Destinations." http://bit.ly/1nJv4k4.

Phoenix RV Park. "Interesting RV Facts You May Not Have Known." http://bit.ly/1l40a1v.

Porges, Seth. "6 Things You Didn't Know About Airstream Trailers." *Forbes*. May 29, 2013. http://onforb.es/1nJv7wf.

The Recreation Vehicle Industry Association. "RVIA Main Site Home." Last modified November 15, 2013. http://bit.ly/1l40fST.

WBCCI.org. "History About WBCCI." Last modified September 17, 2012. http://bit.ly/1mQVETH.

White, Carolyn. "Vintage Airstream Trailers and Modern Owners Keep Dream Alive." ThurstonTalk. http://bit.ly/1nJvpDn.

Chapter 24: Woodturner

Arcadesj. "Zinzulation." *Urban Dictionary*. Last modified September 13, 2011. http://bit.ly/1q1BbyL.

American Association of Woodturners. "Background." Last modified 2014. http://bit.ly/1tayeRF.

eBay. "A Beginner's Guide to Woodturning." Last modified August 20, 2013. http://bit.ly/1ntU4w4.

Gaude, Henry. "What Is a Wood Turning Lathe?" wiseGEEK. Last modified June 2, 2014. http://bit.ly/1nJS7N6.

Lloyd, John, John Mitchinson, and James Harkin. *1,227 Quite Interesting Facts to Blow Your Socks Off*. New York: W. W. Norton & Company, 2013.

Scarpulla, Gary. "History of Woodturning." Woodturning Gallery and Ornamental Woodturning Gallery. Last modified June 3, 2014. http://bit.ly/1qFH1uQ.

Chapter 25: Backpacker

Lemon, Candi. "Top Five Famous Trails in the U.S." http://bit.ly/1rq9dhc.

Pacific Crest Trail Association. "Media Fact Sheet." Last modified 2014. http://bit.ly/1rJaT93.

Peakbagger. "Idaho Twelvers." Last modified October 25, 2011. http://bit.ly/1rMtqQh.

Stephens, Mark. "Did You Know? 20 Fascinating Hiking Facts." *Adventure Parents* (blog). Last modified July 19, 2012. http://bit.ly/1k2cZyn.

Stevenson, Jason. "The Wrong Way: Top 52 Hiker Mistakes." *Backpacker Magazine*. Last modified March 2011. http://bit.ly/1l4WNrd.

US National Park Service. "National Trails System: Visit the Trails." Last modified February 24, 2014. http://1.usa.gov/1rMtFL9.

Chapter 26: Dancer

AARP. "The Healing Powers of Dance." http://bit.ly/1khwSBX.

Abrook, Paul. "Paul's Dance Quiz." Paul's Quiz, Freiburg Germany. http://bit.ly/1pkfawj.

Dance Steps. "Popular Dance Styles and Dance Genres." http://bit.ly/1nvuIxX.

Fun Trivia Quizzes. "Dance—Fun Facts and Information." http://bit.ly/WYTtse.

Madrone, Eli. "Dancing Your Way to Health." *Examiner*, August 9, 2013. http://exm.nr/UD3LMN.

SalsaCrazy. "A Salsa Dancing Guide for Women: 19 Easy Ways to Attract More Men to Dance with You." http://bit.ly/1q46Yz0.

Sowerbutts, Elisabeth. "Important Facts About Dancing." *EzineArticles.com*, http://bit.ly/1lJyNtO.

The Art of Dance. "Fun Facts About Dance!" http://bit.ly/WYTJrl.

"Top 10 Facts About Dance." *Express* (UK), April 29, 2013. http://dexpr.es/1owd79e.

Tucker, Ian. "Peter Lovatt: 'Dancing Can Change the Way You Think.'" *The Guardian*, July 30, 2011. http://bit.ly/1rJbhVf.

Chapter 27: Softball Player

10 Facts About. "10 Facts About Softball." Last modified 2010. http://bit.ly/1xk6JCN.

AARP. "Senior Softball Players Athletes Compete in the Winter National Championships in Fort Myers, Florida." *AARP Bulletin*, November 11, 2009. http://bit.ly/1q47FIK.

Eastvale Girls Softball Association. "Softball Fun Facts!" Last modified 2014. http://bit.ly/1mRZxrI.

Fun Trivia Quizzes. "USA Softball—Untimed Quiz." Last modified January 1, 2012. http://bit.ly/1tcDxjl.

Senior Softball. "Senior Softball-USA." http://bit.ly/UD4LAu.

Team USA. "USA Softball." http://bit.ly/1rMw6NU.

Chapter 28: Target Shooter

Freeman, Clayton. "Outside: Barrels of Fun at Jacksonville Skeet and Trap Club." *The Florida Times Union*, January 27, 2014. http://bit.ly/WINMyK.

Fun Trivia Quizzes. "Skeet Shooting." http://bit.ly/1ziMfNC.

Hobby Helper. "How to Shoot Skeet." Last modified 2010. http://bit.ly/1tcF3BX.

Lauten, Ryan. "World Record Clay Shoot Trailer." *YouTube*. January 27, 2013. http://bit.ly/1tcFa0w.

PBS. "Gun Timeline." *History Detectives*, PBS. http://to.pbs.org/1tcFe0d.

Statista. "Participants in Target Shooting in the U.S. 2006–2012." Last modified 2012. http://bit.ly/1ziMpEC.

USA Shooting. "History of USAS." Last modified 2014. http://bit.ly/1nKNVga.

Chapter 29: Triathlete

Fitzgerald, Matt. "Transition Workouts: When to Run After a Ride." Active.com. http://bit.ly/1qGdroN.

Kent, Hazen. "Thinking About Doing a TRI?" Tri-Newbies Online. Last modified 2011. http://bit.ly/WYWdWv.

Quinn, Elizabeth. "The Bonk During Exercise." About.com, Sports Medicine. Last modified April 10, 2013. http://abt.cm/1tPOnJB.

Squillace, Mary. "10 People over 70 Who Are Fitter Than You." Fitbie. Last modified 2014. http://bit.ly/1rMwVpP.

Total Triathlon. "Triathlon Distances." Last modified 2014. http://bit.ly/WINTKI.

USA Triathlon. "Demographics." Last modified April 2013. http://bit.ly/1rqdUHN.

———. "Swim Conduct: Wetsuits." Last modified 2014. http://bit.ly/1rV5rNY.

Acknowledgements

I pitched the idea for this book to my former boss, Doug Covey, over a hamburger and a beer in a Phoenix restaurant. Doug was wildly enthusiastic and I deeply thank him for his unwavering belief and support in me throughout this project.

My special thanks to each one of the talented and engaging interviewees who told their stories and generated the energizing spirit of this book. I thank them for their time, enthusiastic support, and the camaraderie that fueled my progress throughout this publishing journey.

It doesn't matter if you rock with the Stones, or roll with the Beatles, we can all agree Ringo had it right when he sang, "I get by with a little help from my friends." A special tribute to my friends who volunteered their talents and generously gave their time. Thanks to Carol and Joe Anesko for their comments and critique. Thanks also to Pat Rodriguez for her dedication and her knowledgeable language skills that sharpened the focus and delivery of this book. A special thank-you to polymath Bob Risedorph for his continuous support and masterful insight on what constitutes a good read.

My gratitude to Barbara Aronica for creating a dynamic book cover that captures the spirit of this book. Thank you to Sue Balcer of JustYourType.biz for her wonderful layout design work. Finally, thank you to Rachelle Mandik, equal parts advisor, counselor, and mechanic, whose skillful editing brought out the very best in my work. Together, these people were indispensable in helping me to create this compilation.

Index

A

A Year in the Life of a Beekeeper, 25, 32

AARP TriUmph Classic, 346

ABA Checklist, 40, 361

ABCs (and Ds) of Medicare, 171

Adler, Stella, 123

Administration on Aging, 216, 370–71

Aesop, 207

Affordable Care Act, 172, 177

Airstream
- caravans, 278
- company, 277–78
- costs, 282

Amateur Radio Relay League (ARRL), 261

Amateur Softball Association (ASA), 323, 332

Amateur Trap Shooting Association, 342

Amazon
- associates program, 232
- book distribution, 133
- retirement books, 1

America's Got Talent, 119

America's Promise, 224–25

American Association of Retired Persons (AARP), 180–81, 346, 357, 376–77

American Association of Variable Star Observers, 19

American Association of Woodturning, 288

American Beekeeping Federation, 31

American Bird Conservancy, 39, 41

American Birding Association (ABA), 33, 40, 44, 361

American Brewers Guild, 249

American Hiking Society, 308

American Homebrewers Association (AHA), 241, 246, 249–50,372–73

American Motorcycle Association, 269

American Red Cross, 160, 169–70, 252, 368

American Rivers, 55

Anderson, Kelly, 232, 371

Angelou, Maya, 195

Apiculture, 23

App Resources
- Amateur astronomer, 21
- Backpacker, 308
- Birdwatcher, 44
- Blogger, 238
- Calligrapher, 97
- Craft beer homebrewer, 250
- Crossword puzzle constructor, 109
- Dancer, 321
- Disaster volunteer, 170
- Fiction writer, 143
- Motorcyclist, 275
- Mushroom hunter, 69
- National park volunteering, 192
- Performing arts usher, 131
- RV traveler, 286
- Softball player, 332
- Stone sculptor, 155
- Target shooter, 343
- Triathlete, 357
- Vlogger, 239

Asian calligraphy, 87

Assisted–living facilities, 207–08, 210, 213

AstroAlert service, 19

Astronomical League, 11, 17, 20, 360

Astrophotography, 18, 20–21

B

Baby boomer statistics, 2

Backpacking, premier spots in the United States, 309

Ballet, 127, 130–31, 311, 367

BAMONA, Butterflies and Moths of North America, 55, 58, 362

Bankers Life and Casualty, 5, 359

Barker, Bob, 121, 171
Bee Culture magazine, 24, 31–32
Beer
classification and style, 245, 373
production, 245–246
Berra, Yogi, 323
Beetle, mountain pine, 190, 369
Bighorn sheep, 185, 190, 369
Binoculars
Amateur astronomer, 14
Birdwatcher, 38
Bird conservation, 34
Blackgunners, 340
BMW Million Miler Club, 364
BoardSource, 196, 198, 200, 203, 205–06
Boys and Girls Clubs of America, 224
Brew clubs, 246
Brewers Association, 245, 249
Brokaw, Tom, 102
Buffett, Jimmy, 1
Bureau of Labor Statistics, 195, 369
Bush, President George W., 172
Byam, Wally, 277–78

C

Calligraphic styles, 87
Carlin, George, 277
Carrara marble, 150, 152
Cascade Mycological Society, 61–62
Catholic Charities, 160, 169
Centers for Disease Control and Prevention (CDC), 4, 360
Central New England Woodturners, 288, 295
Certified Wildlife Habitat Program, 49, 51, 58
Charlie Elliott Astronomy Club, 13, 16
Christian Service Charities, 197
Christmas Bird Count (CBC), 42, 45
Cisco Corporation, 203, 205, 369
Citizen Science, 41, 45
Classes
Beer homebrewing, 249
Dance, 312, 321
Fiction writing, 143
Stone sculpting 154
Target shooting, 342
Woodturning, 295
Clinton, President Bill, 103, 106
Clothing, special
Backpacker, 302
Beekeeper, 28
Dancer, 316–17
Magician, 118
Motorcyclist, 271–72
National park volunteer, 188–89
Performing arts usher, 126
Softball player, 328
Target shooter, 337
Triathlete, 352–54
Woodturner, 292
Clues, creating crossword puzzle, 104
Colleagues of Calligraphy Guild, 91, 94
Colony collapse disorder, 30, 32
Community Emergency Response Teams (CERT), 160, 170
Convergent thinking, 319
Convoy of Hope, 160
Copperplate calligraphy, 88, 92, 98, 365
Cornell Lab of Ornithology, 40, 42, 44
Corporation for National and Community Service (CNCS), 174, 217, 223, 225, 371
Coubertin, Baron Pierre de, 334
Crane symbolism, 36, 362
Cruciverb.com, 104, 108, 366
Cruciverbalist, 99

D

Dance, choosing your dance style, 312
Day, Mrs. Geraldine, 330
de Young Museum, 147, 367
Dexterity in magic, 115
Disaster
Action Team (DAT) 162
deployment, 163

Hurricane Sandy, 164–65
North Dakota flood, 166–67
Services, 160–61
Divergent thinking, 319
Dutch Observatory, 16, 20

E

Earning money from your blog, 232
Earp, Wyatt, 333
Earthwatch, 40, 44, 56, 362
Engrosser, 90
Equipment
Amateur astronomer, 14
Backpacker, 303–05
Beekeeper, 28
Birdwatcher, 38
Blogger, 232
Calligrapher, 92–93
Craft beer homebrewer, 243–44
Crossword puzzle constructor, 103, 105
Dancer, 216–217
Fiction writer, 140
Habitat restorer, 53
Ham radio operator, 257–58
Magician, 118
Motorcyclist, 268–71
Mushroom hunter, 64
National park volunteer, 188–89
RV traveler, 281–82
Service dog trainer, 76–77
Softball player, 328
Stone sculptor, 149
Target shooter, 337–39
Triathlete, 351–54
Vlogger, 233
Woodturner, 290–91
Esquire magazine, 111, 366

F

Farrar, Margaret, 102
Fascinating Facts
Amateur astronomer, 20
Backpacker, 307
Beekeeper, 31
Birdwatcher, 43
Blogger/Vlogger, 237
Calligrapher, 96
Craft beer homebrewer, 248
Crossword puzzle constructor, 108
Dancer, 320
Disaster volunteer, 169
Fiction writer, 142
Habitat restorer, 57
Ham radio operator, 231
Magician, 121
Medicare counselor, 180
Motorcyclist, 274
Mushroom hunter, 68
National park volunteer, 191
Nonprofit board director, 204
Ombudsman for elder care, 215
Performing arts usher, 130
RV traveler, 285
Service dog trainer, 81
Softball player, 331
Stone sculptor, 154
Target shooter, 342
Triathlete, 356
Woodturner, 294
Youth mentor, 225
Federal Communications Commission (FCC), 254, 256
Fidelco Guide Dog Foundation, 73–74, 76, 78–80, 82–83, 364
Fine, Dr. Philip, 101
Finlay, Trevor, 263
Foster Grandparent Program, 217–19, 222–23, 226
Freedman, Marc, 218, 223, 226, 371
Fugate, The Hon. W. Craig, 251
Fungi, 59, 62, 68–70, 363–64
Fungus festivals, 67–68

G

Galax, 50
Garden habitat restoration, 50–51
GEARS program, 273
Gibran, Khalil, 23
Ginseng, 49–50

Global positioning system (GPS), 64, 155, 304–5
Google AdSense, 232
Google Analytics, 232, 235, 237
Graham, Martha, 311
Great Backyard Bird Count, 42, 45
Great Smoky Mountain National Park, 50, 191
Growth of craft brewing, 241
Guide dog, 72, 79–81, 83, 364

H

Habitat
  cover, 52
  food sources, 51
  loss, 34, 47, 363
  places to raise young, 52
  restoration, 48
  water supply, 51
Habitat for Humanity, 160, 170
Half Ironman, 346
Ham radio
  call sign, 256
  "Elmer," 254
  emergency response, 252
  global reach, 251
  regulations and licenses, 254–55
Harley–Davidson, 263, 271, 274–75, 374
Harvard Study of Adult Development, 4
Hawkins, Margaret, 346
Health
  care, 172
  insurance, 173
  maintaining, 4, 215, 318, 356
Health benefits of dancing, 318
Hennessy, Terry, 324
Hill Museum & Manuscript Library, 95, 98
Honey, 26–27, 31, 361
Huffington Post, 202, 237, 368, 370

I

Idaho Hiking Club, 305
Idaho's *Twelvers,* 306, 376
Identity loss in retirement, 3–4
Illumination, art of, 90, 94–95, 97, 365
Indian calligraphy, 88
International Association of Master Penmen, Engrossers and Teachers of Handwriting (IAMPETH), 90, 97
International Brotherhood of Magicians, 114, 121, 367
International Crane Foundation (ICF), 36–37
Iron Butt Rally, 267–68, 275, 374
Ironman, 346
Islamic calligraphy, 88

J

Jackson, Donald, 95
Jobs, Steve, 87
Johnson, President Lyndon Baines, 159
Johnson, Robert, 263, 374
Jones, Chris, 111, 366
Journal of Aging and Physical Activity, 318

K

Koch, Jim, 241

L

Legion of Honor, 146–47, 368
Leukemia & Lymphoma Society's (LLS), 346, 348–49
Life list, *See* ABA checklist
Lovatt, Dr. Peter, 319, 377
Lowell Observatory, 19, 22
Lutheran Disaster Response, 160, 170

M

Madrone, Eli, 318, 376
Magic by Bill, 122
Magic Café, 116, 122
Mandela, Nelson, 217
Maquettte, 151
Mayo Clinic, 351
Medicare

fraud, 177–78, 181
program, 171–172, 180–81, 211
MetLife Mature Market Institute, 2–3, 359
Michelangelo, 150, 154
Michigan Medicare Medicaid Assistance Program (MMAP), 173, 180, 368–369
Mind of the Triathlete, 350
Mint.com, 232
Mohs hardness scale, 150, 368
Morse code, 253–54
Motorcycle
endurance trips, 267
types, 269–70
Motorcycle Industry Council, 263, 374
Motorcycle rallies, 275
Muir, John, 33
Mullins, Sasha, 263
Museums, famous calligraphy, 98
Mushroom
myths, 60
toxins, 65
varieties, 66
Mycelium Running: How Mushrooms Can Help Save the World, 62, 363
Mycology, 59, 363–64

N

NASA–JPL Solar System Ambassador, 17
National Audubon Society, 33–34, 42, 44, 69, 362
National Historic Trails, 299–300
National Honey Board, 27, 32, 361
National Institute of Health, 4
National Mentoring Partnership, 217, 224, 226, 371
National Oceanic and Atmospheric Administration (NOAA), 55, 57, 169
National Park Service, 49, 183, 192, 308, 363, 369, 376
National Recreation Trails, 299–300, 308
National Rifle Association, 338, 342
National Scenic Trails, 299
National Shooting Sports Foundation (NSSF), 339, 343
National Skeet Shooting Association, 342
National Sporting Clays Association, 339, 342
National Trails System Act of 1968, 299
National Voluntary Organizations Active in Disasters (NVOAD), 159, 170
National Wildlife Federation (NWF), 47, 49, 51–52, 57, 363
NATO phonetic alphabet, 261
Nature Conservancy, 56–57, 363
Negro Baseball League, 330
Neonicotinoids, 30
New England Journal of Medicine, 318–19
New York Times crossword puzzle, 99–101
Newman, Stanley, 102, 109
Newsday, 102
Night Sky Network, 15, 21
Nonprofit board director
composition, 198
duties, 196
good qualities, 199
questions before joining, 202
North American Mycological Association, 65, 69

O

Oakley, Annie, 336, 341
Obama, President Barack, 107, 169, 172, 330
Observatories, 21–22
Office of the State Long-Term Care, Ombudsman, 207
Olympic
softball, 331
target shooting training center, 333
target shooting competition, 334, 342
triathlon, 346
Ornamental penmanship, 91–92
Orvis, 338, 343

P

Pacific Crest Trail, 307, 376
Paige, Satchel, 6
Pairing beer and food, 249
Palmer method, 92
Parkinson's disease, 319, 321
Penn & Teller, 111, 121
Permit requirements for mushroom hunting, 63–64
Pheasants Forever (PF), 56–57
Picasso, Pablo, 145
Plato, 11
Poaching, 49–50
Pointed pen styles of calligraphy, 88–89
Poisonous mushrooms, *See* Toadstool
Powell, General Colin, 224
Prime Time: How Baby Boomers Will Revolutionize Retirement, 218, 226, 371
Project Feederwatch, 42, 45
Psychology and magic, 113–14
Purpose, in retirement, 5–6

Q

QSL cards, 259

R

Radner, Gilda, 71
Ramp, 50
Reading Resources
  Amateur astronomer, 21
  Backpacker, 308
  Beekeeper, 32
  Birdwatcher, 44–45
  Blogger, 238
  Calligrapher, 97–98
  Craft beer homebrewer, 250
  Crossword puzzle constructor, 109
  Dancer, 322
  Disaster volunteer, 170
  Fiction writer, 144
  Habitat restorer, 58
  Ham radio operator, 262
  Magician, 122
  Medicare counselor, 181
  Motorcyclist, 276
  Mushroom hunter, 69–70
  National park volunteer, 193
  Nonprofit board director, 206
  Ombudsman for elder care, 216
  Performing arts usher, 131
  RV traveler, 286
  Service dog trainer, 83
  Softball player, 332
  Stone sculptor, 155
  Target shooter, 343
  Triathlete, 357
  Vlogger, 239
  Woodturner, 295
  Youth mentor, 226
Red Cross, *See* American Red Cross
Research on mentor participation, 223
Retired & Senior Volunteer Program (RSVP), 173–74, 181, 218, 225
Retirement
  finding purpose, 5
  importance of good health, 4–5
  importance of planning, 1–2
  transition, 3–4
Reuters Health, 4
Robinson, Ken, 287
Rocky Mountain National Park, 186, 189–90, 369
Rondelles, 149
Rose, Ed, 112–13, 122
Rhythmic Souls, 314

S

Saga, Spencerian, calligraphy workshop, 90
Salsacrazy.com, 318, 376
Salvation Army, 160, 170
Samuel Adams, 241
Scott, Dave, 345
Search Engine Optimization (SEO), 234
Self–publishing, 141
Senior Corps, 174, 181, 217, 225
Senior Softball USA, 324,

332, 377
Service dog
breeds, 72
demand for, 80
multiple services, 71–72
placement, 79
puppy names, 77
retirement, 80
training, 75–76, 79
SHIP Volunteer Program, 173
Shortz, Will, 100–1, 108–9, 366
Shrooms, 62
Simmons, Hubert "Bert," 330, 332
Skeet, 336
Skew chisel, 291
Slot dance, 314
Society of American Magicians, 114–15, 122, 366–67
Softball
senior league modifications, 326–27
tournaments, 328, 332
Software for
astrophotography, 20
blogging, 237
crossword puzzle construction, 109
Solar System Ambassador, 17
Spencer, Platt Rogers, 89–90, 92
Spencerian calligraphy, 88–89, 97
Sporting clays, 337
Sports & Fitness Industry Association, 345
Sprint, 345
St. John's Bible, 94–95
Stamets, Paul, 62, 69, 363
State Health Insurance Program (SHIP), 173, 175, 180, 369
Stegner, Wallace, 183
Stewart, Terra Brie, 60, 364
Strategic Bird Conservation Framework, 41
Strunk & White's Elements of Style, 140, 144
Sturgis Motorcycle Rally, 274–275
Sull, Michael, 90–91, 93, 97
Swarms, bee, 27

T

Task force on systemic pesticides, 30
Team In Training (TNT), 346–49
Teller, 111, 114, 121–22, 367
Textile clothing, 271
The Magician's Oath, 116
Theme, of crossword puzzle, 102–3
Thoreau, Henry David, 299
Toadstool, 65
Tools, *See* Equipment
Toy Soldiers Forever, 234, 238
Transition,
in retirement, 3
to a senior facility, 214
triathlon stages, 345, 356, 378
Trap shooting, 336
Trekking poles, 303–4
Tribe Group, 350
Truffles, 66–7
Truman, President Harry S., 171
Tundra, 186, 191
Twain, Mark, 106, 133, 142

U

UK's Bee Farmers' Association, 30
University of
Buckingham, England, 101
Georgia, 24
Hertfordshire, England, 319
Michigan, 277
Oregon, 66
Urban astronomy, 11–12
US Census, 2, 370
US Fish and Wildlife Service, 33, 50
USA Shooting, 333, 339, 343, 378
USA Triathlon, 345–46, 349–50, 356–57, 378

V

Vermeulen, Greg, 202, 370
Video Resources
Amateur astronomer, 21

Backpacker, 308
Beekeeper, 32
Blogger, 238
Calligrapher,
Craft beer homebrewer, 250
Crossword puzzle constructor, 109
Dancer, 322
Disaster volunteer, 170
Fiction writer, 143
Habitat restorer, 58
Ham radio operator, 262
Magician, 122
Medicare counselor, 181
Motorcyclist, 275
Mushroom hunter, 69
National park volunteer, 192
Nonprofit board director, 206
Ombudsman for elder care, 216
Performing arts, 131
RV traveler, 286
Service dog trainer, 83
Softball player, 332
Stone sculptor, 155
Target shooter, 343
Triathlete, 357
Vlogger, 239
Woodturner, 295
Youth mentor, 226

Volunteers-in-Parks (VIP) Program, 183, 192

W

Wall Street Journal, 263, 374
War on Poverty, 218
Website Resources
Amateur astronomer, 20–21
Backpacker, 308
Birdwatcher, 44–5
Blogger/Vlogger, 238
Calligrapher, 97
Craft beer homebrewer, 249
Crossword puzzle constructor, 108
Dancer, 321
Disaster volunteer, 169–70
Fiction writer, 143
Motorcyclist, 275
Mushroom hunter, 69
National park volunteer, 192
Nonprofit board director, 205
Performing arts usher, 130–31
RV traveler, 286
Softball player, 332
Stone sculptor, 154
Target shooter, 342–43
Triathlete, 356–57

Wendling, Bob, 345
West coast swing, 313–14
Western calligraphy, 88
Weston, Dave, 318
White, Betty, 99
Wisconsin Mike and Key Club, 253
Wordplay, 101, 109, 366
Writing
contests, 140, 143
critique, 139
genres, 133
workshops and conferences, 137

Wynne, Arthur, 99, 366

Y

YMCA of the USA, 225–26, 312, 357
YouTube, 235

Z

Zappa, Frank, 241
Zinzulation, 294
Zoning regulations for beekeeping, 25
Zuckerberg, Mark, 204, 229
Zymurgy, 248, 250

About the Author

Photo by Fernando Aguila

Having worked since she was twenty-two years old, Christine Sparacino retired from a varied career as a teacher, corporate trainer, and grant writer. She considers writing and publishing "pure pleasure."

Christine calls retirement the start of a winning trifecta, pursuing three perfect pastimes: creating new friendships, learning new things, and writing about the journey. It's time to shed the manacle of your past job identity and use your time to explore and jump into your new identity. This is the core message of her book, *Energize Your Retirement: Stories of Passionate Pursuits*. Retirement is all about connecting with family and friends, maintaining good mental and physical health, giving back to the community, and discovering new passions.

Christine writes from her home in Northern California, which she shares with her husband. They have two grown sons, and for years, the only TV channels watched had either a baseball, basketball, or football game in progress. Having little choice, she became a rabid Pac 12 football fan.

Visit **ChristineSparacino.com** to share your passionate-pursuit story. You'll find the website filled with lots of resources, and informative blogs on all things having to do with enjoying retirement.

Speaking engagements: Christine enjoys speaking to audiences, both large and small, about the passionate pursuits of retirement. It is an opportunity to share the energizing stories of retirees, the fascinating facts uncovered through her research, and buckets full of resource information on how to begin your new journey. Contact Christine through her website: **ChristineSparacino.com**

Made in the USA
San Bernardino, CA
28 December 2014